OUR WOMAN
IN HAVANA

ABOUT THE AUTHOR

Sarah Rainsford has been a BBC foreign correspondent for over fifteen years, beginning in Moscow, where her team's coverage of the Beslan school siege won the SONY Gold Award. She has since been based in Istanbul and Madrid, and worked in Afghanistan, Iraq and Ukraine. She was posted to Havana in 2011. This is her first book.

@sarahrainsford

OUR WOMAN IN HAVANA

REPORTING CASTRO'S CUBA

SARAH RAINSFORD

ONEWORLD

A Oneworld Book

First published by Oneworld Publications, 2018

This paperback edition published 2019

Copyright © Sarah Rainsford 2018

The moral right of Sarah Rainsford to be identified as the Author of this work has been
asserted by her in accordance with the Copyright, Designs, and Patents Act 1988

ISBN 978-1-78607-580-2
eISBN 978-1-78607-400-3

Every effort has been made to trace copyright holders for the use of
material in this book. The publisher apologises for any errors or omissions
herein and would be grateful if they were notified of any corrections that
should be incorporated in future reprints or editions of this book.

The Publisher is especially grateful to the Graham Greene Estate for permission
to reproduce copyright material from: correspondence, diaries and journals held at
Georgetown University Library; correspondence held at John J. Burns Library, Boston
College; *Ways of Escape* (Vintage Classics); *Our Man in Havana* (Vintage Classics);
Reflections (Vintage Classics); *Collected Essays* (Vintage Classics); *Getting to Know
the General* (Vintage Classics); *Graham Greene: A Life in Letters*, ed. Richard Greene
(Little, Brown); quotations from *The Other Man* by Marie-Françoise Allain (Penguin);
and quotations from *The Life of Graham Greene* by Norman Sherry (Penguin).

Maps © Erica Milwain 2018 (Havana map data © OpenStreetMap contributors)

The names and identifying characteristics of some persons
described in this book have been changed

Typeset by Hewer Text UK Ltd, Edinburgh
Printed and bound in Great Britain by Clays Ltd, Elcograf S.p.A.

Oneworld Publications
10 Bloomsbury Street
London WC1B 3SR
England

Stay up to date with the latest books,
special offers, and exclusive content from
Oneworld with our newsletter

Sign up on our website
oneworld-publications.com

MIX
Paper from
responsible sources
FSC
www.fsc.org **FSC® C018072**

For Kester

CONTENTS

Maps   ix

Endings   1

Part I

1 Without Haste   13

2 The Ruins of Havana   25

3 Confessions of a Martini Drinker   37

4 Consumption Anxiety   52

5 Connecting Cuba   67

6 The Sleeping Faith   81

7 Red Lines   96

8 Entertainments and Commitments   106

9 Condoms and Cricket   122

10 Adela   130

11 The Forgotten Reporter   141

12 Ways of Escape   155

Part II

13 Film Crews and Firing Squads   171

14 Love Not Money   182

15 Enemies and Allies   199

16 Cuba Libre   218

17 Athenian Forum   226

18 Sympathetic Visitor   241

19 The Case of Oswaldo Paya   254

20 Exile   270

21 Let's Dance   282

22 The End of the Affair   293

23 Nice Girl from Vedado   308

24 Sierra Maestra   325

    Slow Erosion   337

    Acknowledgements   349

    Notes   351

    Index   361

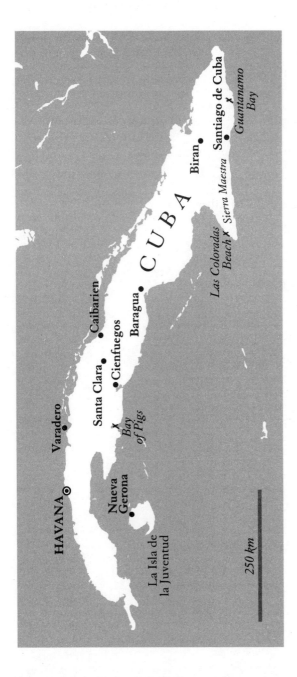

HAVANA

Varadero

Santa Clara
Caibarien
Cienfuegos
Baragua

x
Bay
of Pigs

Nueva
Gerona

La Isla de
la Juventud

C U B A

Biran

Santiago de Cuba
x

Sierra Maestra

Las Coloradas
Beach x

Guantanamo
Bay

250 km

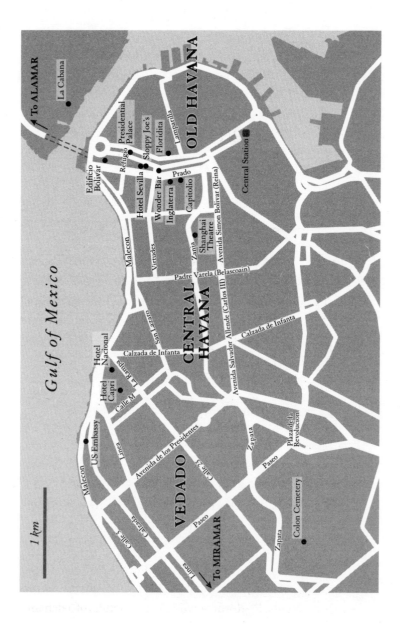

ENDINGS

There is a *frentecito frio*, a little cold front as Cubans call it, but it's still warm for an Englishwoman so I decide to walk all along the Malecon to Old Havana. As the waves crash against the sea wall and curl over, cascading onto the path, I cross the road. A tourist trying to take a photo gets a soaking. It's December 2017 and just over a year since Fidel Castro's death but some things haven't changed. Men *pssst!* as I pass and try to match my step. 'Where are you from?' is the usual opening line as they draw alongside, but they soon drop away unoffended.

I reach the beige block of what's now the US embassy, one side still obscured by a forest of giant flagpoles erected in 2006 when the building housed the US Interests Section. The Americans had begun running an electronic ticker tape across the front pronouncing the ills of communism so the Cubans flew black flags to conceal it. It's more than two years since presidents Raul Castro and Barack Obama restored formal relations, broken after the revolution. The rusting poles now stand empty, but on the Anti-Imperialist Platform down below the letters of a defiant slogan remain bright and clear: *Patria o Muerte, Venceremos!* Fatherland or Death, We will Triumph!

The Interests Section became an embassy in the summer of 2015 and the following spring Obama became the first serving American president to visit Havana since the 1959 revolution. Cubans crowded the streets to welcome him and the message he brought: that it was time to bury the differences and disputes of the Cold War. The make-up with America sparked a rush of tourists as travel articles began hyping Havana. There was a surge of Europeans first, eager to experience Cuba 'before the Americans came' and made Havana just like anywhere else. Americans followed swiftly after, many for the same reason, as the US government relaxed its travel restrictions and direct commercial flights resumed. Returning to Havana myself, I began to see cruise liners docked near my former office and packed open-top tourist buses looping their way around the city. Before a groundbreaking USA–Cuba football match, I heard a man in a Stars-and-Stripes T-shirt pronounce that he was glad to visit before Havana got a Hooters.

On the Malecon a small fleet of beautifully restored 1950s American cars passes me by, passengers dangling over the sides snapping photographs. December is high season but I notice fewer tourists this time and friends in the Cuban travel business have confirmed a fall. The brief optimistic surge that followed Obama's visit has faded since he left the White House, though I still spot the odd American on the seafront, conspicuous by the huge water bottles they clutch as if they're heading into the desert.

I come to Havana as a tourist too these days but the city was once my home. I was Havana Correspondent from late 2011, reporting for the BBC from inside one of the world's last communist-run states. I hadn't been sure about taking the post when it was offered, wondering whether heading for a country of limited breaking news and restrictions on reporting was career suicide. Friends were baffled by my hesitance, picturing only Caribbean sunshine and cocktails. In the end my deep curiosity about life in Castro's Cuba won out.

There was also the chance of being there for that one big story. Though Raul Castro had been president since 2008, and in charge for two years before that, his elder brother Fidel remained a powerful presence. The iconic revolutionary was in his mid-eighties and seriously ailing when I arrived in Havana, and just a week into my posting a rumour spread on Twitter that Fidel had died. An editor called asking me to check it out, sparking what I described later in my diary as 'slight panic'. I fretted that I wasn't ready to cover such a big moment. How could I interpret Cubans' responses when the only locals I knew by then were my new colleagues? Luckily, the rumour had been started by wishful-thinking or mischief-making exiles in Miami and soon faded.

It was the first of many false alarms and each time I'd have to scramble to prove Fidel was still alive, just in case. That wasn't easy on a secretive island. After decades as the energetic, obsessive leader involved in everything, by my time in Cuba Fidel was barely seen. At one point he disappeared for ten months until the Communist Party newspaper *Granma* reported he'd attended a six-hour launch of his latest book. Cuban state TV eventually released images and I saw an animated Fidel addressing an invited audience, jabbing his long forefinger in the air and talking quickly as if to defy the rumours of his demise.

When he first fell ill in 2006, and nearly died, foreign editors all but banned their Cuba correspondents from leaving the island. The assumption was that the revolution would expire with its *Comandante* and reporters based in Havana dreaded missing the moment. But by 2011 Raul was firmly in control and he had one priority: saving the socialist revolution Fidel had launched six decades earlier from collapse.

It was a time of fundamental change. A few months before I landed in Havana, Raul released the Communist Party's guidelines for reform, known as the *Lineamientos*. Cuba would remain a one-party state where all organised opposition was outlawed but some of the resented economic restrictions were being lifted. Cubans were free to buy houses and cars for the first time and, crucially, the government was making it easier for people to open their own businesses in the hope of removing hundreds of thousands from the vast state payroll. Raul described it all as an 'updating' of Cuba's socialist model, but in reality he was attempting to ease the strain before it reached breaking point.

Much of my work would follow the progress of these reforms as the island slowly opened up. I was one of a small group of foreign correspondents permitted to work in Cuba, a status that earned me a large laminated ID card marking me out as an officially accredited journalist. No state employee would agree to be interviewed without seeing it, and that meant a huge number of Cubans. There were practical problems to overcome before I could start, like how to file news to London with an Internet connection barely powerful enough to open an email. But finally I made it on air. 'Now it's over to Sarah Rainsford, Our Woman in Havana', the presenter announced down the line – and the label stuck.

Back in Havana now, walking by the waves, it's odd to recall just how tough it sometimes was to work here. Reading my diaries, I realise they contain little description of the charm of the city, its warmth and real beauty. The pages are filled instead with frustration as I struggled with the pace and peculiarities of my new posting. Writing to a friend in Madrid, the busy news patch I'd come from, I admitted that I 'hated' the lack of information in Cuba and missed 'being on TV every day'. Needing official permission to film almost anything, I wailed in my notebook that I felt 'hemmed in' and wanted to scream or explode.

The Malecon was always my consolation. As this walk draws closer to Old Havana I remember how I used to drive the stunning route to and from my office in the colonial heart of the city. I'd wind down the window to smell the sea and soak up the sight of a place whose faded grandeur was so enchanting. Then I'd turn on the music. As well as salsa, I developed a taste for reggaeton with its pumping beat and infectious tunes. The words were so distinctly Cuban, and so rude, I'd sometimes have to ask my producer to translate. One of the biggest hits then was a celebration of masturbation. The shared-taxi drivers would paint the lyrics on their rear windows, and schoolchildren wearing headphones would sing along with the recording playing on their mobile phones. *Kimba Pa' Que Suene*.

* * *

There are a few more pictures of Fidel around Havana now he's gone. He never allowed a cult of personality to flourish while he was alive and I doubt that will happen now, but on my walk I see posters taped to windows and a few murals too. *Fidel es Pueblo.* Fidel is the People.

I left Havana in late 2014 for a new posting to Russia and the challenge of figuring out Vladimir Putin. The crunch came when I was watching colleagues reporting from Kiev where protestors were being shot. In Havana that week I got a call from the British ambassador to announce that Tom Jones would be the guest of honour at the annual cigar festival. But almost as soon as I left, the sleepy island began making major headlines. US–Cuban relations were restored, Obama paid his historic visit and the same ambassador got to host the Rolling Stones when they played the biggest concert Havana had ever seen. Then in November 2016 a BBC newsflash on my phone woke me in Moscow with a jolt: Fidel Castro had died at the age of ninety.

It was the moment I'd learned to be geared up for, but when it came I was forced to watch the coverage unfold from nearly six thousand miles away. On TV I saw myself climbing through the lush mountainside vegetation of the Sierra Maestra, the cradle of

Fidel's revolution. It was one of a series of reports I'd filmed shortly before leaving Cuba and filed to London to run when the day arrived. Watching the obituaries roll I regretted missing the story, but I also knew that Fidel's passing would not provoke the immediate political earthquake that was once anticipated.

Now my curiosity about what will become of Castro's Cuba is pulling me back to Havana. I'm curious too about the fate of those I've met over the years: the true believers and the open dissidents, the entrepreneurs full of hope and the disillusioned trying to leave however they could, all swept up in one man's giant social experiment.

As I approach number 161 on the Malecon I remember how I once met a man there called Jose Ramon in his derelict home. I fear his building can't possibly have survived the hurricane which tore through the region a couple of months before, killing ten people in Havana. I've heard stories of waves breaking against houses and a balcony plunging four storeys to crush a bus. Rounding a slight bend I see that Jose's house is still standing but cordoned off with iron sheets. Behind them, his entrance-way has been cemented shut.

A couple of doors down there are figures moving about in the shadows so I head towards them through a gap in the metal barrier. By the time I hear a man's raised voice and children crying I'm already committed. A woman tells me everyone was evacuated before Hurricane Irma hit and they have no idea where Jose went. As she talks I scan the scene. The family appears to be squatting among the ruins.

At a bar a little further along the seafront, waitresses sing along to a reggaeton hit, trying to lure in the tourists. The building was a famous brothel before such places were banned after the revolution and it's like a mini castle, complete with corner turrets. On an earlier visit a man at the door had told me it was being painted beige, replacing the previous lobster pink, to restore 'authenticity', but that anodyne shade is already flaking to reveal the lurid layer below. I use the bathroom, which has no water, but as I emerge the attendant points firmly towards his saucer for a tip. Outside, a Spanish customer leaps up from his table to have his photo taken with the women dancing behind the mojito bar. *Soy negro, soy feo, pero soy tu asesino.* I'm black, I'm ugly, but I'm your assassin, the middle-aged chorus chants along with the recording. *No es la cara ni el cuerpo. Es mi palon divino.* It's not my face or my body. It's my divine rod.

It's partly moments like this, moments that make me smile, that keep me coming to Havana. I've been twice a year since my posting ended, frustrated when I was based here but now reluctant to let the Cuban 'story' or my connection drop. As I watched the American tourists return after Obama's visit, my mind was thrown back to descriptions of the days when Havana was their tropical playground. The crowds would pour across the Florida Straits to a Caribbean Las Vegas, filling the bars, cabarets and casinos run by American gangsters. The mob was paying hefty backhanders to Cuba's brutal president Fulgencio Batista for the privilege. It was that corrupt world and US domination that Fidel Castro set out to dismantle. Now he was gone, and the Americans coming back, it felt like Fidel's political project was slowly unravelling.

* * *

On my return trips, I've been guided by the writing of another English visitor seduced by Havana. Graham Greene came to

Cuba regularly from the early 1950s, first walking these same streets in the hedonistic days of Batista's rule and then during the early stirrings of revolution. His travel journals and letters are a window on the city that so appealed to him: a Havana of cabarets and sex-shows where 'every vice was permissible' and everything and everyone was for sale. By 1957 he had turned sympathetic witness to Castro's struggle as the uprising against Batista's regime grew. Greene began meeting the rebels and even helped them in their cause as Cuba became one of his commitments.

Our Man in Havana, published in 1958, captures the moment as the island's pleasure era was 'creaking dangerously to its end'. Though Greene claimed that Cuba was no more than an exotic backdrop to his spy novel, the ruins of Havana he describes are uncannily familiar even on this walk. Sixty years later, with Fidel gone and Raul preparing to leave power, the revolutionary era Greene saw born is coming to a close. As I've drawn my own portrait of that moment, I've looked back to Greene's writing during Cuba's last major upheaval: I wanted to see how Havana was then to understand how it is now and what it might become. So I've used the novelist's piercing gaze alongside my own as I explore the making and the unmaking of Castro's Cuba.

* * *

Every time I come back to Havana I'm drawn to the seafront with its long, low wall. It's where Cubans come to flirt and dream, to catch fish and hustle tourists, or just to walk, like me, observe and absorb. The stretch I've reached is where Greene had his own 'man in Havana' walk, the vacuum cleaner sales-man turned spy Jim Wormold. He passed bars full of girls with brown eyes and lovely faces, 'beautiful buttocks leant against the bars, waiting for any life to come along the sea-wet street'. Heading through those same colonnades, I pass a young couple kissing, oblivious to all. A pensioner advertises mobile phone credit for sale from the window of his living room and a man leans against his doorway, plucking a quiet tune on his guitar. Down side streets the old cars shine more brightly after the winter rain and the emerging sun picks out the pastel paintwork of the buildings, each one of them different.

Part I

1

WITHOUT HASTE

'*Pssssst! Papa quiere?*' I jumped as the man passing me hissed suddenly under his breath. Do I want a Daddy? I wondered, confused as the man beckoned. It was the middle of the day in a busy street so I calculated that this stranger wasn't about to force 'Daddy' onto me and I followed. Round the corner he thrust a lumpy carrier bag towards me and named his price. Inside were a couple of kilos of potatoes, or *papas*. It clearly wasn't only Cuban Spanish I needed an induction in, but how to shop.

The man had approached me outside the best farmers' market in Havana: the socialist, not the hipster sort. When we made it inside my husband was accosted by a tall black transvestite in a skin-tight top calling him *guapo* near a table displaying a pig's head split in two. She persisted in trying to lure him away until the pork sellers took pity and disentangled him.

The markets were one of communist-run Cuba's earliest liberalising economic experiments, freeing up farmers to sell some produce direct to customers and not just the state. The

stalls were heaped with giant avocados, mangoes and more, depending on the season, but I could never find potatoes. I eventually discovered that what didn't go to the all-inclusive tourist resorts was usually diverted to the black market. On the rare occasions potatoes did make it to the shops there'd be enormous queues and even fights. The deficit spawned a very Cuban joke when Pope Benedict visited the island in 2012. 'Papa's arrived!' people would say. 'How much per pound?' was the reply.

The dearth of potatoes was one of the many mysteries of Cuba I had to adjust to when I arrived to report from the island. I'd landed in Havana on a sweltering Christmas Eve to an airport full of border guards in short skirts and extravagantly patterned tights. As they flicked unhurriedly through our passports, the women teased and called out to one another as *mi amor*. One of them, perhaps the girl with pink-dyed hair, then handed our documents back and waved me and my husband through. *Welcome to Cuba.* After encountering my first communist entrepreneur in the Ladies' – requesting 'notes please, not coins' for a square of toilet tissue – we were soon squeezing through the crowds into the street.

The drive was my first sight of Havana, a sprawling city of over two million people or around a fifth of Cuba's population. On the outskirts we passed low-rise houses in bright clashing colours and a maternity hospital shaped like a woman's ovaries when viewed from above. Overtaking the hulking 1950s American cars that run through the city as shared taxis, we soon pulled into the upmarket neighbourhood of Miramar. Before the revolution this was where Havana's English-speaking expat community rubbed shoulders with the white Cuban elite. In modern-day Cuba some people were scraping by in cramped rooms down shadowy passageways while others kept neat detached homes behind tall fencing and cactus hedges on Calle 70, a two-lane street that swept down to the sea.

For the first few weeks, as we looked for long-term accommodation, we made our base there in a hotel-cum-apartment complex with a psychedelic paint job. My advance impressions of Havana had been heavily influenced by the steamy *Dirty Havana Trilogy* of Pedro Juan Gutierrez, a novel that gave me visions of a city oozing with sweaty sexuality. Our own dazed and jet-lagged first evening in Havana was spent eating deep-fried cheese sticks dipped in brown sauce in a lobby bar hung with images of Laurel and Hardy alongside Cuba's revolutionaries.

Tranquil Miramar was far from the dirty realist world of Gutierrez. There was a park where children could take horse

rides and teenagers got free martial arts classes. Some week-
ends souped-up vintage American cars would challenge
Soviet Ladas to drag races along a side road lined by a cheering crowd. Walking anywhere at night was an obstacle course
with minimal street lighting and paving stones ripped apart
by giant ceiba tree roots stretching like gnarled fingers. Most
of the manhole covers were missing, presumably taken to sell
for scrap like the metal inscription picked off an unflattering
bust of Yasser Arafat the very first night it appeared on our
street.

I did have ideas of moving out of the suburbs for what I imagined then would be a more 'authentic' Cuban experience. I'd
pictured us renting a flat in a Spanish colonial-era building in
Old Havana with shutters and wooden ceiling fans, and *son*
music floating up from some neighbourhood bar. But the reality
of life in the old city turned out to be less romantic, all power cuts
and tourists and bands strumming 'Guantanamera' on a relentless loop. As a foreign correspondent I didn't have much choice
of accommodation in any case. We had to rent from the state, a
rule I assumed was to help the authorities keep tabs on us as well
as being an easy source of cash. Some journalists would take on
entire rundown houses and spend months repairing and kitting
them out at great stress and cost. When they left, those revamped
homes would revert to the state. With neither the budget nor the
patience for such a deal, we ended up moving into a modern
apartment block reserved for foreigners. Instead of the Buena
Vista Social Club it was the anguished hits of Adele that wafted
up to my balcony.

* * *

Apart from the farmers' markets, the clearest sign of reform in those early days was the privately run house-restaurants, or *paladares*. They first appeared in the 1990s as Cuba reluctantly reopened the island to mass tourism. Prising the economy open to private business was equally uncomfortable for the revolutionary government, but it was forced to adapt to survive. The collapse of the USSR had deprived Cuba of an economic prop worth an estimated $5 billion per year, and the state alone could no longer provide.

In the early days the *paladares* were so encumbered by regulations that many went to the wall. When I arrived in Havana, there were only a handful in my neighbourhood and most served dry fish fillets or pork on oversized plates with a swirl of jam to appear cutting-edge. Over the next three years, the change was dramatic. As Raul Castro allowed the private sector to expand, Miramar got good Italian restaurants, nightclubs and burger bars. On Calle 70, people began selling CDs and offering haircuts on their porches, and one house was partially converted into a gym.

While private enterprise took off, Cuba's centrally planned state economy remained inefficient and underfunded. It was also struggling under an economic embargo first imposed by the US in 1960 and intended to strangle the revolution at birth. Underestimating the impact of all that on daily life, I'd arrived from Madrid with just a couple of suitcases. I then spent weeks scouring Havana's ill-stocked stores trying to replace what I'd blithely left in storage. 'Excitement today as I found sponges in a shopping centre', I noted one day in the diary I kept sporadically.

Hunting for the basics, I also had to get my head round the dual currency system. State workers were paid in Cuban pesos, or CUP,

earning the equivalent of around $20 a month. But all stores sell-
ing anything worth buying operated in convertible pesos, or CUC,
and the prices were at least as high as in Europe. The system dated
back to the 1990s when the government legalised use of the US
dollar so that tourists could inject some hard currency into the
local economy. The dollar was eventually replaced by the CUC,
pegged to the US currency, and by my time on the island almost
everything from cooking oil to clothes was sold in CUC. The
farmers' markets were a rare exception but that didn't make them
cheap. A pound of onions would cost fifteen CUP, roughly a day's
wage for a state worker. When I asked Cubans how they coped,
they'd shrug and smile, and then utter what I learned was the
national mantra. *No es facil.* It's not easy.

My early weeks in Havana continued in a blur of impressions
and shattered stereotypes. There was a trip to immigration to be

fingerprinted for my ID card by cheerful women in military miniskirts and a Jehovah's Witness taxi driver who presented me with a dog-eared copy of *The Watchtower*. There were girls in Lycra leggings printed with the American flag and an elderly Cuban woman wandering Miramar in a 'Crimestoppers UK' T-shirt. Then there was a former Havana correspondent who warned me that I should trust no one, recounting a story about being befriended by a 'spy' who stole his wife's underwear. Back at our state-owned flat, I began to wonder whether the drawer of the cabinet beside our bed was glued shut to conceal a listening device or just because the front was dodgy and would otherwise fall off.

* * *

Early on in my stay I dreamed about a chance meeting with Fidel. 'Offered an exclusive up-close-and-personal documentary', I scribbled down when I woke. 'Excited at the chance of access'. But such dreams were the closest I got to the ailing, reclusive *Comandante*. His brother Raul proved to be only slightly more accessible. I once arrived at Havana airport at 6 a.m. for the chance to see him as he accompanied the Iranian president to his plane after an official visit. I spent three hours drinking grainy coffee in a stuffy room with other foreign journalists before a Communist Party official released us onto the tarmac with stern instructions to conduct ourselves 'respectably' and give a 'good impression' of Cuba.

Our small press pack ended up behind a rope close to Ahmadinejad's plane. 'Shall we take a question?' Raul wondered out loud as the two men approached our huddle, and we all began to shout. 'Ah yes, TeleSur!' he exclaimed, directing his guest towards the TV channel co-sponsored by Cuba and Venezuela, its socialist ally. There was growing talk in the West at the time of tightening sanctions against Iran over its nuclear programme. But the TeleSur correspondent had his own concern. 'How was Fidel, when you saw him?' Assuring the cameras that the elder Castro was 'fit and well', Ahmadinejad was then led off to his plane, my own shouted question left hanging.

Moments later, though, Raul was heading back towards us. Fidel was famous for making long public speeches in his healthy days but his brother usually kept his distance from the TV cameras. This then was a rare opportunity. But just as Raul began to reply to our questions, Ahmadinejad's plane revved its engines and drowned out almost every word. Cuba's leader was soon whisked away by his bodyguards. Back inside the airport terminal I crouched over my recording. I could just about hear Raul joking about his brother's good health over the roar of the plane engines, but when answering a question on economic reform, his comments sounded cautious. For many Cubans the pace of change Raul had initiated was excruciatingly slow and that day their president gave no hope that it would pick up. As Ahmadinejad's plane taxied along the tarmac, Raul told us that change would come 'without pause, but without haste'.

* * *

'Without haste' was a phrase that seemed to sum up my work life in Cuba. A team linked to the Foreign Ministry known as the Centro de Prensa Internacional, or CPI, handled all requests for access or interviews. As the overwhelming majority of activities and institutions in Cuba were still state-controlled, I needed CPI permission to film everything, from farms to dance studios to supermarkets. I soon learned not to promise my editors in London anything until I had most of the footage in the bag.

In my first month I sent a long wish list to the CPI including requests for interviews about an anti-corruption drive. I asked about the restrictions on emigration as one of Cuba's best-known dissidents, the blogger Yoani Sanchez, was repeatedly blocked from leaving the island. I also tried to get comment on new efforts to drill for oil, potentially rescuing the economy from crisis. I was rarely denied access outright; requests judged unsuitable were simply left pending. Meanwhile, I'd get regular emails from the CPI inviting me to events they imagined I might care to cover.

Email Invitation, 15 October 2012

Esteemed colleague:

The Ministry of Construction (MICONS) invites you to participate in a meeting on ... perspectives for production of new
construction systems using expanded polystyrene.

Taxi drivers were among my favourite conversation targets in the early days as I tried to learn as much about the island as I could, though my over-earnest efforts weren't always produc-tive. Attempting to get a Lada driver's thoughts on the new oil rig one day, I realised he was more interested in catching my eye in his rear-view mirror. 'He stared at me and proclaimed, "You're so pretty, you have lovely eyes!"' I recorded in my diary. 'I was only trying to talk about oil wealth!'

There were technical challenges to grapple with too. I was used to broadcasting live using a satellite dish as small as a laptop, but in Cuba that equipment was banned. Two years earlier an American contractor named Alan Gross had been arrested as a spy after smuggling the same technology onto the island. He'd been working to create an unmonitored Internet network for Cuba's tiny Jewish community and was serving a fifteen-year prison sentence when I arrived. Not keen on sharing his fate, I had to rely instead on an ancient piece of BBC kit that worked over the phone line. My image on screen would stutter and freeze until one day it suddenly switched to black and white for an entire live report. Perhaps it was lucky Havana wasn't bursting with breaking news.

As foreign correspondents we were free to travel the island without restriction, but getting access to officials was even more difficult outside Havana. Once in a while the CPI would invite us all on a group trip which theoretically offered rare contact with Party bosses. So in February 2012 I signed up for Santiago. It was shortly before Pope Benedict XVI's trip to Cuba, and as he would visit its second city as well as the capital I thought I could at least pick up some useful pictures of the preparations.

Santiago de Cuba is at the opposite end of the long, thin island from Havana, some 550 miles and a thirteen-hour ride away in a heavily air-conditioned bus. The motorway runs out just where the funding did – about halfway down. The rest of the route is a narrow, often rutted road through the tropical countryside. Trundling along it, we passed faded billboards proclaiming

Adelante!, onwards with the socialist revolution, and a woman on a horse-drawn cart clutching a TV set. At 6:30 p.m. we were plunged into the early winter darkness. 'Potholes emerge from nowhere and force bus to brake fast,' I scribbled in my notebook, recording that one swerve sent a fellow journalist flying into the aisle.

We eventually arrived intact to find ourselves treated more like visiting dignitaries than press. There seemed to be a band playing 'Guantanamera' and someone offering a tray of mojitos every time we clambered off our bus. The entertainment stepped up a notch at the Santiago Communist Party headquarters with an all-female choir in the reception hall. Later, the local Party boss sat at the front of the room while we were lectured at length on city history. As soon as we tried to approach, he shot through a side door at high speed.

Even getting preview pictures for the papal visit was a battle. We were taken to the main city square where workers were erecting a stage for Pope Benedict to say Mass beneath a giant neon image of Fidel. But at the shrine of Cuba's patron saint, Our Lady of Charity, our government guides quickly decided we'd had enough. Insisting that the church needed to close, they escorted us out. I spent the next half hour fuming in the car park as we twiddled our thumbs, church still open, waiting for the rest of our group.

As a newcomer to Cuba there were some useful moments on the trip, including a stop-off at a cooperative farm. Most of the time, though, it seemed our guides wanted to bombard us with statistics and then usher us somewhere to eat. We got big lunches in state restaurants followed by big dinners, more 'Guantanamera' and more mojitos. 'We're not tourists,' I kept protesting pointlessly to the smiling CPI team who'd brought us from Havana. 'If it weren't for the papal visit, we'd be going home with nothing to show other than fatter bellies,' I noted forlornly in my diary.

2

THE RUINS OF HAVANA

Havana looks stunning from a distance but close up much of it is in a pitiful state. Over the years, the official City Historian's office has worked to restore historic mansions, cobbled squares and fountains; it has then installed restaurants and hotels to generate revenue to fund further repairs. The team has big signature projects too, like renovating the Gran Teatro and the giant Capitolio building with its gold-leaf roof. But saving the historic heart of Havana is an enormous task.

Old Havana was already crumbling in the 1950s when Graham Greene began visiting. His woeful hero Wormold felt himself part of the 'slow erosion' of the city and you can see the pockmarked pillars in the opening scene of *Our Man in Havana*. In fact by 1959, when the film of Greene's book was shot, as few as one in six buildings in the old quarter were deemed to be in good condition. Bitten into by the salt-air and scorched by the sun, the colonial heart of Havana had been neglected since the city expanded west, creating grand new avenues and sumptuous mansions. 'Bourgeois' Havana as a whole was then neglected in turn by the revolution.

Looking to the increasingly lucrative tourist market, some Cubans have invested heavily in repairing their buildings at a much faster pace than the City Historian's team could ever manage. I've seen more smart-looking apartments displaying 'to rent' signs each time I've returned, and more cafes and bars too. Greene would have approved of the waiters' T-shirts in one place that declare 'Hemingway was never here.' The American writer moved to Havana in the 1930s and the city gradually filled with plaques and photos in his honour. Another spot now popular with hipster tourists is all exposed brickwork and casually mismatched chairs with a menu offering sourdough bread and pulled pork. Private enterprise, as much as the state, is stalling Havana's slide into decay. It's not clear how much attention is being paid to conservation as a result, but perhaps that's academic when buildings are on the brink of collapse.

The entrepreneurial surge is creating other concerns for the government though. The initial investment often comes from Cubans abroad sending funds to relatives. Families who stayed on the island – arguably the most loyal to the revolution – are getting left behind economically. The problem isn't only the increasing wealth gap. Since most of the original emigres were from the white elite, much of the money being sent back in remittances is going to their white relatives. The worry is that the yawning racial divide which the revolution boasted it had closed is now growing again.

*   *   *

One of the first serious news stories I had to cover in Havana was a house collapse in which three high school students were killed.

At the police cordon, neighbours told me the building had been declared unfit for habitation but that people with nowhere else to go had stayed. We filmed from an intersection as mechanical diggers began pulling what remained of the building to the ground.

About a year later I faced a similar scene in a further-flung suburb. I'd heard talk of another disaster and when we reached La Vibora we found ourselves in front of a huge yellow building with a jagged gap in the middle. It was a former convent that had been converted into a state boarding school after the revolution. Years of neglect had then eaten away at the structure so much that part of a corridor had caved in at some point in the 1990s. The schoolchildren were relocated for their own safety but at least ten families remained in the old building, most of them former staff who'd been given their apartments by the state. Others had moved in later, illegally.

On the morning of the disaster, four storeys of the old convent had come crashing down, burying a 50-year-old woman beneath. By the time we arrived, rescuers had been trying to reach Maria Isabel Fernandez for several hours. 'She'd just gone back into the house when the floor fell through and the whole place collapsed,' one of her neighbours, Yurliany Martinez, told me. 'My daughter was screaming for her Aunty Chabela and I had to grab her and run.'

A group of men had formed a human chain to recover what belongings they could from the parts of the building still standing. On the street, among a mish-mash of furniture, was someone's wheelchair and a cupboard pasted with glossy images of women cut from magazine adverts. Residents told me that a column had cracked in the building the previous week and they'd reported it to the local housing authorities. A meeting had been scheduled but the column gave way completely that very day.

It's unusual for Cubans to reveal what they really think with a camera pointing at them, but that day the crowd didn't hold back. 'No one came before and now they're all here,' a resident called Ismailo commented bitterly, gesturing towards a huddle of local officials and police. At one point a fireman walked past carrying two large rabbits in a crate. They were to be sent into the rubble with thermal cameras for a final check for signs of life.

By the time a Party representative turned up, the rescue operation had been declared a recovery mission and Maria Fernandez was presumed dead. Had the building collapsed any earlier in the day there could well have been more casualties. 'The need for housing is greater than our capacity to build,' the politician Ines Barroso admitted. She said the authorities had tried to help the families in the old convent: when an initial plan to reinforce and save the building was ruled out, residents were offered land and credit to build properties for themselves. 'They've been promising solutions for years,' a furious Yurliany Martinez told me. 'It's all been lies and we're tired of it. Now we've lost a woman who was like a mother to me.'

Yurliany and other residents were moving in with friends and relatives that night with no idea when they might be rehoused. But as they gathered their belongings, and the digger scooped up the rubble of their home, some warned that the whole building should be torn down. They feared others would try to move into the wreckage.

* * *

It was one of the tenets of the revolution that all citizens had the right to a roof over their heads. That was straightforward in the early years as the state expropriated businesses and seized the abandoned mansions of the wealthier Cubans and foreign residents who fled the island. Partitioned up, those buildings became home to multiple families paying a peppercorn rent to the state. But when Maria Fernandez's building collapsed in 2013, government figures put Cuba's housing deficit at some 600,000 properties. Much of the stock in Havana was officially classified as somewhere between poor and perilous.

When I met Mario Coyula, a respected but outspoken architect, he described the situation starkly. 'If nothing changes, Havana may end up with a void in the middle where the city used to be,' he said, as we strolled along the seafront past one long-suffering structure after another. The problem was worst in the central districts where the houses were older and the people poorer. But the picture-postcard Malecon itself is under constant attack by corrosive sea spray, storms and tropical termites. In 1957, the travel writer Norman Lewis described the promenade as a row of millionaires' houses that were like 'wedding cakes turned to stone'. The elements have since bitten big chunks out of those cakes. 'It's impossible to preserve all the buildings,' Mario Coyula warned that day. 'Many will go. We inherited a city we couldn't keep.'

Major overcrowding puts an immense added strain on Havana's housing, with multiple generations living under one roof. Many families have built illegal lofts in an attempt to expand their tiny space but that work, combined with the surplus weight, has had disastrous results. Officials calculate that three buildings collapse either partially or completely in Cuba's capital every single day. I mentioned that statistic to the architect and he clarified that in some cases it was just the tip of a balcony that came off. 'Still, that's why some people walk on the street,' Coyula added. 'On the pavement something could easily fall on your head.'

Exploring Havana's housing situation for one of several reports, I selected an address at random on the seafront and stepped inside with my microphone. Once my eyes adjusted from the glare of the sun, I picked my wary way past a tangle of cables and wooden props supporting the ceiling towards an empty space at the back. Malecon 161 was known as *La Fortuna* but locals told me part of an abandoned building behind had collapsed onto it after a storm some years before, killing one resident and wiping out several apartments.

When I visited there were still twenty people inside waiting to be rehoused. They included Jose Ramon who'd painted the words *Christ is coming, Alleluia!* on his bright blue front door. The inscription was above a little white sticker which meant Jose had been counted in the latest census. Inside his one-room flat I spotted quotes about Jehovah pinned to the walls. Shirtless and wearing ripped jeans cut off into shorts, Jose told me that some neighbours had been categorised as priority cases after the accident and given flats on the city outskirts. But he was clinging to his ruin. He believed the authorities were trying to force the poor out of central Havana to bring in bigger rents and he wasn't afraid to say so: he'd been writing letters to Communist Party officials in protest.

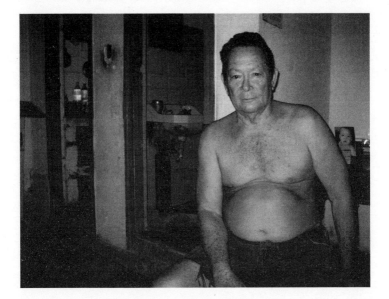

Jose's biggest worry was when it rained. Torrential down-pours transform Havana's streets into raging rivers in an instant, plunging traffic police in water up to their thighs at intersections. Drivers in ancient cars without windscreen wipers are forced to pull over and sit it out. But in derelict buildings like Malecon 161 storms bring real danger. 'I do get alarmed when the rain's heavy,' Jose admitted. 'I sometimes go outside because I'm afraid the building won't hold. I pretend I'm contemplating the down-pour from across the street, but I'm actually keeping my eye on the building in case it collapses.'

Jose's story was far from unique. On a previous occasion I'd filmed further down the Malecon at a former hotel in an even more precarious state. Olga Torriente had lived at number 69 perfectly legally for some twenty years. When it rained heavily she and her husband would pull their bed away from the exter-nal wall, afraid that the long cracks would grow and send the whole building crashing down. A year or so after that interview the building was finally demolished and I could find no trace of Olga. Her former neighbours told me some residents had been rehoused in a suburb while others had taken places in state shel-ters. More than five thousand Havana families were in such temporary housing at the time, and the shelters usually became permanent homes. But I also learned that a handful of people from number 69 were waiting for a replacement building to be finished a few streets away. The flats had been under construc-tion for four years while their future residents waited in the dangerous converted hotel. The man in charge told me too few builders had been allocated to the job and the construction mate-rial kept getting pilfered. But the demolition of number 69 had spurred things on. The new boss was under orders to get the place finished, and in Cuban-socialist style residents were signed off from their regular work to join the building brigade instead.

Meanwhile, the government was trying other measures to solve the housing crisis. A new law permitted Cubans to build their own homes, something that had not happened since the revolution. Next, the state began offering the poorest people financial help to buy construction materials. I met one family of four who'd been squeezing into the same bed for years. They were celebrating finally being able to build an extra room onto their tiny house and spread out a bit.

*   *   *

By far the most fundamental change in the housing sector was when the ban on buying and selling property was lifted. About a year later, I watched from the technicians' gallery of a breakfast TV show as a young presenter perched on a high stool read out the details of houses for sale. The set of *Hola Habana* looked like it was trapped in the 1970s, with blown-up photos of Havana Bay stuck to fake windows, and lots of wooden panelling, but the TV show was offering a groundbreaking service.

For decades the only way to move home for Cubans had been through a *permuta*, or swap. Officially, no money could change hands but in reality there was a thriving black market. Prohibited property swaps were arranged for payment and you could also buy yourself a speedier path through all the bureaucracy. I heard how people would even get married, transfer a property title for a fee and then divorce, just to get their hands on a better home. Such deals were common but clearly came at a risk. Now, in a country where Fidel Castro once banned commercials, I was watching state television advertising housing for sale.

Hola Habana only had airtime for a few properties, but every weekend one section of a broad city avenue was transformed into an outdoor estate agency for the rest. Before the reform all the trade on the Prado was in property swaps. Now most people thronging the street were there to buy and sell. Some house owners stood with handwritten signs on scraps of paper. Others pinned their adverts to tree trunks. Milling among them were agents who would facilitate both kinds of transaction for a cut. Their business hadn't made it onto the expanded list of approved private trades, so the agents were operating illegally. One of them, who called herself Yolaida, told me she'd first visited the Prado to swap her own flat. Now, wielding a notebook full of the scribbled details of customers and houses, she was doing deals for others. 'Swapping was much more complicated,' the undercover agent explained. 'You could wait up to a year for something that suited both sides. Now people can buy, everything is much faster and simpler.'

The government didn't free up the property market completely. To prevent speculation, Cubans were only permitted to own one home each and foreigners remained banned altogether: the government wanted to stop American developers from swooping and buying up the city. But judging by the crowds on the Prado, the new move was popular. An architect browsing the offerings pinned to a tree told me he was looking to pool resources with a friend and buy a bigger flat. They planned to start renting to tourists to supplement their state salaries. Another young man I spoke to had just secured an emigre visa for Canada and wanted to sell his flat in Old Havana to buy something smaller for his mother before he left. 'The system was crazy before,' he laughed. 'Someone would have had to marry me so I could donate them my flat when I went. At least I don't have to do that now.'

On a stone bench a man in his late forties was holding a piece of cardboard advertising a three-room flat for sale. Eduardo told me he'd been coming to the street market with his sign for two months. His wife had already left for the US and he was selling up to go and join her. 'Before, you had to leave the state everything if you emigrated: car, house – they confiscated the lot,' Eduardo explained. It was partly because all property belonged to the state and partly because for years anyone leaving the island was considered a traitor. Now the law allowed him to sell, Eduardo would have money to start afresh in America.

A few days later I went to visit him at his home. Reparto Electrico isn't Havana's most desirable suburb but the apartment was spacious and Eduardo was selling it complete with fixtures and fittings, including his giant pot plants. He'd already had several viewings, though like many he was coy about revealing his asking price. There was a four percent tax on all housing sales which no one wanted to pay if they could avoid it.

The prices I did hear quoted bore no relation to the meagre salary of a state worker. Estate agents on the Prado told me small flats in the city centre were changing hands for around $20,000. Some of the buyers were musicians or artists who could tour and sell abroad. Others were those Cuban entrepreneurs who'd been running *paladares* or renting out rooms since that was permitted on a limited scale in the 1990s. At twenty to thirty CUC, the going rental rate per night was more than a month's state salary. But much of the money involved in the new property boom was clearly coming from Cubans abroad.

For one man I met in the crowd it was all too much. Andres had sold his own place only to see the price for a replacement leap far beyond his reach. Now, forced to sleep on friends' sofas, he complained that rich Cuban-American exiles were fuelling inflation. An older man perched on a nearby wall had been listening as we talked. A retired construction worker, he told me his pension of two hundred Cuban pesos a month, around eight US dollars, barely lasted the week. 'I don't want to tell you my name,' he announced, chomping on sweets. 'That complicates things.' Still, the pensioner said he wanted to downsize from his two-bedroom flat to release some cash and set up as a street trader. He described the housing reform as the best thing Raul Castro had done. 'He's not like Fidel: *you can't do this, or that*,' the pensioner reasoned. 'People couldn't live that way. It's better to live in one room uncomfortably instead of two, but with some money so you can eat.'

3

CONFESSIONS OF A MARTINI DRINKER

I t was only when I reread *Our Man in Havana* that I realised I shared a street with the hapless spy hero of Graham Greene's novel. My own office was in a grand trading exchange in the old city that dated back to the early twentieth century. At Calle Lamparilla 1, the building was just a short distance from the fictional vacuum cleaner store run by Jim Wormold. The novelist gives the address of Phastkleaners as Lamparilla 37, but I've walked up and down the dusty street before without locating any building with that number. There are no houses at all between 2 and 61, just a small park. This time, though, I'm returning to the search with fresh information.

Calle Lamparilla cuts through the historic heart of the city down to my old office near the dock. Sidestepping a couple of elderly men playing the fool for tips at a restaurant window, I turn into the top of the street. Reggaeton music, catchy but crude, thumps from a window and there's the usual chorus of *oye!* as Cubans greet each other enthusiastically, starting conversations at a hundred paces. A small crowd has gathered to admire puppies for sale in a cage. Arctic huskies are in fashion in humid Havana but this vendor is offering a chihuahua and a poodle with sculpted leg fur. A few steps further down, a man perched on a tall chair is having his head close-shaved surrounded by stalls laid out with bric-a-brac and fake designer T-shirts.

There's a reason for my new-found confidence about finding number 37. On an earlier trip I'd visited a branch of the City Historian's office in a grand stone mansion just back from the waterfront. Inside an icily air-conditioned room piled high with papers I met a researcher named Arturo. He had the film of *Our Man in Havana* somewhere at home and was intrigued by my request to locate Wormold's shop. Eager to help, he started scrolling through spreadsheets and scans of old city plans on his computer. After a while Arturo looked up. 'It seems Lamparilla 37 was originally a house of tolerance,' he ventured, lowering his voice slightly. 'You mean a brothel?' I asked, amused that Greene, who kept a list of favourite prostitutes, should have chosen such an address. But that first map dated from 1881 so Arturo went on with his search.

I described the little park I'd seen where I thought number 37 ought to have been. Such spaces were common when houses collapsed so it was possible the building Greene picked had simply gone. But after much scrolling Arturo unearthed a plan of Lamparilla from the 1930s and peering over his shoulder I realised that the numbering in those days was very different. Number 37 was higher up Lamparilla, much further from my office. There were tailors and cafes marked on the street and a New York bank. The map didn't note any business at what was then number 37 but there was an electrician on the same block and two midwives called Maria. Arturo's map also tallied with a scene in

Greene's book where Wormold's daughter Milly walks home from school along Calle Compostela, right beside that spot.

Lamparilla becomes a little smarter as I get closer to the block Arturo has identified. '*Hola!* Where are you from?' someone tries half-heartedly as I pass. 'You want cigars?' In Greene's day this whole area was crowded with different kinds of small businesses. Calle Muralla nearby was famous for its fine fabric shops, and grand department stores on the edges of Old Havana stocked fashions from New York and beyond. The idea of a vacuum cleaner shop like Phastkleaners was less far-fetched than it seems. Even in the carpet-free tropics the latest household appliances were in great demand. There are more houses than businesses here now, though a few signs on balconies offer private flats to rent. A horse and cart are parked outside one, the driver hoping for custom from tourists.

Further down Lamparilla I see a man propping up the doorway of a house covered in crazy-tiling. Dressed in fluorescent green tracksuit cut-offs and flip-flops, he's calling out to everyone who walks past. '*Como anda, papi?*' he asks one man, who raises a hand back in greeting; to women he throws kisses and compliments. This is where Greene describes Milly walking to a hail of catcalls in his novel. Even the writer himself used to get whistled at in Havana and *piropos* are still part of Cuban life. *Si cocinas como caminas me como hasta la raspa!* If you cook like you walk, I'll even eat the scrapings! When Germaine Greer visited in 1985 for a feminist congress she complained that men beckoned her with a *psst! psst!* 'as if I had been a dog'. I used to feel the same way until the audacity of admirers from high-school boys to pensioners began to make me laugh. Eventually I'd feel affronted if I passed a Cuban man in the street and he stayed silent. There's no danger of silence here with the big man greeting all and sundry from his doorway. Eduardo has lived on Lamparilla for fifty years and tells me he was a supreme court judge before retiring. He breaks off to blow more kisses to a passing girl. 'How are you? Did you have lunch yet?' he asks, and turns to inform me that she's German. I ask about the house opposite, testing the idea that it's the one Greene picked for Wormold's shop. 'It used to be a *bodega* until the sixties,' the former judge says, racking his brain for the name of the old grocery store. 'There was a bar too, and flats upstairs.' I explain why I'm asking and Eduardo displays mild to zero curiosity. He tells me that one of his six children is in London married to a Nigerian and promises to find me his daughter's address if I come back. 'You can contact her and say we met.'

I take some photographs of the building and Eduardo encourages me to go over. The place has clearly been used as apartments for many years. The ground floor walls are painted turquoise and though the building has seen better days it looks solid with columns sculpted onto the facade. No one answers my knock at first. Glancing back at Eduardo, I see him urge me to try again and this time a young man's face appears at a window. His mother's out, he tells me, hair tousled and eyes full of sleep, before disappearing back behind the shutters. A piece of paper strapped to the swirling, rusted window bars announces that the lower floor flat is for sale. I wonder if the owner's selling up to leave Lamparilla and the 'ruins of Havana', like Wormold.

* * *

Our Man in Havana opens at the Wonder Bar as the British sales-man sips frozen daiquiris with a German friend and they watch an old man selling pornographic postcards limp by. Greene has Wormold head up Lamparilla to the bar every morning, face 'anxious and crisscrossed'. His vacuum cleaner business is almost dead amid all the power cuts, and his demanding daughter is adding to his money worries. The morning daiquiri with Dr Hasselbacher is a brief escape from the drudgery: seven minutes to get there, six for drink and 'companionship', then seven minutes back to the shop.

Greene never mentions the bar in his diaries but Wormold's favourite haunt, unlike his business, really did exist. I found it listed in the 1958 phone book just below the Women's Club of Havana: *Wonder – Bar P de Marti 351*. The Paseo de Marti is better known as the Prado and the street numbers have changed, but Greene placed his opening scene at the intersection of Prado and Virtudes.

Once the glamorous heart of Cuba's capital, the Prado stretches for a mile from the former seat of parliament in the domed Capitolio building down to the sea. Some of the shattered mansions that line the avenue are little more than shells now with trees growing inside, though the washing strung up in their windows shows they're still inhabited. Decorated with wrought-iron lions and lamp posts, and with laurel trees packed with noisy birds, the Prado's raised central walkway is inlaid with marble from the days when famously stylish Habaneros would promenade along it. The stone benches are a popular spot to gather and gossip as the heat drops out of the day. Teenage schoolgirls spill onto the street after class and I watch a policeman in dark glasses ogle one as she passes, then swing his head back to follow another in the opposite direction. They grow up quickly in the tropics, as Dr Hasselbacher noted to his friend.

On the west side of the avenue there's a tall, slim building with intricate Moorish-style engraving, but the name on the paving outside tells me it was formerly the Splendid Store, not a bar. Looking up I see that two stone balconies have slid from its elaborate facade. The building opposite has a similar paving stone that marks it out as a pharmacy in a former life. The space has been divided to create a small police station and a one-roomed home for a wiry old man who's plastered his side of the flimsy partition with magazine cut-outs. His paper gallery includes everyone from Barbie to Pope Benedict. The man has lived in the area for many years but can't recall any Wonder Bar. Leaning at his open window he explains that the government moved him here when his old house opposite collapsed. By the look of it the new one is not far behind.

In Greene's day the bars on this side of the Prado were pick-up joints with garish electric signs and police on the doors. The brothels were deeper into the warren of streets of the Barrio Colon. According to one article in 1950, 'chattering, cajoling women' would lean out of their windows there and 'pluck at your clothes' twenty-four hours a day. Down Virtudes now, I see two students walking home and an old American car with a cardboard 'For Sale' sign strung to the back bumper. A man trying to herd half a dozen chicks back to safety from the road tells me the rusty, bright red wreck is from 1952 and belongs to his brother. Now that Fidel's long ban on buying and selling cars has been lifted, the man's asking $9,000 for it.

As I cross the Prado to the opposite side a woman passes in loose navy trousers with a fake logo of interlocking Cs and I remember that, just days before I arrived back, Chanel had turned the avenue into an urban catwalk. Celebrities like Rihanna and Madonna had already begun discovering Cuba, flooding social media with images of themselves posing in classic cars on broken-down streets. Picturesque poverty had become chic but the French fashion house took that to another level. Chanel models were swept into the Prado in a fleet of gleaming, restored limousines to strut against a canvas of crumbling homes draped in clothes that would cost years of a Cuban worker's salary. Surrounding streets were closed off and the police were reportedly paid extra to keep locals away from the VIP crowd. For the after-party Chanel took over an entire central square for almost a week. The government needed the money but one friend thought it a 'monumental' symbolic mistake for a country whose leader had railed against consumerism.

An old man I find on the opposite corner resting in the shade rolls his eyes when I mention the fashion show. Dressed in battered boots and loose, home-stitched trousers that look uncomfortably hot, Ricardo Reyes is selling copies of the Communist Party newspaper *Granma* which studiously ignored the whole extravaganza. Now in his eighties, one wonky tooth protruding, Ricardo can't remember any Wonder Bar either even though he's lived locally most of his life. His family moved to Havana before the revolution when his mother began cooking for a rich family. Ricardo had painted buses for a living using a toxic lacquer that would take your nails off. I bring him an ice-cold Bucanero beer and as we sit sipping from our cans in the shade I watch the crowds and fancy that the old man beside me might once have crossed paths with Graham Greene. He would have been around twenty when the author first strolled these streets and described being pursued by bootblacks, their insistent claims that he'd booked their services turning to abuse as he passed. The former American Club that Greene visited is right opposite us, though its last American members left in the 1960s. As the tourists have begun coming back I wonder whether the businessmen will return too. But for now the US still has its trade embargo and the revolution has its deep suspicion of American cash.

The wall behind us belongs to a smart hotel. The concierge has told me it grew to take over the whole block in the 1990s, when Cuba allowed mass tourism again. As it covers the only corner of Prado and Virtudes where Wormold's favourite bar could possibly have been, I guess whatever replaced it was

swallowed up when the hotel expanded. By deduction, I decide that Ricardo and I must be drinking on the steps of the old Wonder Bar.

* * *

Greene began writing his Havana novel at the Sevilla hotel. 'I've got out some clear foolscap and done the first sentence of *Our Man in Havana* – no, a whole paragraph as though you were in the room,' the author wrote neatly on the back of an envelope dated 8 November 1957 and addressed to Catherine Walston, his former lover. The book was meant to be one of his lighter works, turned out in a matter of months as an 'entertainment', but Greene was reeling from his recent break-up with the American, lonely and depressed. His diary reveals that he was drinking heavily, taking sleeping pills and pestering a taxi driver to find him drugs. He poured his fears for the novel into the letter: he was scared the idea had slipped away; what he'd produced so far was hopeless. But by the time he sealed the envelope his mood had lightened. 'A good opening paragraph', he wrote on the flap. His spirits lifted further when he strolled out into the humid Havana streets, noting later in his journal 'more tarts than ever and lovely ones too'.

Greene admitted to a 'predilection for shady places' and Batista's Havana offered plenty. The first trip he recorded in 1954, the year he turned fifty, lasted two days and included a visit to the seedy Shanghai Theatre for a show 'with three girls'. The venue was notorious for a well-endowed performer named Superman who performed sex acts live on stage. Greene would return to Havana several times: for a manic depressive seeking escape, it was the ideal sin city where everything was available, whether 'drugs, women or goats'. The diary of his 1954 visit, kept in a book marked with Catholic holy days, recorded 'cocaine and marijuana offered' as well as 'two girls and boy', as soon as he stepped through the hotel door.

As he drafted the opening pages of his novel, there was something of the Wormold about Greene himself. Melancholic and worn down, his hero has been jilted by a wife who's left for the US. Steeped in gloom after his own breakup, Greene would head to the Floridita for a lift, not the Wonder Bar, where his favourite drink was a dry Martini. 'Couldn't one write a book on Confessions of a Martini drinker?' he scrawled on a long yellow page of his journal one despondent day. 'The tiny rest from reality which no other cocktail will give. The nearest approach perhaps to opium.' He'd hit the opium pipe hard in Vietnam a few years earlier and would remember the early 1950s as the most manic-depressive, hedonistic time of his life.

I'd always steered clear of the puce-pink Floridita when I lived in Havana. The self-styled 'Cradle of the Daiquiri' is now a state-run tourist joint serving some of the most expensive drinks in town. Standing outside, I look for any lingering hints of what Greene might have seen in the place. A conspicuously smart group of young Americans are snapping photographs on their phones and I see from their name tags that they're MBA students from Miami. One tells me they've come to explore the workings of the communist economy then scurries off before I can ask more, as if there's still something of the forbidden about Havana. On the opposite pavement a girl is selling lurid cakes from a cart and the stall outside the art deco building of a near-empty bookshop displays a comic called *Wankarani: The Robot Assassin*.

Ignoring the shouts from bici-taxi drivers, I make for the entrance and it's immediately clear that Greene is not the writer celebrated here. The Floridita is a shrine to Ernest Hemingway who would head there for double daiquiris, T-shirt still stained with fish blood, after a day chasing marlin at sea. The American's bushy-bearded face now stares up at me from the sign on the door, and his life-sized statue props up the bar at the spot where he once regaled fellow drinkers with his tales. Even when Hemingway was a regular here there was a bust of him on a ledge. Greene spotted it in the 1960s, declared it ugly and complained about a cult of the writer.

The Floridita is heaving and I have to squeeze through a queue waiting to snap a photo with 'Papa' Hemingway cast in bronze. A band is crammed into a small gap beside the entrance and a singer in a leopard-print suit is performing *son* music. I eventually find a free stool between a couple of North American girls and some Colombians. Other tourists behind me sit nursing glasses of six-CUC alcoholic slush and nibbling slices of fried plantain coated in oil and garlic. The sweet, moreish cocktails are produced on an industrial scale by barmen in smart red ties and matching aprons who barely pause in their crushing and blending. A man brings plastic bucket-loads of ice from a basement and the bar staff scoop lemon syrup from a huge vat. In a far corner, chin in hand, a woman stares out at the crowd from a stall stacked with souvenirs that no one seems interested in.

In Greene's day the Floridita was not only the haunt of tourists. A 1940s travel book described it as a 'focal point for Cuban men-about-town' and a clearing-house for all the news and gossip. For Greene, that made it the ideal spot for eavesdropping and inspiration. In November 1957 he may have picked up locals'

thoughts on the mounting political unrest in Cuba and heard expat chatter on their golf and tennis tournaments. He possibly caught the buzz over the latest Soviet triumph dominating the headlines: the USSR had just put Laika the dog into space leaving the US scrambling to play cosmic catch-up. Closer to home, Havana society life that month included a *guajiro* party at the British Rovers Club to which well-to-do guests had been encouraged to come dressed as local peasants. One couple duly arrived on foot 'leading their chickens'. Sipping my drink, I check my notes from Greene's 1957 journal. Unlike Hemingway, who liked to hold court, the English writer preferred to observe: one friend described him as having the 'eyes of a fencer'. On 8 November Greene noted that the lower salon was full of loud Americans. He also remarked on a 'mature whore' at the bar with protruding buttocks. Over his rich food, Greene pondered the relationship between a wealthy American and his younger wife dining unhappily alongside him. Ignoring the elaborate menu, the man was insisting on ordering Welsh rarebit.

That first day Greene ordered stuffed crayfish followed by coconut ice cream served in the shell. Later that week he would enjoy the crayfish prepared au gratin with white truffles, asparagus and peas. He rated the restaurant as one of the best in the world, but it's a struggle today to imagine the Floridita as a culinary mecca. A barman tells me the restaurant was always located on the raised dais at the back so I duck up there past some heavy maroon curtains to flick through the plastic-covered menu. The diners are all tourists, most of them bussed in on organised tours. The prices suggest the restaurant is at the top end of state-run fare, with a platter of shrimp, lobster and fish in white sauce for twenty-five CUC. It is named, of course, after Hemingway.

Back at the bar an optimistic customer wonders if there's any Wi-Fi. The barman smiles and rolls his eyes heavenwards as he crushes yet more daiquiri ice. An ageing hippy gestures that his cocktail is too weak, and he and a delighted friend promptly get a free top-up with big glugs of rum. The girls from the US slide off their stools leaving a hefty tip while a Spaniard who'd engaged the barman in a long chat about Havana life leaves nothing. No wonder many Cubans are keen for the Americans to return.

On the wall by the door I spot a framed 1953 article from *Esquire* magazine declaring the Floridita among the world's top drinking spots, up there with the London Savoy. The article declared it a 'truly honest bar' where 'man's spirit may be elevated by conversation and companionship, not enticed into betrayal by his baser instincts.' The author can't have spotted the prostitutes. There are no sex workers in sight at the Floridita any more, big-buttocked like the one Greene noted, or otherwise. The revolution made it a mission to stamp out the ancient trade, though it has of course resurfaced. The whiff of white truffles, on the other hand, was fully eliminated.

4

CONSUMPTION ANXIETY

Sunshine aside, life in Havana sometimes took me back to my days in post-Soviet Russia. Back then I never left home without an *avoska*, a 'just-in-case' shopping bag, stuffed into my pocket. It was there on the off-chance that some scarce food item miraculously appeared in a store, or I passed a black-market trader with a crate of Pepsi or some bananas. Twenty years later in Cuba the shops were nowhere near as bare as in early-1990s Moscow, but the selection was random, unpredictable and uninspiring.

There was a large, low-rise supermarket at the end of Calle 70 which initially looked promising. Inside, a combination of communist central planning and the US trade embargo meant that the shelves were either half-empty or stacked with a single item. One month, adult incontinence pads filled a whole aisle while the most basic items like toilet paper would vanish for weeks. Another time milk was *perdida*, lost as the Cubans say, but the shop's pasta section displayed what looked like the world's largest collection of Pringles. The fish counter which I'd once imagined packed with fresh Caribbean delights actually displayed a mini stack of canned tuna. But it was at Havana's supposedly finest supermarket that I spotted my personal favourite: cans of partridge in brine at a princely twenty dollars apiece. That display didn't shrink at all in three years. Either one of Cuba's central planners had peculiar taste or they'd ticked the wrong order box.

There was, by contrast, a brisk street trade in items knocked off from state restaurants, shops and even nightclubs. A position in a hotel kitchen or a warehouse was highly coveted and many Cubans would supplement their official salaries by pilfering and selling whatever they could. The range of items was extraordinary, from the fizzy wine of the world-famous Tropicana cabaret to catering-size cans of fruit and bags of lobster, defrosting rapidly. Given that the state could no longer afford to pay a living wage and the shops offered so little worth buying, the shadow trade was widespread.

The island's foreign residents had developed their own alternative shopping system. Anyone leaving Cuba would circulate a list of items for sale: a departing Dutch ambassador offered his massage table, others sold cheese and spices well past their sell-by date and one list included an open box of tampons. Everything was always snapped up. Through this system was how we learned that a certain honorary consul was selling a futon. As we had family and friends lining up to visit, and no spare bed, we made our way over to his house in Havana's most luxurious suburb. It was a wasted ride. Anywhere else we'd have been paid to dispose of what we were presented with, but in Cuba's alternative economic reality the diplomat wanted $150. We made our excuses and left, only to spend weeks searching for an alternative. We wound up with a mattress on the floor at double the price of the honorary consul's futon.

The vagaries of Havana shopping turned all overseas trips into goods runs for foreigners and Cubans alike. Anyone who could travel would return to the island laden not only with food and clothes but electronics and vehicle parts. Visitors to Cuba would come heavily loaded. Our first friend arrived on holiday with an extra case full of the items I'd requested, everything from saucepans to garam masala and paracetamol.

The lack of goods is not something tourists necessarily notice with their all-inclusive buffets and gift shops stacked with fine local coffee, cigars and rum. More intrepid travellers who bus-hop around the island often see Cuba as a blessed break from consumerism, a rare space still largely free from adverts and neon lights and with no elbowing people out of the way down the high street. That is true enough until you need something.

One month the washing machine in our flat broke down. It was not the greatest hardship but when I called the state rental agency looking for a repairman I got a disarming chuckle instead. 'I could send someone to take a look, but there's no point,' a man called Carlos informed me down the line. 'We've got no spare parts.' I was slightly disappointed that Carlos wasn't more resourceful given Cubans' much vaunted ingenuity, an ability to perform repairs with whatever's at hand. But it seemed no Soviet Lada part was going to resuscitate my washing machine like it might a broken-down old Chevy.

For a while I joined the ranks of Havana's hand-washers, grateful at least that I wasn't washing and pegging out disposable nappies like my neighbour. Cubans are fanatically clean, smelling of soap however sticky the climate, but scrubbing to ensure several changes of clothes each day is a time-sucking drudge. One Cuban friend would take his shirts round the back of a hotel where staff ran a washing and pressing service on the side. Eventually I discovered a launderette that was a bit pricier but above board, and gave up asking when my own machine might be fixed. *No es facil* was the best the woman at the state agency could manage as she took my monthly rent cheque.

A self-employed repairman might well have been more inventive. By my time in Cuba the government was actively encouraging state workers to set up shop on their own, though 'private' and 'entrepreneur' were words it never uttered. The new business owners were labelled *cuentapropistas*, those working 'on their own account'. While Fidel had only permitted private enterprise under sufferance, Raul recognised that private trade was an irreversible fact of life, with people engaged in all sorts of shadow practices just to get by. His reforms were meant to bring that economic activity above ground and increase the tax revenue available to fund Cuba's hard-pressed system of free healthcare and education for all.

Many of the new start-ups were fuelled by cash from Cubans abroad. While George Bush was president, Cuban-Americans – these were first- or second-generation emigres – had been limited to sending $1,200 a year back to family members in Cuba and could only travel to the island once every three years. But Obama first reduced and then lifted those restrictions in 2009, prompting a huge surge in remittances. As Cuba's own government began opening up the island's economy, the money was used less for food and basic necessities and more to renovate houses to rent or invest in small businesses.

It was with that entrepreneurial spirit gripping the island that Jorge Pena decided to give up his safe but low-paid job at Havana airport and build a 3D cinema. We met in July 2013 as Cuba was marking sixty years since the storming of the Moncada military barracks, the assault in Santiago regarded as the first act of the revolution. I was profiling a number of Cubans to illustrate how life had changed and Jorge seemed a good example of the island's new breed of businessmen. He'd created the mini cinema in the garage of his family's large home in Vedado, the area described in *Our Man in Havana* as the city's 'white rich suburb'. Racially mixed since the revolution, some in Vedado had been getting noticeably richer again thanks in no small part to the increase in family remittances. 'We're trying to feed this craving for business that we've always had,' Jorge told me between showings at the cinema. It struck me as a curious expression given that he'd been born and brought up under communism, but Jorge told me he'd always wanted to 'do something' with his life.

It took five months to scrape together the initial cash. Helped by relatives overseas, Jorge bought the giant plasma screen in Mexico as well as the 3D glasses. He painted part of his garage black, installed comfy chairs for the audience and added a bar. He named the place El Pirata, gave his staff eye patches, breeches and bandanas and placed ceramic pirates on the lawn. Jorge then draped the fence with giant posters advertising children's films.

After just a few weeks in business, he was hugely enthusiastic about Raul's reforms. 'People here like things that are new and for Cubans everything is new!' he explained, as his mini cinema filled up with children for an after-school screening of *Shrek*. He charged three CUC to get in, the equivalent of about three

dollars, which included a drink. The very fact so many could afford that was a sign that some Cubans were earning significantly more than the average state salary. As we spoke, Jorge referred to his customers, mostly *cuentapropistas* themselves, as middle class. He then checked himself as he remembered that Cuban society is officially classless and I was filming him.

Being his own boss was a big change and Jorge admitted to trouble sleeping at night. But he had grand plans. 'There's only room for sixteen people here, so I'd like to have a bigger place and not just one but two or three!' Jorge said. Then he checked himself again, remembering that running a chain of cinemas, like a chain of restaurants, was banned to prevent new business-people getting too rich. Still, Jorge was sure there was no going back now that the pent-up ambitions of his generation had been unleashed. 'I see the changes here as very positive because they are giving people the chance to progress,' Jorge told me in the careful language Cubans often use when being interviewed. 'You can see that more changes are coming, and that's very important.'

I left Jorge feeling that his story had captured the moment. Cubans were beginning to explore all sorts of new possibilities after decades of tight state controls and seemed more hopeful for the future. For a while I saw more and more cinemas like El Pirata pop up in houses everywhere from the smart streets of Miramar to run-down Central Havana. But the optimistic mood was short-lived. First, government officials started talking about the 'banality' and 'frivolity' of what was being shown on the privately run screens, complaining that films were being chosen for profit rather than the cultural enrichment of their audience. Then, in November 2013, four months after Jorge Pena opened El Pirata, all home-based cinemas were ordered to close with immediate effect. The government maintained that it was not banning the businesses since they'd never been explicitly permitted in the first place. The screens had operated under licences for children's entertainment and those papers were now deemed invalid. Unmoved by complaints that the cinemas had cost a small fortune to set up, the government warned that anyone tempted to resist closure would face 'decisive action'.

The shutdown came soon after some twenty thousand thriving, independent clothes stalls had been ordered to close and it raised serious questions about the government's commitment to reform. Officials declared that the stalls were violating permits issued to sell handmade clothes, not items hand-carried into the country. But the suspicion was that the private sellers had been luring customers away from Cuba's drab and expensive state-run stores. Given until the end of the year to sell off their stock, the traders slipped back onto the black market. Cuba's state-run clothes stores remained uninviting and unpopular.

After pushing hard to get someone from the Labour Ministry to discuss the clampdown, I was shocked to learn that an interview had been approved. 'Miracle of miracles!' I declared in an email to a radio editor in London, but I celebrated too soon. Half an hour before our appointment I got word that the man from the ministry had been rushed to hospital and we were never allocated a replacement. Instead, a stern government statement informed the nation of the changes. 'This is in no way about taking a step backwards, quite the opposite,' it read. The statement pointed out that some 440,000 *cuentapropista* licences had been issued by then and vowed that Cuba's economic reforms would go on. But the government stressed that the process was only possible 'in an atmosphere of order and discipline'. I thought of those words the next time I passed El Pirata in Vedado. The cheeky ceramic pirates had vanished and the neon light over Jorge's garage turned cinema door had stopped flashing for good.

* * *

In his 1953 guide to Havana, W. Adolphe Roberts declared that few places could equal the city for 'agreeable restaurants'. But whatever the achievements of Cuba's socialist revolution, culinary excitement was not among them. When we told people we were moving to Havana, those who'd been there on holiday could enthuse about most things except the food. The rise of the *paladares* would gradually change that, as some of the restrictions on operating the house-restaurants were relaxed as part of Raul's reforms.

Getting clearance to film in state-run enterprises was a pain but *cuentapropistas* could decide for themselves whether to meet me. Many were nervous about risking their licence if they spoke out of turn, but others I met, like British-Sri Lankan Cedric Fernando, were happy to chat. With his Cuban wife, Oyaky, he'd launched Cuba's first curry house in 2012 and called it Bollywood. The *paladar* took over the couple's home and their lives.

Cedric's tour of Bollywood began in the family dining room which now housed the restaurant's deep freeze, a coffee machine and the accountant whose papers occupied most of the dining table. The living room and small front terrace had both been set with tables and the tiny kitchen was now catering for an entire restaurant. I watched through a serving hatch as a young man fried lobster masala on a two-ring stove. Cedric had around ten staff altogether, young Cubans with degrees and excellent English who found they could earn considerably more waiting tables than in state-sector jobs requiring a high level of qualifications.

Drawing customers to Bollywood was a challenge. Ordinary Cubans were not allowed the Internet in their homes and Fidel had banned advertising. So with no billboards, online ads or TV and radio spots Cedric had rediscovered the humble SMS. He paid a company overseas around £10 to text special offers to a thousand numbers at a time. Another method produced one of the stranger sights of Havana as Cedric dispatched a Cuban employee dressed in a traditional Indian outfit to distribute flyers. Sweating in his turban, the man would hang around hotel and supermarket car parks until he was chased away by security. Cedric did his own bit for publicity, too. Every time he flew in from London he'd walk the aisles of the plane handing out adverts and was delighted one night when the whole Virgin flight crew showed up for dinner.

Like El Pirata, the curry house was in Vedado, but tucked away in a corner that was harder to find. The man in a turban was posted at the gate to guide cars in, though he'd whip off the outfit and disappear at the earliest possible opportunity. Cedric tried everything he could think of to boost business, from generous helpings of free rum to hiring Cuban girls to belly dance on the tiny terrace, though we journalists didn't need persuading to return. The owner told me a senior revolutionary in his eighties had once dropped by and tried a samosa. Colombian government officials were also regular visitors during their drawn-out peace talks in Havana with insurgents from the Marxist Farc.

Slowly, word of the curry house spread and tourists began turning up with a *Lonely Planet* tucked under their arm. But not everyone made it. Cedric discovered that many *paladares* operated a double-menu system, offering a 'hard' copy with higher prices to foreigners and a 'soft' one to locals. Restaurant owners would pay taxi drivers a fixed sum for every customer they brought in and then claw back the cash on the hard menu. It was a game Cedric would not play. As a result, customers told him that taxis at their hotels would refuse to take them to Bollywood, claiming it had closed.

As his chef flipped the spicy lobster, flames blazing, Cedric pulled open a cupboard to show me another headache. Inside were big pots of bay leaves, chilli and turmeric, none of which featured on the central planner's list of food imports. Like all *paladar* owners I met, Cedric had one major complaint: with no wholesale markets, the restaurants had to buy what limited ingredients were available in state shops at retail prices. They then faced spot checks by inspectors who would search for anything bought on the black market without a receipt and impose heavy fines.

Cedric found a way to 'resolve' his supply problem like any local. 'We ask anyone who comes from England to bring things,' he told me, though he described hand-carrying poppadums, lentils and rice as a nightmare and admitted to relying heavily on old friends at one of the embassies. As we talked, Oyaky drifted in and out with a baby in her arms and a young child trailing close behind. Despite the difficulties, Cedric had plans to develop a roof garden and move the restaurant tables up there to reclaim the living room for the family. 'It's a great success,' he told me, surveying his business with a beaming smile. 'There's no other spicy food restaurant in Havana. It's hard work, but we're on to a small winner!'

* * *

As Cuba's burgeoning *paladar* scene and other ventures needed produce, there was a surge in a separate business to supply them from abroad: the *mulas*. One afternoon I arranged to meet one of those human mules in a local park to find out how it worked. A chunky middle-aged man in a baseball cap, 'Eduardo' didn't want to describe the black-market business on camera but he agreed to give a radio interview if I changed his name. He told me he'd started off by bringing over small parcels for individuals, mostly gifts from relatives in Miami, but the boom in small businesses meant that most of his clients were now *cuentapropistas*.

Eduardo was a Cuban-American and able to travel to Havana freely from the US on his Cuban passport. He worked for an agency that booked him onto a charter flight every fortnight, part of a network of couriers importing everything from food to clothing into Cuba. They were filling in the major gaps in state supply. High-tech goods like mobile phones and laptops were big business. There was also a growing call for cash-mules as other Cuban-Americans sent funds to their relatives for investment. 'There's demand for everything,' Eduardo said, as we talked while sitting on a giant fallen tree trunk in a park near my house. After decades of communism he told me that Cubans had consumption anxiety. The trade Eduardo was engaged in was illicit. Commercial imports to Cuba were not permitted under communist rules and the US embargo restricted official exports to the island. Busting both policies, the mules' deliveries had become the lifeblood of Cuba's expanding private sector. It was how the manicurist got her nail polish, the phone repairman found spare parts, and those renting out flats got new taps, toilet bowls and towels.

'I pay $130 towards my ticket and the agency arranges it all,' Eduardo explained. The resumption of commercial flights to and from the US was still some way off at the time, and the short charter flight to Cuba cost over $500. 'I carry twenty kilos of luggage for the agency and have other clients who request things I can bring in my hand-luggage,' Eduardo said. The process of placing orders was just as unorthodox. As most customers had little or no access to the Internet, they would view the shopping catalogue in Cuba's ingenious offline alternative. The weekly *paquete* was a booming business, produced by those who could get online and download everything from popular TV series to glossy magazines, news and shopping sites. All the material was then bundled into 'packets' for resale on the street. Cubans would bring a flash drive and purchase the offline content by the giga-byte, including the catalogue of goods available to order from the human mule service. For just one CUC you could get hours' worth of the latest TV shows and films from Miami.

When it came to food, couriers like Eduardo were making the most of a loophole in customs regulations. In 2008, after a series of devastating hurricanes, passengers had been permitted to bring unlimited amounts of food into Cuba duty-free. It was a temporary measure intended to allow families to receive help from relatives abroad, but it was soon being exploited by those made wily by a lifetime of shortages and restrictions. When we met, Eduardo's business was about to be squeezed as new rules would require all food to be weighed and taxed at Customs like everything else. The mules were planning to abandon heavier items from their parcels for lack of profit, sending the *paladar* owners who relied on them into a panic.

As the deadline for the new rules approached, I headed to Havana airport to see what was happening. At Terminal 2 I found a last-minute scramble as Cubans rushed to get as much as possible onto the island. Charter companies had doubled the number of flights from Miami and laid on separate planes for the excess luggage alone, and it was chaos. An airline official told me that most of the additional baggage was food.

'We don't agree with this move,' a woman called Delia complained when I asked about the new rules. She was struggling to wheel an airport trolley into the car park, piled high with parcels. All around, hordes of people were lugging similarly big bundles, clearly marked as food. 'Maybe some people are doing business this way, but we're just bringing food for our families,' Delia told me. 'With all their problems, it's not easy. And these parcels were a big help.'

At moments like these, Cuba's reform process felt like it was moving the country one step forwards, then scuttling back. It made the existence of the island's new business owners highly precarious. Even so, the email from Bollywood came out of the blue. I was away in Ukraine reporting on the build-up to war when a message from Cuba popped up in my inbox. It was headed 'Our Man in Havana is leaving'. For all his early optimism, Cedric admitted that his *paladar* had become more trouble than it was worth: he was struggling to get ingredients, staff had been stealing his limited stock, and even guaranteeing basics for the business was a battle. For six weeks the restaurant had been using 'nicely cut' toilet roll as serviettes. But the final nail in

Bollywood's coffin had been the tax. The authorities had made an assessment of the restaurant's likely turnover based on its busiest night and sent Cedric what he judged to be an astronomical bill.

Maybe Bollywood's attempt to sell spicy food was always doomed in Cuba, where most locals find even black pepper too *picante*. The obscure location was probably a bigger factor. A new Indian restaurant would open in the heart of tourist Havana a few years later, a move Cedric had talked of but never made. In the end, though, it was the day-to-day grind of doing business in Cuba that defeated him. In March 2014 Cedric and his family took off for the UK and Havana's first ever curry house closed its doors for good.

5

CONNECTING CUBA

In February 2013 I signed up for another organised press trip out of Havana, this time to Cienfuegos on Cuba's southern coast. I decided to go along despite my earlier frustrations in Santiago because the itinerary promised a visit to an oil refinery co-funded by Cuba's socialist ally, Venezuela. Its president Hugo Chavez was then in a Havana hospital dying of cancer – though no one was admitting it yet – and with Cuba so dependent on Venezuelan oil I figured the refinery was worth a look. It was also another chance to get close to senior Party officials.

The start of the trip didn't bode well. After a three-hour coach journey we were ushered into the provincial Communist Party headquarters for a lecture on the 'development of the province'. The designated official read the statistics directly from the screen, unembellished. Among the highlights we learned the number of home phone lines in the province (few, but growing) and how much concrete was produced per capita (a figure I failed to jot down). Cienfuegos itself is beautiful, an early-nineteenth-century city that prospered on the back of a sugar boom. We got a look inside

the main theatre which had been painstakingly restored thanks to tourist cash and later, wandering the main boulevard, passed a bronze statue of the singer Benny More, the city's most famous son, with his trademark stick and wide-brimmed hat. This time, though, I noticed that our official itinerary was far less focused on city attractions. 'They're not tourists,' CPI officials from Havana chided our local guides several times.

At the oil refinery senior officials were open to questioning and we stopped off at an estate formed of a hundred or so *petro casas* donated by Venezuela, prefab buildings made of plastic for refinery workers and other families in need. There was a model hospital and farm to tour, but in a diversion from the usual themes we were taken to an exhibition of satirical cartoons. In one a man with his mouth screwed shut faced three outstretched hands holding microphones. A sign announced that the artists were addressing issues such as 'the official media discourse, eternal bureaucracy and the limited or zero access to cyberspace'.

Internet access was something we foreign journalists wanted to address too. The suspicion was that the government was stalling on unleashing the Internet to maintain its tight control over information. It would occasionally deny that, with talk of infrastructure problems or lack of cash, but the days of decent connectivity seemed to get no nearer. In Cienfuegos we planned to raise the issue again.

The first night brought an impressive show at the local mini Tropicana, but the second promised to be more useful than fun as the local Party bosses joined us for dinner. Over meat, rice and cabbage, we learned that regional politicians were in the midst of being 'reprogrammed' by the Party. They were all being sent on three-month courses at university for training in the reforms introduced by Raul Castro, the *Lineamientos*. The Party bosses, both women, told us the aim was to change official mentalities. When I asked the Party Secretary for her thoughts on the post-Castro future, she was confident. 'We survived until now and we'll go on surviving,' she told me, the glint of commitment in her eyes. Although well into her forties, the former teacher described herself as part of the young generation of revolutionaries intent on ensuring that the Castros' system endured.

After a creamy pudding and more earnest chat we were called through into the bar where the hotel's own cabaret was in full flow. There we were confronted by young dancers in frilly nylon trousers tossing female partners through the air with a Spanish version of 'I Will Survive' pumping through loudspeakers. A crowd of sun-frazzled tourists had gathered to watch, many of them Canadian retirees who spent several months each winter living all-inclusive at the fairly basic hotel. I'd stumbled on the Canadian equivalent of the Costa del Sol.

Someone had reserved a row of metal chairs at the front of the bar for our group and I found myself sitting next to the Communist Party's Ideology Chief for the province. He was responsible, he told me, for keeping people 'on the right path'. In one pause between extravagant dance routines on stage we discussed whether all critics of the government could possibly be mercenaries, as Cuba claimed. The Cienfuegos Ideology Chief was sure they could. The booming music and the official's reticence made conversation challenging but I kept trying, eventually moving on to ask about the Internet. The Party man assured me that the restrictions did not mean Cuba was afraid of getting connected. 'Information gets in anyway, and anyone with a flash drive can spread it round in half an hour,' he pointed out, referring to the Cuban *paquete*. The sale of Internet downloads was big business by then. Getting everyone properly online, the Ideology Chief assured me, was just a matter of time and money.

But it was already two years since a fibre-optic cable had been laid to Cuba from Venezuela. When the line arrived on the island in February 2011, officials had hailed it as a breach in the US embargo. They'd always pinned blame for the lack of Internet access on the US, arguing that its trade restrictions had prevented Cuba from hooking up to other cables. But after initial celebration, all talk of the new line had stopped. There were whispers of a corruption scandal, but the loudest rumours suggested a split within the Party over the wisdom of connecting Cubans to the outside world.

* * *

Email to programme editor, 19 January 2012

Can't believe how hard it is to file for TV from here. I'm at the mercy of the worst internet connection in the world. I will have torn all my hair out soon.

Cuba claims to have its citizens' welfare well covered. Public healthcare, free schooling and free housing are still guaranteed, though increasingly hard to fund and fraying around the edges. But communism has never succeeded in quelling the consumer instinct. Soviet children grew up dreaming of prohibited Levi's jeans and American chewing gum, and Cubans were now entering their teens wanting a smartphone hooked up to the Internet. Access is considered a basic requirement of life in many places, even a human right, but Cuba has been very slow to provide it.

When I first moved to Havana in 2011 the island was largely living offline. Government statistics from two years earlier suggested that just fourteen in every one hundred Cubans were connected. Of those, only a small fraction would have had access at home. The Internet was delivered to Cuba via an expensive satellite link-up and at that point was only publicly available in hotels. The service was costly – up to eight CUC an hour – slow and liable to collapse. Some days I could eat through three hour-long cards just sending one TV report back to London. I'd sit in the lobby with the Laurel and Hardy pictures near my flat and watch the feed stutter repeatedly and fail. As a foreign correspondent, I was entitled to Internet access in my flat but initially that meant a next-to-useless connection via a screeching dial-up modem. I could make coffee in the time it took to open an attachment and the cost was exorbitant. Sending TV reports from home was impossible.

For Cubans, though, getting online was far more complicated. One day I was working in a small central Cuban town and needed to send a photograph back to London urgently. My producer asked around until he found the one local journalist who was allocated a few hours online each month. She agreed to let me use an ancient desktop computer in her living room where I tried to make my photo as small as possible. The connection dropped out so many times I had a horrible feeling I used up her entire allowance.

Like everything in Cuba, wherever there's a restriction there's a way. Just as I could see illegal satellite dishes hidden behind water tanks on roofs bringing uncensored TV from Miami, I discovered that Cuba had an equally thriving under-ground Internet service. At its most basic, people who were permitted a certain number of hours' access by the state would sell part of that ration to others *por la izquierda*, on the left, as Cubans describe any black-market transaction. I met one woman who bought ten hours' access a month that way for twenty CUC. Anorys, as I'll call her, had the computer keyboard rigged up to a TV in her living room. She would perch in front of it on a little stool and dial up using a stranger's account name and password. The day I visited it had been raining and the connection was shakier than usual, but even on a good day Anorys told me she didn't have time to browse much beyond email. She would copy the content of any message she got onto her desktop to write her replies offline before logging back on to send them.

The state phone company had recently warned those with

authorised Internet accounts that they would be held responsible for any black-market users on their line, so Anorys was worried about losing her connection. She was renting a room to tourists and the online bookings went to her brother abroad who then passed on the details via email. She was doing up another room to rent as well and had been sourcing furniture on a website called *Revolico*. The shopping site was blocked by the government but Cubans who could get online accessed it via a proxy. As Internet payments were impossible, items were posted along with a phone number and buyers completed their transactions via an old-fashioned phone call.

As Anorys and I chatted, her teenage daughter wandered in and I asked if her mum ever let her on the Internet. The teenager told me she could get online at school and I was surprised, asking if they had a computer club. The girl laughed. She and her friends were paying one CUC a month to someone who lived near the school and left his Wi-Fi connection open for them to connect.

An older couple I knew were also buying a black-market Internet service and, like Anorys, feared their connection would soon be severed. The couple had children overseas and that halting, limited line had become their prime way of keeping in touch. Before that they'd gone thirty years on the waiting list for a fixed phone line. This highly educated pair told me they were fed up with feeling like 'fifth-class citizens' in their own country. 'It's all about information,' the woman burst out one day. 'They just don't want us to have it.'

* * *

Whenever we journalists could challenge government officials, which was not often, they insisted that the only restrictions to getting Cuba online were physical or financial. But the popular uprisings that began sweeping the Arab world in late 2010 had also made the government nervous. Speaking at a revolution anniversary event in 2012, Raul Castro vowed that events in Cuba would not follow those of Libya or Syria where he said 'foreign forces' were fomenting unrest.

The role of social media in the Arab Spring protests partly explains the hard line the government took against independent bloggers like Yoani Sanchez, whose critical chronicles of daily life on the island became famous abroad, won prizes and were translated into multiple languages. Her blog, *Generacion Y*, was blocked in Cuba and her activity on Twitter limited by the difficulty of getting online. Even so, state TV programmes periodically attacked Yoani as an enemy agent and a traitor, and the government deployed a whole army of its own bloggers to troll her. The official connections of those users were clear not only from their insults but from their otherwise impossibly good 24-hour access to the Internet.

One soaking wet June morning, I went along to a meeting I knew Yoani would be attending. The event was called 'Click' and the organisers insisted their focus was technological not ideological, an attempt to educate people on the use of social networks. But government trolls and state media had been furiously slamming the gathering as subversive, tweeting photographs of participants and claiming they were agents of the United States. It was a 'meeting place for counter-revolutionaries conspicuous for their mediocrity', the news website *Cubadebate* raged.

The venue was the garden of another young activist not far from my own flat. In Havana, all known dissidents have surveillance cameras installed outside their homes so that the authorities know exactly who goes in and out. Undoubtedly a number of those attending the gathering of bloggers were undercover agents. In Cuba you're never quite sure who you can trust. Inside, I found around forty people squeezed into an outhouse beside a half-empty swimming pool. Perched on plastic chairs, looking more geeky than dangerous, they were sharing online experiences and practical tips.

The star attraction Yoani Sanchez was petite with an old-fashioned taste in clothes and a thick dark plait that dangled below her waist. When I caught her in a break, she insisted that the Cuban government was afraid of the Internet. 'It's a question of political will,' she said. 'They don't want us to find out what's going on inside and outside the country.' According to Yoani, the closed Cuban system would prove very fragile as soon as the 'light of information' was shone on it. 'The Arab Spring showed that whenever there are young people with a phone in their hand, they can change the world.' But at that point, young Cubans' phones were 'dumb'. Without Internet access the small number of active dissidents were reduced to tweeting via SMS. Yoani called it blind tweeting as there was no way to reply or interact, and the audience on the island for such messages was limited.

It was around this time that the US government agency USAID created an offline social network using text messages. Documents obtained by the American AP news agency revealed that the network was known as Zunzuneo and was intended as a vehicle for subversion. According to the AP, the plan was to attract young users with harmless messages about sport and culture and then get political, pushing them towards dissent. The ultimate aim was to provoke a 'Cuban Spring'. The White House confirmed the creation of Zunzuneo but insisted that it was only ever intended to help the 'free flow of information' on the island. The service ended abruptly in 2012 without the forty thousand subscribers ever being aware of its origin.

* * *

As access to the Internet in hotels and via the black market grew during my posting in Havana, Cubans were starting to get online in increasing numbers. The government's monopoly on information had been broken. But without better access a whole generation was at risk of being left behind by the rest of the world. In 2013, two years after the fibre-optic cable arrived from Venezuela, the state telecoms firm finally announced that it had begun testing its capacity. Etecsa warned that rollout would be gradual: only a quarter of homes in Cuba had a phone line so the infrastructure needed investment. But that summer the firm took the first step and opened dozens of 'Internet navigation' centres. The usual pages were blocked: Yoani Sanchez's blog, anti-Castro sites in the US and gambling. The BBC and other news pages opened freely for anyone who cared to look. The real restriction was the price: at 4.50 CUC per hour the service was too expensive for most. There were also fewer than five hundred terminals across the whole island.

The next stage came in March 2014 when Etecsa announced that customers could sign up for email on their mobile phones.

The service was a home-grown Cuban account known as *nauta*, not Internet access, but the offer was cheap and popular. A couple of weeks after it was introduced I found a queue several bodies thick outside the telecoms company office in Old Havana. A couple at the front told me they'd been waiting seven hours to sign up.

Etecsa had seriously underestimated demand and didn't have enough staff trained to install the email software on people's phones. Everyone I spoke to in the queue told me they had relatives overseas they wanted to communicate with. When I wondered whether they were happy just getting email or wanted full Internet access, someone snorted in response. 'It's like asking a child if he wants milk. You don't ask that kind of question. You just give it.'

Others began chipping in. 'It sounds good to the outside world,' a phone repairer told me. 'They say, "Look, Cubans have Internet access!" But we're far from it. The cost for one hour is a third of a state salary for a month.' Despite the tiny official salaries, I noted that everyone around me had a smartphone which suggested that perhaps not all Cubans were struggling on $20 a month. That's true, I was told, though many of the phones were probably gifts from abroad and most of their functions were useless without a connection to the Internet.

A 21-year-old who said his name was Alejandro told me that his generation was desperate to get connected. He was a dentistry student and could only access Cuban intranet pages at university. His wife was in Spain and he was spending a fortune he didn't have to talk to her on email, so he was trying to sign up for the new *nauta* service to cut costs. A couple of days later I collected

Alejandro from his medical school as he'd agreed to a TV interview. As we drove he wondered whether talking to me on camera would cause him problems. I didn't think so and he seemed relaxed enough, so he changed out of his dentist's coat and we headed for a local cafe to set up the camera beside the bougainvillea.

The interview was a disaster from the off. 'Why did you want to get email on your phone?' I began by asking as the cameraman filmed, but Alejandro would no longer meet my eye. Switching tack completely from our previous talk, he told me that he didn't want or need the Internet. Then he jumped up and began pulling off the mic and borrowed T-shirt. 'I can't do this, I'm sorry.' Seeing the once-chatty young student panic, I was saddened. The last thing I wanted was to make trouble for him and I didn't believe there'd be repercussions. Alejandro clearly wasn't so sure. As soon as the microphone was safely removed, he disappeared.

One thing Alejandro had told me, though, was that some Cubans were managing to get online for free. There were a number of open Wi-Fi spots around town where users had unwittingly left networks unprotected. The student told me one of them was close to Havana's main business centre and as I rounded the corner there I saw a huddle of people on phones and laptops in the street. There were problems connecting that afternoon, but a man told me he'd been using the 'guerrilla' Wi-Fi at the same spot for weeks, surfing the Web at no cost and with no censorship.

*   *   *

In late 2016 I turn on the television in my Havana hotel room and the familiar old-fashioned signature tune of *Mesa Redonda* blares out at me. It's Cuba's take on a round-table discussion where all the guests espouse the exact same view. That day's topic is the fortieth anniversary of a terrorist attack which the government blames on the CIA. Another day I catch the news headlines: an ageing Party boss touring a coffee plantation, Latin American students railing against the US trade embargo, and a Foreign Ministry official castigating Barack Obama for failing to overturn the 'blockade'. A year after Cuba officially reconciled with the US, state TV sounds just as it did when I lived here. Just as it has for decades.

Out on the streets I see that things have been moving faster and further. Young Cubans don't watch those TV programmes. A friend's 14-year-old describes the latest black market in passwords to crack hotel Wi-Fi networks. Around town I see a new piece of subversive street art: an image of Jose Marti, the hero of Cuba's nineteenth-century fight for independence from Spain, stencilled onto walls wearing a T-shirt reading 'I "heart" free Wi-Fi'. The biggest change is the authorised Wi-Fi spots. In designated zones around Havana you can now pay to get online by the hour, with accounts that can be topped up by wealthier friends and family abroad. Parks that were once the realm of pensioners doing keep-fit classes and children playing baseball have filled with Cubans of all ages and their phones. Squeezed onto benches, leaning against tree trunks and perched on the kerb, they're all hooked up to the Internet.

Judging by my own friends, Cubans are using their new-found freedom to rent out flats, advertise their *paladares* and keep in touch with family overseas. They're already as obsessed as anyone with posting photos on Facebook, posing on the beach, with

cocktails or at concerts. There has been no major outburst of Internet activism or protest. But it is a technological revolution. A couple of decades late and still a work in progress, the arrival of the Internet marks the end of any lingering isolation for the island. Cuba is now connected.

6

THE SLEEPING FAITH

'Drove to Vedado and ... took photos of the American school where Milly goes', Graham Greene noted in his journal on 11 November 1957, describing the convent school which Wormold's daughter attends in his novel. It's only when I begin hunting that I realise how many churches there still are in Havana. Exhausted from trailing round the grand classical buildings one by one in the sun, I'm eventually directed to San Juan de Letran. Climbing the steps, I see that the church is filled with life-sized statues of the saints, Spanish-style, and shining pews. There are two ornately carved traditional wooden confessionals at the back and tall stained-glass windows above the altar.

San Juan's is also a working monastery. The porter runs through names in his head and tells me that the order currently has a not-so-grand total of eight monks, including two in the central Cuban town of Trinidad. One promptly appears in a flurry of cream robes and with a beaming smile. When I tell Fray Rafael about the old school I'm hunting for, Milly's convent, he doesn't hesitate. 'They were American Dominican Sisters but they all left after the revolution when their property was seized,' he says, identifying the only non-Spanish convent school in Vedado when Greene had visited. The monk gestures to follow him through the cloisters past a huge tree filled with singing birds. In the sacristy, where two young priests are changing their robes for Mass, he makes a call and confirms that the convent presumed to be the one photographed by Greene no longer exists. But he gets an address.

It's already dusk by this time and the air has cooled at last as I walk a few blocks south, hunting for the spot I've jotted down in my notebook. Even in relatively smart Vedado, Cubans are constantly in the street. Porticoed buildings that originally housed one wealthy family are now shared by several who have far less. Only the grandest apartments have air conditioning, so adults sit and gossip on their porches or walls while children run free around them. Music wafts from windows, sometimes a summer pop hit, sometimes salsa. A couple of groups are playing loud games of dominoes. *Hola, linda!* one man calls out to me, trying his luck. *Hola!* I reply cheerfully and he stumbles over a step. 'Careful!' I laugh, and walk on.

As I reach the corner of Quinta y C I see the park Fray Rafael has told me about, a dried-up pond at its centre. Sprawled under a tree nearby is a barefoot man in rags, fast asleep. I can't see anything that could ever have been a convent. My heart sinks. I take photos of nothing much before admitting temporary defeat and then walk on.

*   *   *

It was only back home in Moscow that I managed to get online and trace what appeared to be the model for Milly's convent. 'The address of our school in Vedado was Quinta y D,' Sister

Lucy Vazquez wrote from Florida, where I made contact after numerous Google searches and emails. Fray Rafael had been one street out.

The daughter of a successful Cuban businessman, Lucy Vazquez attended the American Dominican Academy until 1960 and describes her schoolmates as similarly 'upper middle class', at least ninety percent Cuban and all white. They were sent to the Academy by parents who wanted their daughters to learn English and emerge as ladies. The students were bussed to the school each morning from all over the city. 'Each bus had a driver and a chaperone and we were expected to keep silence,' Sister Lucy remembers. Classes were taught in English from the age of twelve and students were banned from speaking Spanish even outside the classroom. 'Most of us resented that,' Lucy recalls, but she admits that the rule served the students well since so many later left Cuba for the US.

In Lucy's childhood most of Havana's private schools were run by religious orders, but she confirmed what Fray Rafael had said: the Dominican Academy was the only convent in Vedado run by Americans. The order was then known as the Dominican Sisters of St Catherine de Ricci and its nuns had three schools in Havana. Aged twelve at the time of Greene's visit, Lucy Vazquez may well have been in class that day. I haven't located the picture he took, so I can't be sure, but Greene would have seen Lucy's schoolmates in smart black skirts and white blouses, hats embroidered with the school initials. The Dominican Academy was just for girls though; in *Our Man in Havana* there are boys in Milly's class, one of whom she sets fire to.

Lucy didn't get to finish her education at the convent. A year after the revolution her parents sent her out of Cuba in what became known as Operation Peter Pan, a covert and controversial programme under which the Catholic Church helped evacuate thousands of children to the US. Their parents believed that the socialist revolution they opposed could not last, and that the painful separation would be temporary. Some never saw their children again and Sister Lucy, like many of the evacuees, has never been back to Cuba.

The next time I visit Havana, in May 2017, I'm armed with the nun's emailed memories. Now I spot her old school immediately, a simple two-storey building with columns along the front creating a long porch. Stone bas-reliefs at a side entrance confirm I'm in the right place: one is an image of the Virgin Mary with Jesus and the other appears to be the school badge. There are big chunks of plaster missing from the low surrounding wall and the arched windows of the old chapel are covered with metal sheets. As I take photos from the pavement to send to Sister Lucy, I see a man watching from the patio.

'Whose head is that?' I ask, to break the ice. I'm pointing at a big bust of a man with a drooping stone moustache that's in a corner of the old school garden. 'That's Maximo Gomez!' he replies, surprised at my ignorance of a national hero, a general in Cuba's nineteenth-century war for independence from Spain. I tell the man I'm curious about what happened to the convent and he lets me in and up to the old chapel door. When my eyes adjust from the bright sun, I realise that the pews have given way to sewing machines and there are seamstresses working on both sides of the chapel, cooled by industrial-sized fans. At the far end a man measures out cloth on the old altar as light streams through the stained glass behind him. Topping the whole scene is the

elaborately painted wooden ceiling of the former chapel, decorated with blue and brown flowers. The convent building was
transferred to the Culture Ministry after the revolution and used
at first for dance studios. It's now home to a variety of state-run
businesses, with a hat-maker inside somewhere, in one of the old
classrooms.

'It breaks my heart to see the dilapidation,' Sister Lucy writes
when I email my photographs. She remembers her school as
beautiful and carefully maintained by the nuns, but the pictures
bring a flood of happy memories too.

Lucy's father owned seven cinemas in Havana over the years
as well as a film company and several properties, putting her
family a social cut above the Wormolds. I remember that it was
Milly's aspirations to be like the other convent girls – to own a
horse and join Havana's country clubs – that had prompted

Wormold, 'a poor non-believing father with a Catholic child', to take up spying on the side.

In the park outside the old convent school a group of young adults with Down's syndrome are having a dance class in the shade of a huge tree. Two men nearby varnish household chairs in the sunshine. Like Greene I watch a while, take my photographs and move on.

* * *

I'd never imagined that a papal visit would be one of my first big stories in communist-run Cuba, but the island's relationship with Catholicism is complex. That much was clear just by glancing out of my office window towards the giant stone statue of Christ towering over the placid bay. Dressed in long robes and with one hand raised to bless the city, the white figure was completed just before the revolution and never removed. Before Benedict XVI arrived it was carefully renovated.

The pope travelled to Cuba in March 2012 as the island marked the 400th anniversary of its patron saint. Cuba's cardinal called it a mission to revive the country's 'sleeping faith', sorely tested by decades of state atheism. But the Church itself occupies a unique position in Cuba. An independent institution that can lay claim to millions of followers, at least nominally, its churches are the only place where a creed other than communism is preached openly to a large audience. It all takes place under close watch. One Havana priest told me he could spot the intelligence agents in his congregation easily because they sat at the back and left after his homily.

Fidel Castro himself was baptised and educated as a Catholic but his would be an atheist revolution. Hundreds of priests fled overseas in its aftermath and others were confined to notorious labour camps. Challenged on that record much later, Fidel could only counter that at least in Cuba 'there was not a single priest executed.' Worship was never banned but the Church was barely tolerated in those years: no practising Catholic could join the Communist Party and those who did continue to worship were black-marking themselves with the authorities.

The situation for believers only began to improve in 1992 when the constitution was changed to define Cuba as a secular rather than atheist state. That gave all religious organisations and faiths more breathing space and paved the way for a historic encounter. In 1998 Fidel invited Pope John Paul II to the island. The Polish pope, who embodied the fight against communism more than anyone, was received warmly, particularly after he denounced the 'ethically unacceptable' US trade embargo. He also spoke of Cuba's 'material and moral poverty' which he blamed on 'limitations to fundamental freedoms'. But officials viewed the visit as a success, proof that the US had failed to isolate Cuba despite decades of pressure.

Ahead of Pope Benedict's visit, though, the government seemed nervous. A full-page *Granma* editorial claimed that anti-Castro forces in Miami were intent on disrupting the event. A headline in bright red ink accused opposition groups abroad of sending money to dissidents along with instructions on what action to take. The aim, *Granma* claimed, was to portray the Cuban people as repressed and abused and pressure the pope to criticise the revolution.

As the visit approached, the Damas de Blanco began calling on the pope to press for more political freedom. A rare opposition group, the Damas formed in 2003 after their male relatives were arrested in a drive against dissent. Many were Christian activists, so after every Sunday Mass the women began marching to demand their release. Now the Damas wanted 'one minute' with Benedict in Havana. 'We want the pope to know that there is opposition here, that there are dissidents,' their leader, Berta Soler, explained to me. 'The repression of human rights activists has increased but the government doesn't want him to see the reality.'

The anniversary of the men's arrests fell a week before the pope's arrival. That morning dozens of the Damas were detained by police as they set off for their usual Sunday march. When those who did make it attempted to move beyond their normal route and head for downtown Havana, police emerged swiftly from the backstreets. 'We sat down on the street, they pushed us around, then they took us by bus to the police station', Magalys Otero Suarez told me when she was eventually released hours later, with a warning not to attend the papal Mass the following week.

In the end Benedict met Fidel during his visit, not the dissidents. But he did have some uncomfortable words for the Cuban government on his plane from Rome. He declared that communism had failed and talked of the need for 'new models' to move towards a society in Cuba which was 'fraternal and just'. The government responded that it would listen to the pope's ideas 'respectfully'. Benedict expanded on those ideas from the moment he stepped off his plane in Santiago, urging Cubans to seek 'authentic freedom'. Watching on a screen from Havana, a local journalist laughed at a Church he said had 'barely evolved in two thousand years' urging change in Cuba. 'There will be no political change in Cuba,' the Economy Minister Marino Murillo repeated emphatically when asked to respond to the pope's words during a rare press conference. 'What we're talking about is updating the Cuban economic model to make our socialism sustainable. That is for the well-being of our people.'

The main open-air Mass in Havana came on the final day of the visit and I arrived on the Plaza de la Revolucion well before dawn for the security checks. A huge Vatican-yellow stage had been installed beneath the towering monument to Jose Marti, the spot where Fidel had once delivered marathon speeches. Facing off across the plaza were two giant icons: the Interior Ministry had a huge Che Guevara on its facade and the national library directly opposite had been draped in an image of Cuba's patron saint.

State employees were given the day off and the square was already busy at 5:30 a.m. By 9 a.m., tens of thousands had gathered, carrying umbrellas to shade themselves from the sun. I've reported from papal Masses elsewhere, surrounded by throngs of joyful Catholics, but while the crowd on the Plaza de la Revolucion was large I didn't feel quite the same energy. Many people left following the sign of peace and the rest were on the move immediately after Communion. A group of boys in tracksuits told me they'd been bussed in from school, but they were neither Catholic nor particularly interested. As the crowd cleared, a mound of Mass sheets near where I was filming remained largely untouched. The Damas de Blanco who'd wanted the pope to hear their protest were nowhere to be seen and their mobile phones were blocked for the duration of his visit.

*　*　*

One Sunday I turned into a quiet street lined with coconut palms on the edge of the suburb of Alamar. In the middle of a row of otherwise identical bungalows was one with a large wooden crucifix fixed to the front. Following the sound of singing, I emerged onto the back patio of the house and into the middle of Mass. The area had been cleared of mango trees and then covered over to create the main body of a church. That morning some two hundred people were squeezed in for the service.

'Religion was never supposed to start here,' Fr Isidro told me later as his parishioners cleared away the wooden benches. Across the bay from the old colonial city of Havana, Alamar looks like a mini USSR-by-the-sea. Built from scratch after the revolution with functional, prefabricated apartment blocks – though painted in very un-Soviet bright colours – it was where Che Guevara's 'New Man' was supposed to emerge. As that man was expected to put his faith in socialism and not God, Alamar was deliberately designed with no churches.

But even in this utopia Fr Isidro said religion was never entirely eliminated. 'A Cuban priest began visiting families and holding meetings in houses and nobody stopped him.' As we talked a woman parishioner wandered over to join us. 'In the old days, if you said you were Catholic at work it was like a sin, so you kept it quiet,' Mayra told me. 'But you had your faith.' The house was now officially registered and allowed to operate freely, but the parish still couldn't get permission for a purpose-built church. Tolerating Catholicism is one thing; encouraging its growth quite another.

The Church's role in social welfare has been increasing, though, and Fr Isidro was keen for me to see that in action.

He drove me across Alamar to a housing block painted a faded shade of pink with a Batman-style black Cadillac parked outside. Up in an apartment, a parishioner called Juan ushered us into his tiny kitchen. All Cubans have a *libreta*, a ration book, which allows them to buy some basic food items each month at heavily subsidised state-run stores. The rations were once substantial and an important supplement to state pensions and salaries. Now that money is impossible to live on and the *libreta* barely stretches a fortnight. So Fr Isidro's parishioners were busy cooking up lunch for twenty hungry pensioners.

'It's not only Catholics we offer food to, it's anyone – believer or not,' Juan explained as his sister stirred a pot of juicy black beans on the stove. 'We choose the most needy.' That day the family were dishing up hot dog sausages and chunks of pork as well as slices of succulent avocado. As they cooked, the small living room filled with men and women chatting and laughing. 'It's like coming to an oasis in a desert!' a lady called Dalia told me between leading the group in bursts of song. 'Everyone arrives here with an extraordinary number of problems. But then the door opens and the jokes start.'

'They say it's important to have *fe*,' Fr Isidro commented, as the group waited for their plastic pots of food. The Spanish word *fe* means 'faith' but the letters also stand for *familia en el extranjero*, family abroad. For those without overseas relatives to send money, Church charity projects are increasingly filling the gaps. 'The government used to be very protective; they didn't like people entering what they saw as their domain,' Fr Isidro explained. 'But they're fine about centres like this now. They know that a lot of people are in need.'

*   *   *

Fr Isidro was baptising at least fourteen babies a week on his makeshift altar, but he knew that most of the families would never set foot in his church again. Many of those seeking baptism were in fact followers of Santeria, the syncretic religion that originated with Africans trafficked to the island as slaves and forced to convert to Catholicism. They conserved their Yoruba faith in private and the two gradually merged. One ritual of Santeria involves being baptised in the Catholic Church.

But at the time of Benedict's visit in 2012, around sixty percent of Cubans described themselves as Catholic. Although only a fraction practised that faith, the Church enjoyed an influence and privilege in Cuba that extended beyond the pulpit. Certainly no one else was allowed the freedom I found behind the heavy doors of Havana's old seminary. There, in lecture halls along sand-coloured stone cloisters once filled with trainee priests, the Catholic Church was giving classes in capitalism. The young rector Fr Yusvany told me the month-long course was in huge demand with state workers looking to make the leap to the private sector. The Church tried to keep its small business course low-profile, wary of provoking the government. For a long time Fr Yusvany wasn't keen on me reporting on it at all, and when he did agree it was on the condition that I came without a camera. One of the organisers described the course as 'weak and defenceless, like a recently born child . . . easy to gobble up'.

Anywhere else such training might sound normal, even dull. But Fidel had shut down all Church schools after the revolution and what I saw in the old seminary, like the social work in Alamar, seemed part of a quiet, careful comeback. 'We believe it's necessary to create an atmosphere where anyone can express their ideas or any ideology and debate that freely,' Fr Yusvany explained, describing an attempt to help shape the new Cuban society as it evolved. 'If you don't create free space, you can't produce anything good.'

One of his graduates, Sandra Suarez, had rented space for her new business in a house close to Havana Cathedral. The owners moved their sofa and TV into a back corridor so that Sandra could display her handmade soaps in their living room. She arranged the little bars in wicker baskets, named the place *Brujas*, Witches, and decorated it with spiderwebs and pointy hats. 'The course was really good for me; they give you advice for free,' Sandra enthused. She'd been a special needs teacher before, earning the equivalent of twelve dollars a month. 'The organisers don't ask if you're a believer or not and I think that's good. What does it matter if it's the Church running the course? It's a service that people here need.'

Stepping out from her shop into the busy Old Havana street, I headed down the cobbles towards the large, dark stone cathedral. As the Church attempts to claw back some lost ground, critics – mostly off the island – argue it's more concerned with its own position than pushing for basic freedoms and human rights. Catholics on the island believe that working from within, nudging Cuba towards change, is more effective.

That may be why Cuba got another papal visit just a year after I left for Moscow. Francis was the third pope to travel to Cuba in under two decades, remarkable for an island where religion was supposed to wither away. By then it had emerged that the Vatican had intervened directly in the US–Cuba reconciliation, playing host to secret talks on restoring relations.

As for the earlier visit of Benedict XVI, that did have one immediately tangible effect. All along the route he took through Havana the potholes were filled and fresh lines painted on the tarmac. The improvements, though, stretched only as far as his passing eyes might see. Had the pope's cortege been diverted by just one street, his car would probably have hit a crater.

We journalists arguably did better. Cuban officials had long insisted that the only reason for poor Internet connectivity on the island was technical, nothing to do with control and censorship. And yet when a crowd of correspondents from all over the world descended on Havana and headed for the papal press centre, they were met by a connection working at Western speed. Outsiders didn't bat an eyelid, but for those of us based on the island it was a minor miracle. Between monitoring video feeds of Benedict's movements and attending briefings we downloaded as many films, TV series and books as we could and praised the pope.

7

RED LINES

The selection of books for sale in Cuba is generally dire. On one of my recent visits to Havana the window display in one of the better shops included *Arterial Pressure* and *Eye Illnesses in Infancy and Adolescence*. The second-hand stalls on the cobbled Plaza de Armas occasionally do better, though their prices are pitched for tourists. I once found a photocopied edition of *Our Man in Havana* there and you sometimes spot a classic of Cuban literature or some Hemingway. But it's mainly chunky hagiographies of the revolutionaries and the odd Danielle Steele recovered from a hotel room. Quality contemporary literature is hard to come by.

The dearth stems from a decision after the revolution that Cuba would stop importing most books and set up its own publishing houses. It was partly an attempt to ensure that literature was cheap and easily available in a mass literacy and educational drive. But the other aim was to control what citizens were exposed to. In the better economic climate of the 1980s, Cubans had a rich diet of classical world literature with writers like

Dickens or Balzac widely available at heavily subsidised prices. But regular access to contemporary foreign literature stopped with the revolution as the government couldn't or wouldn't pay for the publishing rights. Cuban readers grew out of touch with what was going on elsewhere but the hunger for good literature has survived.

In February 2013 I joined a long stream of people heading to the annual book fair. The event is held across Havana Bay at La Cabana fortress. Inside its turreted walls I found the paths, rooms and marquees heaving with readers. There were talks, literature readings and seminars to choose from but most visitors made straight for the stalls. The glossy offerings for children were immensely popular. There was also a long queue for a Mexican publisher with titles ranging from trashy romances to Alan Greenspan's musings on economics. The only quiet unit was the one occupied by a left-wing British firm who'd brought works on Marxism and revolution all the way to Havana.

Cuba's best-known contemporary novelist, Leonardo Padura, appeared at a spillover venue back in Vedado where people waited hours to get their hands on one of his books. 'This happens whenever one of his novels is released: it sells out in an instant,' a student called Jorge told me, nodding at the long line snaking towards the white plastic table where Padura sat. The author was signing his latest work, based on the story of Trotsky's assassin. A few hundred extra copies had been printed specially for the fair but it was nowhere near enough to meet demand. 'We've been queuing since early morning to get one,' Jorge explained, though he complained that the book was 'a bit expensive'. The chunky novel he was clutching was priced at a heavily subsidised thirty Cuban pesos, or just over a dollar.

Now in his early sixties with a grey bushy beard and kindly eyes, Padura still lives in the house where he was brought up in the southern Havana suburb of Mantilla. One day during the book fair I drove out to visit him there and we talked at length, sunk in large wicker chairs in his spotless living room.

The author began his career in 1980 as a journalist. He worked first for a cultural magazine and then for the communist youth paper *Juventud Rebelde* in the days when Padura says it published real journalism and investigations. It was 1990 when he began writing the first of his *noir* detective series featuring a hero known as Mario Conde. The author chose the genre specifically to allow him to explore the margins of Cuban society. Working at the height of the 1990s economic crisis, after the Soviet collapse, writing saved Padura from 'madness and despair'. A passionate and engaging conversationalist, he joked that there were just three problems in the so-called Special Period: breakfast, lunch and dinner. He set his first books a little before the crisis because he realised his detective-hero would be physically incapable of chasing criminals in a city with few working payphones, even less public transport and minimal street lights.

The author sees the social and economic meltdown of those years as a turning point for Cuban literature. 'In the 1990s, paper, electricity and ink all disappeared and Cuba just stopped publishing books.' Providing food became the greatest priority for the government. But the fact the state could no longer support writers ultimately allowed them to cut loose. 'This rupture created a distance, a space, which was gradually filled with freedom,' the writer explained. 'First we began writing differently, then we began finding publishers abroad.'

His own literature tackles once-taboo subjects such as the cultural repression of the 1970s and the revolution's persecution of gay men. Some still criticise Padura for avoiding direct criticism of the Castros. But the literary liberation the author describes is perhaps best reflected in his heavy-drinking hero. 'I think the most critical point in my work is what happens in characters' minds, especially Mario Conde,' Padura explained, describing something I've since heard from other Cubans whose faith in the revolution was shattered in the 1990s. 'I think Mario Conde's discovery that so much sacrifice has been in vain is the most controversial,' the writer admitted of his alter ego. 'His sense that time has passed and he can't get that back, and that he and his generation are left with nothing.'

Since he secured a foreign publisher Padura's books have all appeared in Cuba, too. The Spanish firm waived its rights so long as the novels came out unaltered, and they have. The print runs are small, supposedly for cost reasons. But Padura says he's kept nudging at the limits of his new freedom ever since.

Beyond fiction, the author concedes that doublespeak is still a reality of everyday life and that the Cuban press is utterly partisan. Books by searing critics of the revolution who went into exile, like Reinaldo Arenas or Guillermo Cabrera Infante, still only circulate in photocopied form or second-hand. The government won't spend scarce funds importing or publishing its ideological opponents. But Padura argues that just as people in the street are now looser with their critical tongues, so too are artists and writers. Cuban cinema delivers hard-hitting depictions of the daily struggle, as do musicians. Padura suggests that culture has been allowed to develop as an outlet to critique the social crises that politicians and the press play down or ignore.

I wondered whether Padura's international profile has protected him and permitted him more freedom. Perhaps lesser-known and younger writers are more wary. But Padura argued that no one in Cuba had a safety net. 'When you have a critical view there's always an element of risk.' All the same, he believed that the appearance of work like his had helped other authors push the boundaries. He felt that the biggest form of censorship for writers inside Cuba today was self-imposed. 'I imagine there are still red lines, but if you read my books you will see that many of them have now been crossed.'

* * *

Pedro Juan Gutierrez has crossed all those lines himself and many more. Probably Cuba's second-best known contemporary author, he has much in common with Padura: both former journalists, they are close in age and both launched their literary careers during the traumatic 1990s. Like Padura, Gutierrez is a disillusioned former believer who describes himself as part of a 'tricked generation, a bit sad, a bit melancholic'. His work can be even harder to find than Padura's in Havana bookshops. It's why copyright violations were the least of the author's concerns when fans appeared on his doorstep, pirate copy of one of his novels in hand, to ask for a signature.

Gutierrez's fiction probes deep into the dark margins of Cuban society. His first novel is grimy, sexually explicit and shockingly direct, a largely autobiographical story of survival set in the author's own neighbourhood of Central Havana. He calls the *Dirty Havana Trilogy* a work of catharsis, written over three years in the dead of night and mostly drunk. It was a very public literary 'striptease' performed as the author's personal life and the political project he once had faith in were falling apart. In the broken-down streets of Havana, the writer who had helped teach Marxism at college watched Cuba's economic collapse morph into a moral one before his eyes. Children turned to begging and women sold themselves to tourists to survive. Most if not all of the characters in his novel are based on real people. For Gutierrez, harsh times demanded harsher prose.

Two publishers from Santiago de Cuba expressed interest in the book when he read a few chapters to them, but then went silent. The manuscript eventually found its way to Spain where it was published in 1998. Gutierrez says the novel sold out in a week. It has since appeared in almost two dozen languages, making the author a big name in what he defines as 'dirty realism'. For all its success and critical acclaim, the *Trilogy* has still never been published in Cuba.

Originally from Matanzas, Gutierrez's father had an ice cream business which was seized by the revolutionary government in 1961, plunging the family into hard times. Pedro Juan spent his early years wheeling and dealing for cash, selling comics first and then ice cream at the docks. He cut sugar cane and worked in construction before eventually deciding he wanted to write. Offered a job in radio, he studied journalism at the same time and began writing poetry and then novels in secret on the side. Like Padura, Gutierrez has chosen to stay and write in Cuba despite the difficulties. But it is his country he is attached to, not its system. He points out that, unlike literature, politics and politicians are not permanent.

I first met Gutierrez at the 2013 Havana book fair. One evening I went to a poetry reading in an old family mansion that now houses the Writers' and Artists' Union. Having read the writer's first risque novel, I was a little nervous of meeting the man himself. That feeling only deepened as we struggled to find a quiet spot to talk in the lush gardens. We ended up hovering under a porch in the dark. But like Padura, the tall, bald-headed author was open, unpretentious and engaging. I discovered that he'd fared worse, though, with officialdom. 'When the *Trilogy* came out in Spain they read it as a political book,' Gutierrez told me. 'I was working as a journalist at the time and they kicked me out of my job.' A career of twenty-six years ended overnight.

Gutierrez went on writing his fiction. 'I carried on publishing abroad and living here, sometimes in peace and sometimes not in peace. But I stayed.' He continued to insist that his shocking portrait of Havana life was apolitical. 'I write literature, not journalism, and I try to exclude politics from my books because it is temporal,' Gutierrez argued on that shadowy porch. But he appears compelled to write what others don't dare to.

As a journalist, he once investigated conditions at a juvenile detention facility outside Havana, only to be told the story was 'too dark' to appear in the Cuban press. So he changed some names and converted the story into a work of fiction. I wondered, then, how he could possibly suggest that his novels depicting prostitution, abject poverty and drug taking were not an act of political engagement. I recalled a warning I once heard from a fellow journalist that reporting on prostitution was a red line for the government. I also had vivid memories of filming as a huge haul of marijuana seized by Cuban coast-guards went up in flames in an old factory furnace, under armed police guard. Zero tolerance was the emphatic message. Gutierrez insisted that he was simply writing about what he saw all around him and what he knew. 'People who think of politics all the time see politics in my books,' he said. 'Those who think of sex all the time see sex. Each person has their own interpretation.'

Some of his novels have begun to appear in Cuba, albeit with small print runs, but the *Trilogy* remains on the blacklist. One official told me the objection was because the novel was 'scato-logical', not because of its politics, though several other equally explicit books have been published. 'I think the stage is slightly more dynamic now and that those who decide what to release have more freedom,' the author argued, predicting that even his most controversial work would eventually appear in Cuba. 'I will go on writing what I want.'

* * *

A few days later I went back to the fair at La Cabana where the crowds were still large but the stalls fast emptying of stock. In the main hall, Leonardo Padura was taking to the stage to warm applause. The author was being awarded the National Literature Prize by a jury of fellow writers, presented by the president of Cuba's official Book Institute, Zuleica Romay. She described Padura to me as a popular winner who'd given voice to the concerns and aspirations of Cuba's people. When I questioned whether the prize was a sign of increased tolerance she put it differently. 'You say this is tolerance or an opening but those words have political connotations. I think we are simply interested in the social function of literature which is something it has always had.' Even children's books touched on themes including corruption and emigration these days, she pointed out. 'It's about having a closer connection with the problems of the people.'

Padura told his audience that he'd faced criticism and 'abuse' over his career, both at home and from Cubans abroad. But on stage, holding his prize certificate in a huge frame, he said the sacrifice had been worth it. 'I have tried all these years to be a man as free and independent as possible,' the novelist explained. 'I have written the books that I have wanted to write, that I have believed that I should and could write, and through literature I have spoken about our reality.'

Even as we reached the end of our own long conversation in his Mantilla home, Padura had allowed himself to be a little hopeful for Cuba's future. He talked of a new mobility in society, of change after decades standing still. 'Imagine, when I was thirteen I was banned from listening to the Beatles. It was the music of the enemy!' he reminded me, adding that his generation had suffered many other sacrifices. 'We've been through so much, that I have to be an optimist. After so many difficult years when so many things were banned and denied us, people here deserve to live better and to have a bit more freedom. To realise themselves as individuals, which is so important.'

8

ENTERTAINMENTS AND
COMMITMENTS

The man swinging back on a metal chair outside the Edificio Bolivar leaps up when I ask to visit the old British embassy. Without a word he heads for the hallway of the art deco tower and signals for me to follow. Its paintwork now slightly faded, this light denim-coloured block is where Graham Greene came to visit Ambassador Stanley Fordham on the first day of his trip to Havana in November 1957.

The embassy moved into the tower on the edge of Old Havana in 1950 as Britain upgraded its mission in Cuba. The diplomats left some thirty years later for a larger property in upmarket Miramar but the Bolivar tower is more subtly stylish. With its simple lines it stands out among the elaborate Spanish colonial architecture all around.

A group of residents have already gathered to wait for the lift when we approach, including a woman with a miniature dog. A sign inside announces eight passengers maximum and someone pats my guide on the belly. 'We're eight and a half with that,' he

says and everyone laughs, guide included. Up on the fifth floor, on a landing full of unexpected curves and hidden corners, he presents me to a woman who appears to be in charge of the building. She looks sceptical when I mumble something about an 'important historic meeting' here back in the 1950s, but waves me on. The embassy used to cover the top three floors of the building, she tells me, but it's all flats now.

Upstairs a wary-looking young man with a beard opens the door and I suddenly feel awkward at the intrusion but he invites me in. The flat has two walls painted bright pink and is unusually bare but it boasts a glorious view. Swerving to avoid a Rottweiler, I step through the full-length glass doors onto a terrace that looks straight across the bay to the lighthouse. To the right I can see over the park towards the ornate turrets of the Presidential Palace. It was here that Ambassador Fordham told

Greene about the deadly attack on the palace that he'd witnessed a few months earlier, when radical leftist rebels nearly succeeded in assassinating Cuba's president.

It was 13 March 1957 and the rebels arrived at the palace in a delivery truck, stormed the building and rushed up the stairs towards President Batista's office. Tipped off, he escaped to safety on an upper floor as his military deployed tanks and anti-aircraft guns. The fighting in the heart of the old city continued for over three hours while residents and tourists cowered inside buildings. An American who ventured onto his balcony at the nearby Hotel Regis was struck by a bullet and killed, one of the casualties reported by *New York Times* correspondent Ruby Hart Phillips who'd been heading to her office in the next street when the ambush began. She described the city centre that night as like an 'armed camp' with civilians barred from the streets and all bars and clubs closed. Fordham told Greene that he'd watched the battle from behind the shutters in the typists' room until a burst of gunfire sent him and his staff rushing for cover. He may well have mentioned the unfortunate American to the novelist: in *Our Man in Havana* a man photographing a beggar near the palace is also killed by a stray bullet, which 'sounded the knell of the all-in tour' to Cuba.

As I thank my guide at the exit of the Edificio Bolivar I spot a small poster of Fidel Castro on the wall. The slogan reads *Fidel entre nosotros*, always among us.

* * *

The attack on the Presidential Palace was the most audacious in a growing catalogue of revolutionary violence. Months earlier, in October 1956, Batista's head of military intelligence Antonio

Blanco Rico had been gunned down at a top nightclub, sparking a wave of repression that saw Havana's prisons fill up with young men suspected of supporting the rebels. New Year 1957 began with a bomb at the Tropicana cabaret. But even after the assassination attempt on Batista in March, the city's main English-language paper tried to play down the disturbances. With tanks in the city centre and shrapnel and blood on the streets, the *Havana Post* carried an interview with Cuba's president declaring that he had 'smashed' the armed revolt and was in full control. An editorial sought to reassure a mainly American readership that it was business as usual. The stylish new Hotel Capri was set to open its doors that November, complete with casino and cabaret, and the Riviera and Hilton were due to follow soon after. But for the American gangsters heavily invested in President Batista and his sin city, the omens were not good.

Greene's own second night in Havana saw the most extensive bombing in a year, with twenty to thirty explosions. He noted the 8 November attacks in his diary a couple of days later when nine cinemas were hit, mostly by devices tossed from moving cars. 'People thought it was an aerial bombardment,' Greene recorded, although he'd been at a live sex show at the time and hadn't personally heard a thing.

* * *

Turning off the Prado at Calle Trocadero, I walk towards the canopied entrance of the Hotel Sevilla where Greene stayed on his 1957 trip. The sound of recorded piano music and thumping feet from the wide-open windows of the National Ballet School opposite has stopped for the day and the dancers have long since

headed home. Cuba's pride, the school is back in its sumptuous historic building following a major refurbishment prompted when a stucco angel plunged from the ceiling.

The Sevilla lobby has something of the Alhambra about it with its blue Moorish wall tiles. *Our Man in Havana* described the hotel's downstairs bar as dark and gloomy when Wormold and his German friend Hasselbacher shared a drink here. Wormold was on his way to meet spy-recruiter Henry Hawthorne in Room 501 to receive his instructions and code number. Today the bar area is light and open. There's a *son* band playing softly in one corner of the patio and next to the musicians I recognise the figurine which Greene was photographed beside on an earlier trip in 1954. There are green ceramic frogs around the bottom, spitting water into a fountain. The combination of statues, bright ceramics and wooden fans turning on an ornate ceiling creates an elegant colonial feel.

Looking round further I see the yellow walls are covered with photographs of celebrities associated with the hotel and I'm pleased to spot a large picture of Greene on one of the pillars. Photographed beside a bookcase, the author looks slightly startled but it's a rare public reminder of the Englishman's link to Havana in a city brimming with shrines to Ernest Hemingway. Sharing the picture gallery with him are Al Capone and Santo Trafficante Jr., the Florida-based gangster who ran the hotel casino.

Just as Greene was beginning to write his novel here, the hotel lobby became the crossing point for a number of writers and reporters doubling up as actual spies. Greene had served in the Secret Intelligence Service, or SIS, during the war, posted first to Freetown and then Lisbon where his boss was the Soviet double agent Kim Philby. His biographer believes he never entirely cut his connection with the SIS, meeting old contacts when he returned from trips abroad.

On his second day in town Greene had drinks with another man with a sideline in intelligence. Ted Scott, a journalist for the *Havana Post* and NBC America, was a New Zealander who reported from Panama before moving to Havana in the early 1950s. His own spy link was Ian Fleming, the creator of James Bond.

Even after the success of his novels, Fleming kept his day job as foreign manager of the *Sunday Times*, commissioning reports from around the world. But he'd worked in naval intelligence during the war and appears to have stayed in the game. He had a particular focus on the Caribbean region, where Jamaica was his second home, and was increasingly interested in the instability in Cuba. Ted Scott was one of Fleming's sources but he didn't share the New Zealander's confidence that Castro's rebellion would soon be stopped. So in December 1957 he deployed another journalist-spy to Havana. The understated English travel writer Norman Lewis had also worked for British intelligence during the war and knew Havana, having lived there briefly in 1939. Lewis saw enough on a journey to the east of Cuba to believe that Castro's forces would not be defeated as easily as Scott and the Foreign Office seemed to think.

Lewis just missed Greene at the Sevilla but Scott was a long-term resident in one of its penthouse suites and the two men met in the hotel coffee shop. Fleming had told him that Scott, a handy boxer in his younger years, was one of four models he'd used for James Bond but Lewis struggled to see the likeness. The New Zealander was 'short and somewhat plump, with rosy cheeks, small blue eyes and the expression of a confiding child'. His hands were small and dimpled and his 'small feet encased in brilliantly polished shoes'. Scott kept a record of his sexual conquests, boasting that they ran into the thousands. Invited up to the journalist's penthouse, Lewis passed a 'quite naked Negress' in the anteroom whom he mistook for a statue until he noticed her goosebumps.

A few weeks earlier Greene had shared a 'long train of daiquiris' with the *Havana Post* man in the bar of the Sevilla. Despite their common interests, he took a violent dislike to Scott. A 'fat, unattractive little New Zealander with an American accent', Greene scrawled in his journal, describing a man who talked constantly of Havana as a 'sex centre' and of 'the availability of girls'. It was enough to 'make one's sex die', he wrote. It seems that's exactly what happened. After the daiquiri session with Scott, Greene headed for Chinatown and the notorious Shanghai

Theatre. As bombs went off outside, he watched a performance in which a gardener character undressed a number of girls until the last one allowed him to 'rub his face in her fur'. Unsatisfied, the novelist emerged into the Havana night with a craving for opium. He signed off his journal limply: 'Home to bed undisturbed'.

Greene would meet Scott again when the ambassador threw a lunch in honour of the famous visitor. When Fordham informed Greene that he'd known Scott for over twenty years, the novelist sneered, 'What a horrible young wretch he must have been.' In return Scott used his newspaper column 'Interesting if True' to make regular digs at the author, sniping about his taste for low dives like the Shanghai.

* * *

But in November 1957 Greene had come to Cuba for more than the 'brothel life'. As he absorbed the sights and sounds that he would reflect in his fiction, the author was working on a plan to travel east and cure his 'ignorance' of the island. He would head for the towns of Trinidad and Cienfuegos first, then to rebel territory in Santiago. With the help of the Cuban writer and revolutionary sympathiser Lisandro Otero, he hoped to meet Fidel Castro himself.

The sheer thrill of the trip would have appealed to Greene, who regularly sought danger to jolt himself out of the depression that plagued him all his life, never more so than in his early fifties. He liked to be in risky places where 'fundamental upheaval' might take place. Preparing to journey to the heart of Cuba's civil war, Greene met US diplomats as well as the British ambassador. He also lunched at the Miramar Yacht Club with the *Time* correspondent. 'A lot of background material', Greene scribbled in his journal. 'But not for my story.'

The front of his notebook for this visit reads: 'Havana Journal. While writing Our Man in – but interrupted'. Towards the end it becomes cryptic, with initials replacing full names. On 12 November 1957 Greene breaks off mid-page with an eerie final observation. 'The pretty girl in the taxi with the policeman: head back: almost fainting. I suppose a street accident.'

Sadly the journal records nothing of his travel east and it wasn't until Greene's 1980 memoir, *Ways of Escape*, that he disclosed more details. The night before setting out he had a 'late party' with a group of Fidel's supporters. Among them was Natalia Bolivar, whose lover had been killed during the assault on the Presidential Palace. Bolivar had been showing a tour group round the Fine Arts Museum right behind the palace when she heard explosions and dropped to the floor. As the battle raged, Bolivar watched in horror as Jose Luis Wanguemert was shot on the street in front of her.

Bolivar now asked Greene for help to get warm clothes and socks to Fidel's fighters in the mountains. He agreed, explaining later that he sympathised with the rebels' struggle. It was also his chance to get closer to Castro.

By then the rumble of revolution was growing steadily louder in the east as resistance to the brutality and inequality of life under Batista increased. Saboteurs cut power lines, blew up bridges and torched sugar cane fields, and rebel troops mounted guerrilla attacks on government forces. Hundreds of suspects were arrested and the bodies of others were found hanged or shot by the side of the road. Arriving in Santiago Greene found the dark streets deserted and Batista's troops on patrol. He sensed the 'smell of a police station' hanging over the city. He was back, he wrote, 'in what my critics imagine to be Greeneland'.

Despite delivering clothes to the rebels, the author's encounter with Fidel never materialised. One report suggests that security was too tight to smuggle the writer up into the mountains unseen. But the trip was not wasted. Tracking down the contacts he'd been given, Greene met some central characters from the revolution. Armando Hart had just pulled off a dramatic escape from a Havana court and when Greene arrived at his Santiago safe house Hart was getting his hair dyed in disguise. His wife Haydee Santamaria was with him, looking like she'd been 'battered into fanaticism' by events. Four years earlier her previous fiance had been captured by Batista's police as he took part in Fidel's disastrous assault on the Moncada military barracks. He was castrated and mutilated. The police caught her brother too and gouged his eyes out with a bayonet. They then forced her to identify the corpses. Speaking much later, Santamaria told one interviewer that she didn't die herself at Moncada but 'left more than my life there'.

For years Greene had visited Cuba as a hedonist, blotting out the background of violence, imprisonment and torture. In 1957 he travelled further and probed deeper, coming face to face with the shadow side of his pleasure island. Hints of that experience appear in his novel. But Greene's attitude to Cuba had been transformed: what started out as an entertainment had become a commitment.

* * *

Greene would later describe Ted Scott as 'one of the nastiest pieces of work' he'd ever encountered. It was some claim given the shady places Greene had been. Keen to know more about this 'James Bond' of Havana, I tracked down someone who'd known both men well. Now in his nineties, Bernard Diederich was a veteran correspondent for *Time* magazine who'd worked all over Latin America. He spoke to me by phone from his home in Haiti, a country he'd once explored with Greene, a friend and mentor. Diederich had met Scott on reporting assignments in the region, including in Havana, and confirmed with a chortle that the journalist was most definitely a 'ladies' man' and reputedly a spy. He also described his fellow New Zealander as somewhat 'mad'. In one incident in Santo Domingo, Diederich recalled Scott almost drinking himself to death. 'They thought he had malaria but no mosquito could bite him and survive!' When I wondered why Greene took such a violent dislike to Scott, Diederich laughed. '[Scott] was a wart! A nice wart when you got to know him. But he was a type that Graham could not stand and Greene was very particular in his friendships.'

Heading past the photo wall at the Sevilla towards the lift, I'm now on the territory of both men. The hotel PR man tells me that Room 501 from Greene's novel is occupied so I can't go in, but he assures me it's just like all the other rooms. Emerging onto the sixth floor, like Wormold when he tried to give a drunken Hasselbacher the slip, I then take the stairs back down to the fifth. The rooms are arranged like 'prison-cells round a rectangular balcony' as Greene noted; the one he chose for his MI6 agent is tucked in an obscure corner.

On the dark red wall outside 501 is a small plaque with Greene's name. It notes simply that the writer 'located one of his characters in this room at the end of the 50s' and makes no mention of the fact that the writer himself stayed at the hotel.

The PR man tells me the hotel's guest records from the 1950s were lost long ago so there's nothing left to indicate whether 501 was actually Greene's room. I like to think it wasn't a random choice though. Perhaps the author began working on *Our Man in Havana* behind the cream slatted door here in front of me. He was a creature of routine who would start writing between 7 and 8 a.m. and turn out five hundred words each morning regardless of how much he'd drunk the previous night. The novelist would then have emerged from the Sevilla into the midday sun, brushing past the bootblacks to make his way to the Floridita for lunch.

If Greene's presence in the Sevilla is marked, albeit modestly, Ted Scott is a long-forgotten guest. Climbing higher in the lift to the top floor, I discover that his former penthouse has been converted into a bar, fitting for the brash *bon viveur*. This is the place Scott described being hit by shells in 1957 during the raid on the Presidential Palace. The dapper reporter wailed in his column that one fragment of shrapnel had 'cut through my wardrobe' and that his best brown tropical suit was among the casualties.

The bar is empty when I walk in and the only member of staff is half-watching Telesur. The long polished wooden bar is lined with Spanish tiles and the walls dotted with more pictures of American gangsters. Turning the TV down, the barman informs me that everyone on display is linked to the hotel's history in some way. As I'm sure he won't have heard of Ted Scott, I ask about Graham Greene but he looks blank.

A window by the bar looks all the way down the Prado to the coast. A block back from the sea, cranes marked with lights are still moving as builders work through the night to finish another new hotel, right next to the Edificio Bolivar. It's two months since Obama's visit and Havana is bracing itself for an avalanche of Americans and other tourists. The barman has already noticed more visitors, especially Europeans rushing to see Cuba 'before it changes'.

In the old days the Americans would come for sex, he informs me rather surprisingly and unprompted. He explains that there was an establishment right next to the Sevilla where women would 'attend' to men. Said to be among the most luxurious in the Western world, the Templo de Marina was stuffed with period furnishings and plush draperies. Accounts from the era describe clients being handed refreshments by staff in white coats. 'Perhaps your writer went there,' the barman suggests, given what I've now told him about Greene, whose list of favourite prostitutes included such characters as 'Russian boots' and 'Real tough buggerer'. But if Greene ever did visit the brothel next door, he didn't record it. The building now houses a staff training centre for the hotel and a snack shop.

I wonder if the barman can make me the author's favourite dry Martini but he shakes his head. 'We used to know all those cocktails but we've forgotten them,' he tells me regretfully. 'We only know the ones based on rum.' My husband asks for a shot of Santiago rum instead but the place is sponsored by Cuba's other big brand, Havana Club. The display bottle of that is empty so we settle for beer.

* * *

Greene finished writing his novel in the spring of 1958. He referred to it dismissively in a letter to a writer friend as 'a rather hack job'. Still, it made the money he needed to fund his expensive ways of escape. He sold the film rights for $100,000 and his next trip to Cuba was on a recce for locations with the film director Carol Reed, just a week after *Our Man in Havana* was published.

On the initial leg of his flight, first class from London to New York, Greene met a 'mysterious and pretty English girl' dressed in mink and sable reading his new novel at the bar. In a letter to his former lover Catherine Walston on 12 October 1958 he described how the girl had asked whether the legendary sexual showman Superman was worth seeing. She was, Greene wrote, 'passionately fond of Havana, blue films and brothels'. On an earlier trip the girl's lover had wanted to watch her have sex with the first six men to show up at a brothel, one of whom 'had to be a negro'. The titillating conversation helped Greene pass the time to New York, where the pair shared a Benzedrine pill to give him energy for a meeting with Columbia Pictures ahead of his flight to Havana the next day.

By the time the writer arrived in Cuba, Castro's rebellion was so far advanced that he was confined to Havana. Even the main roads were prone to ambush. Greene left few notes of this trip, although he did manage a visit to the Tropicana. He sent a postcard of the club's famous crystal arches, informing Walston that he'd won seventy dollars on the slot machines with just one twenty-five cent piece.

He also appears to have met contacts among the rebels who sought his help to stop the British government selling fighter jets to Batista. London was acting on the basis of poor intelligence from the embassy in Havana that the overthrow of Batista was unlikely. The rebels declared Law Number Four of the Sierra Maestra in protest, calling for a nationwide boycott of British products including Gordon's gin and 'English' whisky.

On 24 October, just two hours after arriving back in the UK, Greene wrote to Labour MP Hugh Delargy. He told him that the activities of Captain Ventura, Batista's 'chief torturer', had intensified and victims' bodies were being 'flung out by the wayside'. Greene was appalled that Batista would be using British planes to bomb his own population. Contrary to intelligence from the embassy, the author judged from his own trip east that the region sided with Fidel almost entirely. He also wanted to prevent anti-British feeling on the part of the man he believed would probably be the next ruler of Cuba.

On 12 December 1958 the Foreign Office belatedly recognised the rebellion in Cuba as civil war and implemented an arms embargo. Just two weeks later Batista fled the island. Almost immediately Greene wrote to *The Times* pouring scorn on the British government's 'extraordinary ignorance of Cuban affairs' in ever considering the sale of fighter planes. Ambassador Fordham later admitted that he'd misread the significance and scale of the unrest. 'We are expected to be right when all around them are wrong,' he wrote woefully to the prime minister. For Greene it was confirmation that his send-up of the Foreign Office and intelligence services in *Our Man in Havana* was fully justified.

* * *

It's December 2017 when I next drop into the Sevilla, looking for a drink and a moment's respite from the sun. Visiting Cuba exactly sixty years earlier, Norman Lewis saw the hotel as a place of calm. 'No-one would have dreamed that Havana was in a state of revolutionary ferment,' the writer recalled, and it's still a pleasant retreat from the bustle and dust of the city.

Making for the patio I glance towards the pillar with the photo of Greene and realise it's gone. I scour the walls for a while, thinking it's been moved, but don't find it. 'It's OK, he's perfectly safe,' a new woman on the public relations desk assures me, when I enquire after what appears to be the only picture of Greene in Havana. She explains that the hotel had a visit from the former French president Francois Hollande and they'd had to remove some 'old' photos to make way for new images. 'It's hard to fit everyone in,' the PR woman reasons and promises the writer will make a comeback.

As she walks off I scan the wall of fame again. Across from the ex-president of France, a former hotel worker turned Havana vagrant is still on display. Nearby, the founder of Alcoholics Anonymous has also made the cut that ousted the English novelist from his spot. Ted Scott, I suspect, would have been amused.

9

CONDOMS AND CRICKET

Extract from diary, 19 June 2013

Normally as a foreign correspondent the first task in the morning is to check the headlines in the local paper, watch the TV news. Here I often forget even to open the paper. Yesterday's headline was the sixth anniversary of the death of Raul's wife. Absence of news means anniversaries are news. Apart from the day of my favourite headline in *Granma*. 'Vaginal dryness. Causes and symptoms'.

The thing about news is that it's very often negative. Death, disaster and destruction grab headlines around the world. Cuba's news bulletins by contrast prefer to focus on anniversaries, festivals or meeting the milk quota. Until a little constructive criticism was permitted on the state airwaves towards the end of my stay, the media were so busy depicting the socialist utopia that the difficulties of daily life were largely ignored.

As a foreign correspondent, exploring those difficulties was part of my job. Emigration, collapsing houses and the lack of

Internet were the topics I covered because they were issues that affected the people I met. But Cuba was also a place of charm and energy, music and laughter, and occasionally I'd produce stories just because they were fun.

That's how I came to be filmed walking through the streets of Old Havana in early 2013 with the British ambassador. It was a time when you couldn't take two steps in Havana without seeing people wearing the Union flag and we wanted to discover what was behind the sudden craze. There were children in Cuban school uniform with British-flag bags, clothes stalls piled high with flag vests and trainers stamped with the red, white and blue pattern. I spotted girls with British flag manicures and two young boys with the Union flag shaved into the backs of their heads. Filming them, I got a local band to play on the cobble-stones, segueing from a Cuban tune into 'Rule Britannia'.

This particular ambassador wasn't your stereotypically stiff Foreign Office type. He learned to dance salsa and later helped bring the Rolling Stones to Havana. That was a major event in a country where the older generation once listened to *Los Rollings* in secret because the revolution banned rock 'n' roll. The pre-concert party the ambassador threw at the official residence with the band had expats fighting furiously for an invite.

The flag fashion had started in 2012, which happened to be the 250th anniversary of the brief British occupation of Havana. But there was no deep message behind the trend. It was linked to the Olympics in London which Cubans had followed avidly: the car park attendants at my office block had congratulated me personally for hosting a good games. The ambassador took the craze as a sign of 'Cool Britannia' but when he wondered what else the flag-wearing Cubans had picked up about Britain one

suggested 'James Blunt' and another asked whether the diplomat might help him out with the cost of a flight there.

There were other stories that made me smile. Quite early in my stay I realised I was wary of asking interviewees' names because I could rarely understand the response. I seemed to come across few Juans or Miguels; more often, the people I'd speak to had names like Yumilsis or Mileidy. Following a surge in Fidels and Ernestos after the revolution, imaginations had started to fly in the 1970s. That's when the letter Y, rarely used in Spanish, became popular. Parents invented new names like Yulieski or Yohandry and even altered 'normal' names like Daniel to Yaniel. Some saw it as a small assertion of autonomy in a country where so much else was under state control.

A language expert I consulted had uncovered names like Dayesi, covering yes in three languages. People would write names backwards to create new ones, like Otrebla for Alberto, and most recently parents had begun merging their own two names for their children. But my personal favourite was a woman called Meylin I met one day on the street: she said her mother had named her after the canned meat she used to get on the ration book.

Fortunately, the local BBC producer went by the far more traditional name of William, a man with whom I one day found myself shopping for condoms. I don't remember where I'd first heard there was a deficit of cheap contraception, but a quick chat with some women waiting for their bus from work confirmed the rumour. One told me she'd tried to stock up recently with no luck. 'You'll have to sit tight,' her friend laughed. 'Or have a cold bath!'

I decided to check out Havana's chemists and took William with me. We must have made a peculiar sight, me and a man well into his sixties dashing all over town desperately seeking condoms. They were heavily subsidised by the state as part of its safe-sex policy and a pack of three was normally available for just one Cuban peso. At that price they doubled for balloons at parties. But that month even state-run cafes, which usually listed condoms on their price boards next to the soft drinks and pork sandwiches, had run out.

A newspaper in another city tried to make light of the deficit there, informing readers that the Ancient Egyptians had used knotted animal intestines for contraception. Meanwhile, a night-club owner in Santa Clara personally travelled thirty kilometres to find a village chemist that still had stock.

When the reason for the shortage emerged it was bizarre. A major delivery of Chinese condoms had arrived in Cuba stamped with an expiry date that had already passed. The manufacturer insisted it was a mistake and Cuba's own condom quality controllers confirmed that. Teams were then set to change the date on every single packet by hand, but they'd been unable to keep up with demand.

Another occasion found William and me deep in the countryside watching the raunchiest maypole dance I've ever seen. Baragua looked like a typical provincial town: sugar mill at its heart and surrounded by cane fields, streets lined with brightly coloured low-rise houses and crowded with bicycles, horses and carts. But if you listened to the locals, you'd hear a smattering of English among the Cuban Spanish. The English speakers were descendants of hundreds of people from British colonies in the West Indies who'd headed to Cuba for work almost a century before. In those days many sugar mills on the island were run by

Americans. Many of the new arrivals to Baragua came straight from building the Panama Canal. They intended to earn some money and then leave but a good number ended up settling in Cuba and raising large families. Decades on, their children and grandchildren were trying to keep the community's traditions alive. The English-speakers were once served by five churches of various denominations. When I visited, only the Anglican St James's still opened its doors on Sundays and numbers there were dwindling. The parish priest had left years before and an elderly deacon now led prayers for a congregation made up primarily of pensioners. The choir, once the pride of Baragua, had been replaced by a tape recorder. After the service, the wonderfully named Ethelbert Scantleberry, whose own parents had travelled from Barbados in 1920, was in wistful mood. 'The churches used to be full,' the 86-year-old remembered, chatting in sing-song English. 'It's not like today, with only a few of us.' Black-and-white photographs pinned up at the back of the church showed packed pews and children in their Sunday best.

'In this vicinity everyone spoke English in the street because we all grew up together and went to the English school,' a younger woman named Olivia Adderley Berry explained. She told me the school was closed down after the revolution and the community's grasp of English had been fading ever since. Even the church service had switched to Spanish and the old English-language prayer books were gathering dust in a passage. Olivia's mother was Jamaican and her father from Barbados, but although she still spoke to her own children in English they all replied in Spanish.

There was one English tradition, though, that the younger generation were keen on. Baragua's cricket team practised on the edge of town where the grass was long and the ground bumpy. 'The bats are no good,' match umpire Henry Paris Jordan told me with a shrug, as yet another home-made creation cracked loudly and split in two. There was no state funding for cricket, as it isn't classed as an official sport, and the team's own resources were very limited.

Getting a good match could be as hard as getting good bats. There were few teams to compete with in a nation of baseball fanatics. One player told me there were other British West Indian communities in Las Tunas and Guantanamo but the nearest was three hours' drive away. 'Sometimes there's no fuel for the truck to get them here,' the cricketer explained. As we spoke, a man passed the pitch with a large pig on a rope and no one but me batted an eyelid.

First-hand accounts of the British West Indians' history in Cuba are fast disappearing. When I visited Baragua there was just one survivor from the original wave of migrants. The family of Ruby Ellis told me she was 106 years old. Her house was a few streets from the cricket pitch and when we arrived she was sitting in a wheelchair in the doorway, watching the world go slowly by. Ruby had arrived by ship from Jamaica in the 1920s and met her Antiguan husband in Baragua. They had nine children and 'plenty' grandchildren, as she told me with a sudden broad smile. Ruby had never been back home, but others had left Cuba over the years. 'Plenty Cubans in Jamaica now', she said, in slightly broken English. 'All those here gone to Jamaica.' Nowadays it's those elsewhere in the West Indies who are the wealthier ones, sending money back to relatives in communist Cuba.

The West Indians are gradually losing their distinctive names as well as their English. Henry Paris Jordan tells me his children are called Eutileisy and Danay and he himself prefers to be known as Enrique. Nobody knows exactly how large the community is these days and its members' migration stories have never been recorded. But the Baragua West Indians have managed to preserve one more thing from their heritage.

That evening after cricket a group gathered in the shadow of the sugar mill in the *barrio* where their families originally settled. The white mill managers had all lived on the opposite side of the tracks, upwind of the smoke and the smell. In front of me, the men and women in bright green spotted costumes began to move around a maypole, threading ribbons in an increasingly energetic routine. The pole itself was then dismantled for the dancers to limbo beneath it, never missing a drum beat.

For once this was a story with a happy ending. Soon after our feature story was broadcast I started to get emails from cricket enthusiasts in Sweden, Canada and Pakistan all wanting to send bats to the Cuban team. In the end it was an American who came through for them. With no direct postal service between the US and Cuba, William picked up the two new bats in person when he was next in Miami and we drove them down to Baragua. The team was delighted.

10

ADELA

It was pretty early for a party, almost as if the organisers wanted the LGBT marchers off the streets before too many people noticed. But this crowd stood out even by Cuba's extravagant standards. One man wore nothing but tiny silver-sequinned pants and a tattoo snaking up his chest while another danced frenetic rumba in high heels and blue curly wig, mini-dress tassels whirling madly as his friends cheered. By 10 a.m. several hundred revellers had gathered at the end of La Rampa, just up from the seafront, many carrying rainbow-striped umbrellas to shade their exposed skin from a sun that was already beginning to burn.

Last to take her place behind a banner at the front was Mariela Castro. In her early fifties, the director of the sex education centre Cenesex is a prominent spokeswoman for LGBT rights in Cuba, where her own father Raul led the military that sent gay men to labour camps in the 1960s. Surrounded by foreign TV cameras as the procession began, Mariela proclaimed the slogan of that year's march as 'No to Homophobia!' and the theme was spelled out on posters all around. The very existence of the event since 2008 is proof of progress on that front, as is a whole month of government-sponsored activities across the island in support of gay rights. Mariela herself secured one of the most progressive victories for transgender people when she campaigned successfully for sex-change surgery on the state health service. As she joined the colourful crowd on La Rampa, she admitted that she was struggling in her latest battle – to legalise same-sex marriage. 'I'm sure it's possible,' the president's daughter assured me, by far the most modestly dressed person there in jeans and a T-shirt, rainbow flag draped over her shoulders. 'The time will come. The biggest challenge is the prejudice we still have to overcome.'

There was no sign of that prejudice during the parade as locals looked down from their balconies and a small crowd lined the route to cheer the procession led by drummers and dancers on stilts. 'We just want to be recognised as equals,' Amanda explained as she shimmied up La Rampa, a prime gay cruising area before the revolution. A woman carried a painted sign declaring 'I've got a gay son and he's amazing!' Further up, a man had his own child perched on his shoulders. 'I wanted to show support for this cause,' Rogelio Diaz told me. 'LGBT people are not attacked like before. In schools and at work they're no longer expelled for their sexual orientation. But there is still a lot to do.'

A few others on the march waved placards and drawled the official slogan, *No a la Homofobia!*, but most concentrated on whistling and dancing the conga. They had to make the most of it as their annual street party ran for just three short blocks before veering right and out of sight beneath the concrete mass of the Pabellon Cuba exhibition centre.

As the music inside blared and the festivities continued, I hung on for the interview with Mariela that she'd always found reason to avoid in the past. Now, as we set up our camera in the least noisy corner we could find, she appeared in a floppy straw hat along with a short, heavily built woman with bleach-blonde spikes and hooped earrings. Adela Hernandez had recently achieved celebrity status in Cuban LGBT circles as the first transgender person elected to public office. She'd been voted onto the local council, the Poder Popular, in her tiny northern fishing village of Caibarien and Mariela was eager for us to meet. 'This is an important example of how things have changed, including people's mentality,' she enthused, with Adela clutching a mini rainbow flag by her side. 'People overcame their prejudices and voted for her.'

When I put a couple of questions to Adela her answers were stilted, perhaps because she worried about saying the wrong thing to a foreign reporter in front of a Castro. But she seemed genuinely proud of her status as Cuba's poster girl for LGBT rights. 'When people have confidence in you and you represent something important to the revolution, it's not difficult,' Adela told me solemnly. 'Cuba is demonstrating that there is democracy. People need to see that we've had difficulties, but we've overcome them.'

* * *

A little earlier I'd watched Mariela grab a megaphone down on the Pabellon stage to rally the crowd. *Homofobia, no! Socialismo, si!* she shouted, eliciting a fairly feeble response at first. The venue was full of admirers, including a good number from abroad. I met a gay fireman from London bursting with enthusiasm for the revolution and the ration book in particular. He looked crestfallen when I told him it barely covered the very basics for a fortnight. There was also an elderly Italian who'd come to film a video clip for his latest single. 'When I first came here homosexuals feared the police,' the singer told me, explaining that he'd been visiting Cuba for some twenty years. 'Now it's free here like in Spain and Italy. It's marvellous and Mariela is doing wonderful work.'

'Helllloooo to the Cuban LGBT-H community!' the woman herself called down from the stage. 'That's "H" because I'm here with you too. There are loads of heterosexuals here!' she announced, to mini whoops from below. Mariela's work on improving gay rights is high profile and has been effective but she's also come in for plenty of criticism, mostly from abroad. The Cenesex group she heads is an official body and the only organisation advocating gay rights that's permitted; independent groups of all kinds are banned. Mariela's critics want to know why, if she's liberal enough to champion LGBT rights, she doesn't challenge her father on other fundamental issues like free speech, free elections or even the right to stage a protest.

The president's daughter instead sticks to one approved topic in public, mixing talk of sex-change operations and gay marriage with denunciation of imperialist domination. At Havana Pride she began her speech by praising the Cuban Five, a group of intelligence agents arrested in the US whose fate had become a national cause. 'The LGBT movement has fought with total sincerity for the freedom of the five heroes unjustly imprisoned in the USA,' Mariela declared to those scattered around the pavilion in a riot of rainbow

Mohican wigs, wedge heels and spangles. 'From their unjust prison the five have sent a greeting to all of you and us here today!' *Homofobia no, Socialismo si . . . Viva!* came the dutiful reply.

Backstage I bumped into Jeffrey Weeks, a renowned British sociologist and expert on sexuality, who declared himself 'rather amazed' by the changes he'd seen in Cuban society. 'Everything I've heard about what's happening suggests that people are ready to make amends [for the past] and be much more positive about sexual diversity,' he said, sharing his first impressions of gay rights on the island.

That past is what I wanted to discuss with Mariela, but questioning official figures in Cuba is a painful process and an acquired skill. I didn't have much time with Mariela but I began by asking her about the things we both wanted to talk about, such as her campaign to legalise same-sex unions. From there we discussed the achievement of Adela Hernandez in getting elected. I then moved on to more difficult, and for me intriguing, ground: given her views on gay rights, did Mariela believe that Cuba, her own family, had done enough to acknowledge the repression of homosexuals in the past?

She instantly went on the defensive. 'Why do people demand that Cuba be at the vanguard, ahead of the whole world?' she wanted to know, pointing out that the island wasn't the only place with a history of discrimination against sexual minorities. 'The suffering and discrimination of LGBT people at the start of the revolution has been inflated. That's partly because everyone expected the Cuban revolution . . . to do away with all the bad and bring all the good things,' she continued. 'But it was no hurricane, it was a revolution!

That's why I sometimes ask myself, why is everyone so demanding of Cuba? It was a process the whole world was going through.'

But not every country set up forced labour camps that imprisoned homosexuals, so I asked Mariela if Cuba needed to recognise that error more clearly and in public. The strident gay rights advocate became evasive. 'I think the whole world should call a convention to recognise its errors of discrimination. In all topics. The rich countries will have to recognise their errors of discrimination in colonial systems, and in the current neo-colonial systems of domination.' I told Mariela what I wanted to know about was Cuba, her own country and its past, but she pulled the entire planet and every issue into her response.

'Let's convene the whole world and make everyone say a mea culpa for the barbarities committed in the world,' she retorted. 'But I think the world is not ready for that. We want to continue with our experiment, with Cuban socialism. And for people to leave us in peace.'

* * *

'It was like I was alone, facing the lion,' Adela Hernandez remembered as we talked about her childhood in rural Cuba. It was a couple of days after the Pride parade and we'd met up away from the crowd, noise and official escorts. I wanted to learn more about Adela's story of coming out in a small fishing village far from Havana.

In a high-rise behind the city baseball stadium, she and a friend were getting ready to go clubbing. Adela was dressed in a bright blue boob tube and stonewash jeans, arched eyebrows

carefully painted onto her tanned face. Now almost fifty, Adela told me she took her female name from the local sugar mill. She started to dress as a girl from a very young age. 'My dad beat me a lot for that,' she said. But high school was even tougher than home. Adela felt that she was seen as a 'monster' and she was verbally abused and mocked. 'I wanted to leave that first year. I cried and suffered a lot, then one day I decided to push back.'

A year before Adela was born as Jose Agustin Hernandez, Cuba launched *Operacion P* against 'pimps, prostitutes and poofs'. The revolutionary government saw homosexuals as morally corrupt and ideologically suspect. The modernist writer Virgilio Pinera was among those rounded up by police for effeminacy and spent a night in custody before powerful friends intervened to secure his release.

It was in the early 1960s that the notorious network of labour camps known as the UMAP appeared, Military Units to Aid Production. Thousands of people judged socially deviant by Cuba's macho, militaristic revolution were detained and sent to the camps to work. Homosexuals, religious believers, prostitutes and 'layabouts' were all targeted for failing to fit the mould of Cuba's 'New Man'. Even the future cardinal of Cuba served time. Young men called up for military service had to parade before the recruiting sergeant and if their gait was 'too gay' they were redirected to the UMAP.

I once passed a spot on the road to the beach outside Havana where I was told the 'delinquent' detainees were gathered prior to their journey east. There was nothing left to see but I remember a colleague assuring me that the camps were essentially an alternative military service system, not forced labour. He implied that the UMAP was for gay men's own good, to protect them from the rigours and potential abuse of military service. Those detained didn't see it that way. A Canadian journalist who managed to visit one of the camps near El Dos de Cespedes in 1966 described how 120 inmates aged from sixteen to sixty were kept in guarded barracks behind barbed wire. They had strips of sacking slung between wooden posts for beds. 'Inmates who didn't work, didn't get fed,' Paul Kidd wrote, noting that reports of physical brutality were widespread. The men were to serve three years, usually cutting sugar cane or quarrying for stone by day and subjected to doses of ideological indoctrination by night. The poet Jose Mario remembers a sign outside his own camp declaring that 'work will make you a man.'

The UMAP network was eventually disbanded following an international outcry. But the 1970s saw a purge of homosexuals from education, culture and the Communist Party itself, labelled 'degenerate' and a corrupting influence. Fidel later claimed that his own visit to the UMAP had made him aware that the original plan had been 'distorted'. Arguing that the camps were created as an 'opportunity to work, to help the country' at a time of major military mobilisation and external threat, Fidel conceded that the system had discriminated against homosexuals. He blamed a lingering machismo and prejudice from pre-revolutionary days, insisting that he harboured no such feelings himself.

Fidel went further in a lengthy interview for Mexico's *La Jornada* in 2010, describing what happened as a great injustice. 'If anyone is responsible, it's me,' he admitted. Even then, he stopped short of an apology. 'We had so many terrible problems, problems of life or death, you know?' Fidel explained, citing the Bay of Pigs invasion, the October 1962 missile crisis and multiple attempts on his own life among other more pressing threats he was then contending with.

I mentioned all this to a Cuban friend one day and he erupted with an anger I'd never seen before. He told me his own colleague had been condemned to the UMAP and then black-marked for life. The man eventually committed suicide. 'Fidel needed to apologise to the Cuban people, not foreign journalists,' my friend insisted. He wanted that apology printed on the front page of *Granma*.

In Adela's case, it was her own father who turned against her. She was in her late teens when he handed her over to the police in the misguided hope that time in prison would make a man out of his only child. She was charged with 'pre-criminal dangerousness' and sentenced to four years behind bars. 'It was a terrible experience. I don't even want to remember it. You could be dead in twenty minutes because there were all kinds of criminals there. Murderers, thieves. Everything.'

Adela never forgave her father. 'It was his fault I went to prison and he didn't care at all.' His plan to 'cure' her sexuality was obviously doomed. Attracted to men in uniform, Adela attempted to join a military academy when she finished high school but wasn't allowed in. Instead, she was driven to a nearby nursing school where she studied for three years. After graduating she began the period of obligatory social work to repay her 'free' degree, before abandoning that to join a weekend cabaret drag act in Caibarien. Now a technician at the local hospital, she still performs in her spare time, dressing as Haila, the glamorous *mulata* star of Cuban salsa, and singing at a recreation centre for sugar workers.

Adela's election to the local council caused quite a stir in the fishing village as foreign journalists descended. 'When all those foreigners came in their cars State Security called me in because they didn't know what was happening. I told them clearly that I'd struggled and suffered a lot but that now, thank God, we are free,' Adela recalled, keen to stress to me her political loyalty, as she had to the intelligence officials. 'All countries have committed errors and now we've reached the moment of reflection.' I noticed that she'd begun retreating behind set revolutionary phrases, anxious perhaps that her story could be seen as criticism.

For Adela, being elected and accepted as a politician was a watershed moment for gay rights. But she told me she had one other personal ambition. Her official ID still carried her male birth name and a photograph of her as Jose Agustin. When we met, Adela already had appointments lined up with specialists and psychiatrists to begin the long process of assessing her suitability for surgery. 'Many people just want to have breasts, not the operation, but I've had lots of hormones and I already have the breasts,' she explained. 'I want the operation. I want to be, definitively, what I've always wanted to be. A woman.'

11

THE FORGOTTEN REPORTER

I n a glass cabinet inside the Museum of the Revolution there is a typewriter supposedly used by the *New York Times* correspondent who conducted an exclusive interview with Fidel Castro in the Sierra Maestra. The sympathetic account marked a turning point in the revolutionary's struggle for power. But the name on the sign above the typewriter is not that of the newspaper's Havana correspondent. History does not remember Ruby Hart Phillips. It remembers her colleague, Herbert L. Matthews.

It was early February 1957 when a young rebel came to Ruby's office. There'd been no word of Fidel for over two months and Batista's government had declared the revolutionary leader dead. Anxious to set the record straight, Castro's supporters were looking for a Western journalist who could travel to the mountains to meet him. Ruby's first reaction was loud surprise at the news that Fidel was alive. Her next was to turn down the biggest story ever to land in her lap.

Havana correspondents were then operating under what Ruby described as the 'tightest censorship ever imposed', with a government deeply nervous about the rebellion building in the east. She was forced to file copy back to New York in secret, instructing editors to attribute her analysis to 'American travellers returning from Cuba'. Ruby did report Castro's growing 'hero' status and Batista's brutality, but warned that she would be 'deported immediately' were any such thing published under her name. Like many at that point she couldn't be sure the revolution would succeed. If it failed she didn't want to risk being ordered off the island that had been home for three decades. So when she was handed the scoop with Fidel that would have ensured her place in journalistic history, Ruby opted to remain in the shadows.

Instead, she consulted her close friend Ted Scott and the pair hit on the idea of bringing in Herbert Matthews from the US, who could get the story for the *New York Times* and then leave. His starry-eyed account from the mountains is now the stuff of legend. 'Fidel Castro, the rebel leader of Cuba's youth, is alive and fighting hard and successfully in the rugged almost impenetrable fastnesses of the Sierra Maestra,' Matthews wrote. After several hours crouched on a blanket listening to Fidel, the journalist described him as an 'educated, dedicated fanatic' with flashing brown eyes and captivating intensity. He declared that Batista's army was fighting a losing battle against a leader supported 'heart and soul' by thousands of Cubans. Matthews' account was exactly what the rebels had been counting on. Not only proof that their cause was undefeated, it was a romantic portrayal that boosted the revolutionary cause both in Cuba and abroad.

Ruby credited the interview with resurrecting the revolution and ensuring its victory less than two years later. She wasn't the only one. A colleague remembers Matthews' texts prompting a joke that the paper could put Fidel Castro on one of its campaign ads, claiming 'I got my job through the *New York Times*.' Fidel himself teased Matthews publicly on his first trip to the US, revealing that he'd had just eighteen men in his rebel army when the journalist visited. Matthews had never asked, Fidel explained, so he hadn't enlightened him.

It's no surprise then that the *New York Times* correspondent is celebrated at the revolution museum inside Batista's old palace. Among the tired-looking exhibits denouncing subsequent 'enemy' efforts to destroy Fidel's revolution, the typewriter the museum claims, apparently wrongly, that Matthews used is on prominent display. The sign above misspells his name as HEBERT in a slip that would surely have made Ruby smile.

* * *

I try to avert my eyes from the dark slab of liver spread out on the ledge, offering food for flies in the late morning sun. Alongside it is the skinny leg of some unidentified animal, probably goat. Near the meat stall there's a group of men gathered on broken metal chairs, one with a heavily blood-stained T-shirt stretched tight over his pot belly. Just metres from the classical splendour of the former Presidential Palace, Calle Refugio is a typically tattered Old Havana street. The address I'm looking for is past the butcher at number 106, a pale pinky-cream-coloured building squeezed between smarter properties. As I draw closer, Bob Marley's 'Is This Love' drifts from an open window. Directly opposite is an office of the CDR, the committee for defenders of the revolution – or neighbourhood snoops. Up on the terrace of the old

New York Times office, I see a girl pegging out towels on a washing line.

It's May 2017 and I've come looking for another 'woman in Havana' long before that label was ever attached to me. I never heard mention of Ruby Phillips while I lived on the island and only came across the reporter's story as I began exploring Greene's time in Cuba. But as *New York Times* correspondent from 1937 until 1961, Ruby was a major fixture on the Havana scene, and the more I read about her, the more I wanted to know.

I've not found any evidence that Ruby ever met Greene herself, but Ted Scott would surely have moaned about the author to his friend given how much he sniped about him in his newspaper column. It's also quite likely that their paths crossed. Ruby and Ted drank at the Floridita like Greene, and the Englishman's favourite hotel, the Sevilla, was just two blocks from Ruby's office on Refugio.

While other correspondents and writers drifted in and out of Havana over the years, Ruby became a near-daily chronicler of its stories. In 1935 she wrote disparagingly of those 'famous and not so famous writers and journalists' who would waltz into Cuba for a few days and claim to understand it. She herself would typically work from 10 a.m. into the early hours of the next morning, radio blaring and typewriter thumping. In the immediate aftermath of Batista's overthrow she stayed in the office for twelve days straight. Every mass rally at the Presidential Palace was right on her doorstep. The looting of casinos and businesses took place all around her, and among those arrested or deported after the revolution were her contacts and friends.

As I hover outside Refugio 106, safely past the sweaty meat stand, a tall man in jeans and polo shirt emerges. He tells me he only moved in a couple of years back and had no idea that the building once housed an American newspaper. I remember a feature of the place that Ruby described in one of several books she wrote, and the man confirms that the old iron staircase that corkscrewed up to the roof was still in place when he moved in. 'We had to take it out though, it was in a bad state,' he says, polite but a little guarded, so I don't push. A man outside the CDR is watching me, lazily.

Ruby was not only the sole US newspaper correspondent resident on the island, she was also the only female reporter. Because she wrote under the byline R. Hart Phillips, many readers had no idea of her gender and the paper got letters of complaint referring to 'Mr Phillips'. Ruby remembered one visitor who met her several times in Havana bidding her farewell and regretting that he hadn't met her husband, the *New York Times* correspondent.

Reporters don't hide their gender any longer, though there are still significantly fewer women foreign correspondents. In my own twenty-odd years in the field I've met few men happy to dabble in charity work abroad while their wife or partner gets deployed far away at short notice. Fortunately my own husband is a 'portable' writer, content to live all over the world. At the time, Ruby was far more of a rarity in her profession.

By strange coincidence the most celebrated female journalist of the era moved to Havana while Ruby was there, though not for work. Martha Gellhorn, who made her name during the Spanish Civil War, arrived in Cuba in 1939 to live with Ernest Hemingway, whom she later married. But she found life 'hollow and boring' in Batista's Havana. That December she escaped to report from Finland on the start of war 'at nine o'clock promptly'.

Unlike Gellhorn, Ruby fell into her role as a journalist. The daughter of an Oklahoma cattle rancher, she moved to Havana as a stenographer in the 1920s when Cuba was full of Americans and their businesses. She met and married James Doyle Phillips, known as Phil, who ran a printing and translating firm. In 1931 it was her husband who was offered the post of *New York Times* correspondent. Ruby persuaded him to take the job, believing that it would be 'fun . . . and at times dangerous'.

The 1930s were lively years to be reporting from Cuba, with constant armed revolts and their brutal suppression. Ruby's refusal of the Fidel interview was not through cowardice: she dodged bullets during street unrest from the very start of her career. In fact, she complained once that there was 'nothing to write about except shooting and bombings', declaring herself a little 'out of patience' with it all. 'I looked back over my diary today,' she noted. 'Murders, revolutions, hurricanes and disasters.' Ruby's Havana was a world away from the island life I recorded in my own diary. Whereas I had to negotiate at length to interview any state official, invariably unsuccessfully, Ruby would simply wander into the Presidential Palace at the end of her street to talk to her sources. Other contacts, from revolutionaries to government ministers, would wander into Refugio 106 themselves to give her tip-offs. As for dodging bullets, the most dangerous thing to happen to a journalist in Cuba in my time was when a Chinese correspondent crashed into a cow that had gone to sleep in the middle of the *carretera central*, the island's largely unlit central highway.

Ruby's first office in Cuba was in the Manzana de Gomez on the border of Old Havana. On the way to Refugio in 2017 I passed the building, just renovated as a luxury hotel with a gleaming mall beneath. Inside the Armani Jeans shop a man wearing a thick gold chain was holding a glass of something sparkly, and I watched the staff fussing around him and posing for photographs. A woman at the entrance told me he was a salsa singer. Two girls next to me were staring wide-eyed at the glittering window display where the price tag on a pair of sandals was $254.

'It'll cost $1,000 a night in there,' a bicycle-taxi driver told me knowingly as I emerged on the far side of the mall. In fact rooms were considerably cheaper, but still almost two years' state salary for one night. The man smiled and made some joke about his own income. It was just a hustler's line hoping for some business or a tip, but contemplating the cream walls of the glamorous new hotel butted up against near-squalor, I wondered when real resentment might begin to set in.

Ruby worked at the Manzana de Gomez office with her husband until he was killed in a car crash in the US in 1937. After the accident she returned to Cuba with their young daughter and eventually took over Phil's job. For the next twenty-four years Ruby represented the *New York Times* in Havana in a career that spanned no fewer than eleven changes of government. One former president, Ramon Grau, supposedly said that Ruby knew as much about the island as he did, and when Batista spotted her at the back of a press conference the day after his 1952 coup he pushed through to bring her to the front for a photograph.

It wasn't only the government that sought Ruby out. When she moved to Refugio 106, finally defeated by the noise of political rallies, thundering omnibuses and 'spontaneous riots' around the Manzana de Gomez, revolutionaries would drop by her new office with tip-offs. Fidel himself once sent a runner to deliver Ruby a mountain orchid as a gift.

* * *

Ruby Phillips is a footnote to the story of the Castro interview. Though it's a role she herself chose, she deeply resented how she was treated on other stories both before and afterwards. Higher-fliers would frequently swoop in to Havana to scoop the headline pieces, relegating Ruby the resident to the inside pages of the paper. Her feisty character leaps out from her correspondence with editors in New York. In 1954 she protested furiously about a male colleague being deployed to cover elections in Cuba, informing her bosses that the island was her 'territory' and that she objected to being reduced 'to the condition of a legman'. Ruby argued that she had reported on some of the 'hardest hitting stories' to come out of Cuba, and her bosses actually buckled. A few years later came a polite note to the foreign news editor enquiring after a promised pay rise. 'I really need some more money before I starve to death.' In 1959 she had to push for more pay once again, undercompensated by comparison with other journalists on the island, all of them men.

In a January 1959 feature on Ruby that it entitled 'Their Man in Havana', *Time* magazine described the correspondent as an 'enduring, familiar figure', but thought she could make a revolution 'sound like a Long Beach reunion'. *Time* saw that reflected in the journalist's taste in fashion, recording her preferred outfit as a sober 'grey sweater, carmine blouse and blue slacks'.

Such dismissal of Ruby no doubt contained a degree of chauvinism: she was a lone woman operating in what was then a very macho club. But one journalist who knew her was adamant about her limited abilities. I'd found references to Ian Aitken, former *Daily Express* correspondent and later *Guardian* political editor, in Ted Scott's newspaper columns as well as one of Ruby's books. He was frequently deployed from New York to Havana in the 1950s where he became firm friends with Scott and knew Ruby well. As I chased her shadows across Havana, I was talking to one of the last living links to Ruby's world.

Ian Aitken was recovering from a bout of pneumonia and a fall when I contacted him, but the 90-year-old emailed a few times from his hospital bed in England. I was at an all-inclusive hotel in Varadero, a couple of hours' drive from Havana, when I logged onto the Wi-Fi to read his latest short reminiscence. Surrounded by young Canadians ordering slugs of rum for breakfast after another night of non-stop drinking, it wasn't the quiet few days' break on the beach I'd been hoping for and I was bleary-eyed as I opened the message over a double espresso in the lobby bar. 'I never thought much of Ruby Hart Phillips as a journalist, she had no nose for news and couldn't write a story for toffee,' I read. 'Ted Scott used to rewrite her copy before sending it off to the NYT.' Knowing Scott's inclination to bluster and machismo, I wonder whether that's something he claimed or Ian Aitken actually saw. In the *New York Times* archive some of Ruby's script is barely visible beneath the scrawl of corrections, and her own editor admitted she was 'not the best writer in the world'. But Ruby's contacts were unrivalled and her editor praised her work as of 'the highest calibre' during Cuba's many moments of crisis.

Dismissing any notion of her journalistic flair, the former *Express* man instead described Ruby as 'nice, quite good looking and very brave'. The latter was a quality that Scott singled out when he was contacted for his friend's obituary in 1985. 'She was a very brave and foolhardy woman, probably because she didn't have good eyesight,' an elderly Scott told the *New York Times* by phone from Florida. 'She used to stop to put on lipstick before going into action, and that infuriated me.' It was a habit, though, that saved Ruby's life. In March 1952, when Batista seized power, she stopped to do her lips on her way to the Presidential Palace. That pause meant she just missed an 'exchange of machine gun fire' in which four people were killed. Unflustered as ever, she stood behind a concrete pillar until it stopped, then walked on. By contrast Bernard Diederich remembers his macho friend Scott hitting the floor in the Refugio office at the mere sound of gunfire in the street.

Surprisingly, Ruby didn't meet Fidel herself until July 1959. Even then she was accompanied by Herbert Matthews, back on one of numerous visits, and another *New York Times* colleague, Tad Szulc. By then Ruby's dispatches from Havana had become increasingly wary of Castro and his political intentions. Fidel's timetable had slipped as usual and it was 3 a.m. by the time the group headed for the Habana Libre coffee shop, with Fidel hungry after another marathon TV speech. Describing the encounter in 1963, Ruby recalled being annoyed as he'd promised an interview only to arrive and announce that he would speak off the record. 'As usual he talked on and on,' she grumbled. So when Fidel posed rhetorical questions over his steak and potatoes, Ruby jumped in to respond. Matthews later objected to what he felt was her 'hostile' tone as she demanded to know where Castro planned to get all the 'millions and millions of dollars he is planning to spend'. Ruby also informed Fidel that Americans didn't take to him because he was forever denouncing the US and because they feared his links to communism.

The conversation in the hotel continued until 8:30 a.m., but none of the journalists could report a word of it directly. 'I never did get the interview with Castro,' Ruby complained later. 'He apparently did not like to have his questions answered.'

* * *

I've discovered too much about Ruby to give up easily on seeing her old office, so I decide to return to Refugio 106 and ring the bell. The door clicks open and I see the man I'd met before in the street, now at the top of a steep flight of stairs. He invites me up and calls his wife. 'I told people you were asking around and they said not to let you in,' the woman greets me, emerging from a back room in shorts and a vest T-shirt. 'But I thought why not? I have nothing to hide. It's just a house!'

Maura and her family bought the apartment eighteen months ago and they're in the middle of renovating. She's happy to show me round and fascinated by the history of her home. We match what I'm seeing to the office Ruby described in her memoirs. The stairs from the entrance still open onto a corridor which leads into the front salon. That's where Ruby had a TV constantly turned on to catch the news. In 1957 she added a radio with a special antenna to catch Fidel's broadcasts from the mountains. Today there's a computer table and an exercise bike.

The salon is also where a pet parrot named Mickey would hop about during Ruby's later years here. The bird was a gift to Ted Scott from a businessman who left Cuba when the Castro government confiscated his marble quarry. The Hotel Sevilla wouldn't stretch to accommodating animal life so Ted moved Mickey into the office on Refugio. With one wing clipped and no danger of him flying away, the bird was often out of his cage eating through telephone cables, snapping pencils and ripping buttons off coats. He took particular pleasure in trashing Ted's belongings, which Ruby thought was payback for Ted's constant talk of parrot pie. Relations with Sheba the cat were far better. Ted had rescued her from a nearby street with a broken right forepaw and nursed her back to health in the office. Smitten, the ex-boxer devoted several of his newspaper columns to 'the tiniest, cutest little kitten you ever saw'.

Maura has installed wooden doors in the salon that open out onto a small terrace covered in terracotta tiles. She tells me the apartment was one step up from a slum when they moved in. The family own a flat in the next-door building which they rent to tourists and it was that money they used to buy Ruby's old office soon after the ban on property deals was lifted. Finding building materials isn't easy, but Maura's even managed to reclaim original stained glass from other Old Havana ruins for her windows.

Ruby had her office overlooking the patio at the back, and Ted kept a desk and phone in the next room to file his reports for NBC. His style, according to Ian Aitken, was 'strong on drama and very loud'. A third office was converted into a bedroom for use on those late nights when the drive home was too long to contemplate. The layout has barely changed, although Ruby's office is now a kitchen and there's a woman inside cutting up chicken for dinner. Watching her, I imagine Ruby's assistant Sarita Valdes Rodriguez doing the same. I'd read how, between fixing stories for Ruby, she would whip up a chicken stew in the office kitchen when visitors called. Sarita's husband, Raul Casanas, was Ruby's official assistant for the *New York Times*, paid to check news reports and rumours. In May 1959, when Fidel wanted an audience to declare his agrarian reform in the Sierra Maestra, Ruby sent Raul on the arduous trek up the mountain. After the grand signing by lantern-light, the entire hungry press pack had to sleep the night on the floor.

Maura invites me up the wooden staircase she's installed in place of the rickety iron one from Ruby's day. Pushing open a door, she reveals a spacious bedroom with gleaming tiles where Ruby once stored her clippings and files. Maura has grand plans for the whole place. She'd like to make a garden on the street outside but the city authorities say the property would stand out too much from the crowd. Maura wonders if they'd change their mind if they knew its history. 'I don't want them to take the place off me, mind you!' she laughs, imagining a museum here. 'Well, not unless the American newspaper gives me one in exchange in New York.'

Back out on the street, I stand for a while in the shade trying to conjure up life here as the revolution took hold. I picture Ted Scott, still ebullient, holding court on the terrace. He's enjoying a drink and a lewd comment with some visiting reporter from the US while fending off another vicious attack by Mickey the parrot. The *New York Times*' days at Refugio 106 are already numbered. But for now, Sarita is cooking up a stew in the little kitchen as the radio blares from the salon with another of Fidel's interminable speeches. Two cigarettes burning simultaneously in her ashtray, Ruby hammers away on her typewriter out back.

12

WAYS OF ESCAPE

The first time I got a taste of what it was like to be Cuban was when I tried to leave. It was early 2012 and I'd been planning a short break when I discovered I needed permission to get off the island. 'It's OK, we'll do it all for you,' an official at the CPI told me, amused at the look of shock on my face. 'But what if I need to go urgently?' I protested. 'Say someone gets sick?' 'In that case we'd process your exit permit urgently,' the official tried to reassure me. 'It would only take two or three days.'

Having my freedom curtailed even for a few days was a disturbing new sensation, but for me getting an exit permit was mostly a formality and an annoying expense. For Cubans the 'white card' was a powerful tool of control. It was one reason so many had risked their lives trying to leave illegally over the years, taking to the shark-filled Florida Straits on flimsy home-made rafts.

Walking down the Malecon one day with a young British film-maker, Lucy Mulloy, she told me her feature *Una Noche* had been inspired by the experiences of rafters she'd heard about right there on the seafront. 'I was pulled to the story because it's so extreme and yet so many people take that chance,' the director explained. 'I met one person who'd tried to leave nineteen times on a raft only to be forced back by the currents or the sharks.'

Lucy and I had paused for a moment next to a man fishing from the Malecon wall. When he learned what we were discussing he told us his rod had been a leaving gift from a friend who had skipped the country. 'He tried four times on a raft and an inner tube, but he'd get caught.' In the end his friend managed to marry an Italian and left with her instead. The reasons Cubans risk the sea crossing are complex. Fidel restricted the right to travel in 1961 as professionals began fleeing the island in droves and those limits were still in place when I arrived in Havana. An exit permit cost $150 initially and more to renew every month. If you stayed away longer than eleven months, you forfeited all residence rights: free education, healthcare and food rations on the *libreta*. For doctors, athletes and scientists the restrictions were even tighter. The government referred openly to such professionals as 'human capital', meaning those it had trained for free and could not afford to lose. It was an admission that, given the choice, many would leave Cuba for good. Known dissidents were also routinely rejected for the white card. The blogger Yoani Sanchez described the system as her country's Berlin Wall.

The government blamed it all on the United States. Since the early 1960s Cuba's neighbour had been offering asylum to anyone who wanted to 'seek freedom' from Castro's Cuba. Arguing that the US was trying to lure people away and undermine the revolution, Cuba claimed the exit permits were a form of protection from aggression. In 2006 President George W. Bush introduced another policy that infuriated Havana when he allowed Cuban doctors to walk into any US embassy in the world and request asylum. More than forty thousand Cuban medics were working on missions abroad at any one time and some seven thousand defected that way before the American programme was rescinded.

Such policies, coupled with the sheer difficulty of daily life in Cuba, prompted many hundreds each year to try to reach the US however they could. Just like those who defected while abroad, the rafters were condemned by Cuba's government as *gusanos*, worms. Those who made it were banned from returning home.

From the Malecon, Lucy and I took a drive out of the city to where she'd met people practising rowing in preparation for their crossing. I drove gingerly through the long grass down a narrow path towards a scrappy bit of beach where an elderly man was approaching in bright pink leggings. He'd played a small role in *Una Noche* and had just seen the final cut. 'I had my shoes on the wrong feet!' he wailed to the film director in mock protest as they kissed in greeting. 'What a disaster!'

As the three of us talked it became clear that the old man had more pressing concerns than a future career on the big screen. He made a living by floating on a rubber inner tube out at sea dangling a fishing rod and then selling what he caught on the street. As the fine for unlicensed fishing was around four months' state salary, this man and his friends would conceal their equipment in the undergrowth. But the police had grown wise to them. Rather than chasing individual fishermen, they'd simply set fire to the scrub whenever they felt like it and destroy everything. As we talked on the beach the man suddenly pointed behind us. Clouds of smoke were moving through the grass towards my parked car at disturbing speed. Yelping, I scrambled up the embankment, flip-flops slipping from beneath me, to panic-reverse onto the main road. The car cost me a small fortune from the state rental company but I was pretty sure the insurance didn't cover incineration by bush fire.

Like the man in pink leggings, the two young Cubans Lucy chose for the lead roles in *Una Noche* were plucked from the street. When they were flown to an awards ceremony in New York, the couple disappeared as soon as the plane landed. Their decision was no real surprise. During casting, people would tell the director they couldn't guarantee they'd still be in Cuba by the time she made the film. 'Ideally young people would prefer to stay in their own country,' Lucy told me. 'But there's a lot of latent desire and energy here and a real yearning for opportunity and people are looking for that elsewhere.'

As the audience emerged from the premiere of *Una Noche*, some told me they saw the tragic tale as a warning that trying to chase the American Dream in a flimsy raft just wasn't worth it. But one woman in floods of tears on the cinema steps felt differently. Maylil, the sister of the lead actress, understood exactly what drove young people to take the risk. 'It's because of how things are in this country,' she said. 'Young people's material needs, the things they can't get here. That's why so many families are separated and so many people are suffering.'

* * *

The Cuban preoccupation with emigration and separation was clear from the island's art. One month the entire Havana seafront was loaded with symbols of flight and escape as the Malecon was transformed into a giant open-air gallery. The most prominent exhibit in the 2012 Biennial was a large metal frame filled with wire fencing that had the silhouette of an aeroplane cut into it. Further along, where Cubans often sit to watch the sun drop, I found drawings of the sea wall itself as if it were made of barbed wire. Beneath a bridge there was a 1950s Chrysler transformed into a home-made submarine, complete with periscope. I was surprised by the strength of social commentary I was seeing but the exhibition curator told me the arts had always been 'aggressive' in Cuba and prone to reflect the reality of people's lives. 'The Malecon is the site of so many experiences, joyful and sad, where so many emotions have played out,' Juan Delgado explained. 'This is a tribute to that past, the present and the future.'

One of those 'experiences' had been back in August 1994 when an unprecedented protest broke out on the Malecon. Anger had simmered all summer after a group of Cubans hijacked a ferry in Havana Bay in an attempt to redirect it to the US. More than

thirty people on board were killed when the boat was intercepted by Cuban coastguards. A spate of further hijackings followed and on 5 August a protest erupted on the seafront. The clash between the crowd and police was so rare it acquired a name: the *Maleconazo*.

The following day Fidel declared that all those who wanted to leave the island should go: the government would not stop them. He believed that the US policy of taking in all Cubans was encouraging the hijackings, rafters and defections that cast him and his revolution in a bad light. Fidel calculated that a mass influx of immigrants would force the US to toughen its rules and so reduce the numbers trying to leave. Sure enough, when more than thirty thousand Cubans set out to sea in rafts cobbled together from wood and giant inner tubes, the US and Cuba ended up signing new migration deals.

From then on Cubans had to get one 'dry foot' onto US soil to be allowed to stay and become residents. The American coastguard was to repatriate rafters found at sea rather than rescue them unless they claimed 'fear of persecution'. But the new rules did not stop the flow entirely. In 2012 the US coastguard intercepted more than a thousand Cubans in the Atlantic. The number who've died trying to reach US shores is not known.

* * *

In 2013 the Cuban government finally scrapped the hated exit permits. From 14 January, Cubans who wished to travel no longer needed clearance from the government. They could also stay abroad for up to two years and retain their residency rights. It was recognition that Cubans were leaving in droves in any case. Now the government was allowing those who went to return, and in the meantime they'd be able to send much-needed money back to their families from abroad.

For many Cubans the sheer cost of plane tickets meant that foreign travel remained an impossible dream. Almost all countries would still require a visa, bar chilly, distant Russia and a handful more. But the law marked a historic shift in thinking on emigration. Senior medics, athletes and some others would still need additional clearance to travel but, critically, they were no longer banned. Even the sharpest government critics found that the doors were suddenly open. '1 day until the #migrationreform comes into effect and I wonder if the island's bolts will slide back for everyone,' Yoani Sanchez wrote on Twitter the night before the rule change. The answer, when she next tried to travel, was yes.

On the first day of the new system, I made my way to the main immigration office where people were heading to apply for passports. It was early morning but there was already a long queue and several other foreign camera crews jostling for the best shots. Even an official from the CPI had turned up. The guard at the gate was being bombarded with questions and an enterprising salesman was feeding the crowd with paper cones twisted from the pages of *Granma* and filled with peanuts.

A 23-year-old bank teller applying for his first-ever passport told me he wanted to try his luck in America. 'I want to have a good house, good wife and good car and I think it's easier to get that in the US,' Daniel said. His father was a chiropodist who'd left on a raft in the 1990s. Rescued by the US coastguard some twelve miles off shore, he eventually got a job in an American hospital. Now Daniel wanted to take an easier route out to join him, learn English and study medicine. 'I know life's not rosy over there, but with hard work you can achieve things. I want to have the American Dream!'

Another queue up the side of a nearby house led to a man filling in application forms for people on a clattering ancient typewriter. As Hector Duarte waited his turn, he told me his whole family was already in the US. He was so desperate to join them he'd tried seven times by raft. 'It's risky, but what could I do?' He spent three months in prison each time he got caught but it was a vicious circle. His criminal record prevented him getting an exit permit so he'd try the rafts again only to get caught. Now that those permits were no longer required, he could apply for a US visa and go like anyone else.

* * *

There was a joke in Havana that the last one to go should turn out El Morro, the lighthouse symbol of the city. Living in Cuba,

I began to get used to losing friends. When one of them, Juan, told me he was leaving I learned that he'd been planning his getaway for some time. He'd married a childhood friend from Cuba who lived in the US, on the understanding that one day she would help him off the island. Soon after we celebrated his twenty-fifth birthday with a big, sickly cake, Juan was gone.

One day shortly before he left I had an unusually frank conversation with Juan and his friend Julio. 'The changes here don't give young Cubans much hope; we don't see light at the end of the tunnel,' Julio shrugged, his tone defeated. 'We're living day to day. It's all about getting by, not about having plans and ambitions. That's why a whole generation is leaving, voting with their feet.'

That frustration is a large part of what drove Raul's reforms: the government felt it. But for these two young Cubans the changes weren't moving fast or far enough. 'It's like we're babies who have been crying for years and now they've given us milk to calm us,' Juan tried to explain. 'They've rocked us a bit, and now we're going back to sleep.' His friend felt life was passing too quickly not to act. 'It feels hypocritical banging your chest and cheering the revolution when you have no conviction inside. I want Cuba to be a functioning country. I want some elements of socialism to remain. But I want to make a living too, and to be free.'

Very soon after leaving, Juan got a job and he was soon posting photos of himself on social media, posing with big cocktails in fancy Miami hotels and bars. Despite a lifetime spent under communism, he liked fashionable clothes and the latest status symbols as much as any young capitalist. From his messages it seems his marriage of convenience gradually turned into a real romance. The last I heard, he and his wife were expecting a baby.

For another friend, Anailin, the end of exit permits meant her long-held plan to leave Cuba would be cheaper. We met up again when I came back to visit Havana in 2016. It was well past 2 a.m. at La Gruta, one of the city's livelier venues, and the music had switched from salsa to reggaeton. The competitions were over, the crowd of sweat-soaked Cubans was thinning out and most of the salsa tourists had disappeared. But underneath the glitter ball a hard core were still dancing and in the middle was Anailin, ponytail flying and hips rotating non-stop. Excited by the music, she plunged to the ground in the splits. Anailin was on a night shift at a government office nearby but with little to do beyond clocking on, she'd slipped out to meet her friends in the steaming-hot club. Hours later she'd return to the office to sleep until the morning shift arrived.

Anailin was a graduate from one of Havana's best universities but was paid just sixteen CUC a month by the government. The money went nowhere but she kept the job to give her some kind of status. 'It makes you respectable,' she told me once, explaining that the police would see that ID and wave her on. But if the state job was Anailin's cover, dancing was her passion. After someone spotted her at a club one night, she began working with various salsa schools helping faltering male tourists master some basic moves. Dancing was what she'd come to rely on but male students were thin on the ground, and while private salsa schools could charge up to sixteen dollars per person in a group class, most only passed on a fraction of that to the teachers. The Cubans had to hope the tourists were generous tippers at the end of the week, though that wasn't always the case. A friend told me how a group of women had once thrust a big wad of notes into his hand on their last night of classes. Excited, he'd made for a quiet corner to count it, only to discover the notes were all *moneda nacional*, local Cuban pesos, and worth very little.

Watching Anailin fly around the floor it was clear that she danced for the love of it. But salsa was also her way of escape. She'd told me frankly that she hoped to meet and marry a man who would help her to leave Cuba. That route out was far simpler for male dancers. The great majority of salsa tourists are middle-aged women and many are looking to pick up a partner, if only for the holiday. Most of the dance schools try to ban relationships with students on pain of dismissal but it's almost impossible to police. I saw dancers disappear all the time, only to appear on Facebook weeks later somewhere in Europe. Wrapped in more clothes than they'd ever worn in their Caribbean lives, they'd often be pictured alongside a new wife or even a baby. Perhaps some were tales of true love but many hook-ups didn't last long beyond the plane ride.

A day or so after that night at La Gruta, I met Anailin again over a mountain of rice, beans and prawns. It was mid-afternoon and the restaurant terrace was quiet for an hour or so between coachloads of tourists. As we ate, Olivia Newton-John's 'Xanadu' piping through the sound system, Anailin picked up on the thing that was bothering her. She'd hit her thirties and begun to worry that she'd never meet anyone to marry and get her out. She feared she'd be out of work altogether soon, as tourists started requesting a younger partner. 'I couldn't do that, though,' she said, and I followed her gaze towards two girls climbing into an open-top car with some far older men.

Anailin's plans had progressed since I'd last seen her. She'd been researching alternative ways to leave Cuba if she couldn't find a foreigner through dance and had already sold her house to help pay for it. Her favoured option, safer than the rafts, involved paying for a fake marriage to a Mexican. The $10,000 fee included a visa and transport to Mexico's land border with the US where Cubans had special immigration status and were allowed across. I wasn't sure at which point Anailin would get to divorce her new 'husband' or whether there was a whole pool of Mexican men offering this service for cash.

I wondered why she was so anxious to go now, with signs of more freedom in Cuba and more opportunity opening up, and she looked back at me with her big wide eyes. 'It won't happen. Or if it does, it will take years and I'll be forty-five or fifty. My life will be nearly over.'

As usual, we'd managed to find room after all the rice and beans for a slice of *flan*, Cuba's eggy answer to the creme brulee, and as we finished the meal I suggested that life abroad wasn't always easy either. It could be tough with a new language, far away from relatives, working hard to make the rent. Intelligent, ambitious and frustrated, Anailin just wanted the chance to try. 'I would love to stay in my own country, don't get me wrong,' she told me. 'There are a lot of good things here like the human warmth which you can't replace, and your family. But sometimes I just want to buy myself something nice like a new top or a pack of good cheese, and I can't.'

Thankfully, Anailin didn't have to marry a stranger. Around a year later she was introduced to a foreigner the same age who was mad about Cuban music and dance and the two immediately hit it off. Not long after that we all met up in Europe.

Walking along the seafront, as we'd once walked near the Malecon, Anailin told me she'd been honest with her new husband from the start, warning him that she planned to leave Cuba. She'd given him a choice: invite her to Europe to see how it went or let her go ahead with her plan to marry a Mexican. He didn't need telling twice. He got her a visa and before it expired the two were sharing their wedding pictures online.

Heading to visit, I was nervous at first that Anailin may have rushed into things. Perhaps this man wasn't good enough; maybe she'd be overwhelmed and full of regrets. I needn't have worried. She was busy enjoying new food, learning a new language and a new trade, and planning to teach salsa classes for some cash in the meantime. Thanks to the migration reform, she no longer had to cut her ties with Cuba for good. Anailin was an expat in Europe, not an exile, and had already managed to travel home for a visit. 'I miss my friends and the warmth and openness of Cuba,' she told me, as we sat on the rocks looking over the Mediterranean. 'But I'm happy here.'

Part II

13

FILM CREWS AND FIRING SQUADS

The woman on film glides languidly through the water, long dark hair streaming beneath her. When she reaches the end of the swimming pool the camera tilts up slowly towards the skyline and the whole of downtown Havana is revealed. The view from the roof of the high-rise Hotel Capri has barely changed from when that opening scene of *Our Man in Havana* was shot here a few months after Fidel Castro's 1959 takeover. The gigantic green and white FOCSA building looms on one side; once an exclusive residence, its own swimming pool is long since dry with smashed tiles. The bulky grandeur of the 1930s Hotel Nacional stands on a slight incline opposite, its sweeping driveway still lined with slender palms. Beyond that, stretching in both directions, is the Malecon sea wall where people sit and gaze across the Florida Straits lost in thought.

I'd booked a couple of nights at the Capri which features in several scenes from the film of Greene's book. It's also where the stars stayed in 1959 during their month-long shoot. The brash tower was then among the smartest hotels in town, one of several to open in the late 1950s after Batista's government offered loans and casino licences to lure investors prepared to spend big. As the grand hotels and their gaming emporiums went up, US gangsters dreamed of installing casinos and clubs along the whole length of the Malecon. With Batista in their pocket, the money-making potential looked endless.

The opulence did not last long after the revolution. The Capri was eventually nationalised and entered a slow decline as American tourists were first frightened away by the political tumult and ultimately barred by the US from visiting Cuba. But by the time I was reporting from Havana the government had spotted commercial potential in the island's past. The casinos remained firmly shut, as did the brothels, but recreations of 1950s venues were in vogue. The Capri was one of a number of iconic old spots to be renovated, though recapturing the original glamour proved more difficult. In 1959 the hotel was shiny and desirable, with handsome American actor and wide boy George Raft in the casino as front of house. More refined guests, like the newly knighted Alec Guinness, found the place vulgar. Arriving in Havana in a 'rakishly slanted' felt hat to play Wormold, the actor described the Capri as 'very gilded' and 'vastly over-decorated'. His own room put him in mind of an 'ante-chamber at the court of Louis XVI', while his co-star Noel Coward was in a suite decked out like a Mandarin's palace.

There's no longer any VIP accommodation and my own room on the ninth floor is far from palatial. But the angular furniture and period photographs are a definite nod to the 1950s and the small rooftop swimming pool still a major attraction on melting Havana days. Overlooking the pool, Raft's former penthouse is now a blandly styled restaurant.

Down in the lobby, original copper chandeliers shaped like bursting flowers hang from the ceiling, their elegance slightly marred by energy-saving light bulbs. The name 'Capri' is spelled out on the wall in swooping golden font with a star dotting the letter *i* and the area is lined with low-slung suede sofas. The hotel is heaving again, though not yet with Americans, but the days of famous film star guests have passed. At breakfast a mixture of loud Londoners and Spanish package holidaymakers stalk the buffet table, picking through slices of rubbery cheese and sausages.

* * *

On New Year's Day 1959, just over a year after the Capri first opened, crowds poured onto Havana's streets as news spread that Batista had fled. The mood was exuberant, with people wrapped in the red-and-black flags of Fidel Castro's 26th of July Movement. But there were outbursts of violence. A mob turned on the parking meters, wrenching them from the pavements and stripping them of cash. They then smashed and looted shops, particularly those linked to Batista sympathisers. At the Capri, George Raft left the newly crowned Miss Cuba in his penthouse bed to rush downstairs as a crowd intent on smashing up his gaming tables broke in. The actor used all his charm and the Capri escaped with no more than broken glass, but other casinos were destroyed as Cubans vented their fury on a powerful symbol of Batista's corruption. As many as thirteen people were killed in the rioting and hundreds of tourists evacuated from Havana as Fidel's rebel army made its triumphant journey towards the capital.

Just three months later, director Carol Reed had to convince the backers of *Our Man in Havana* that filming in Cuba could proceed as planned, assuring them that Greene's connections with the rebels would protect their investment. The new government did agree to the production; in fact, it was offended that Reed's team even renewed its request, which seemed to place the revolutionaries on a par with their repressive predecessors. So in April 1959 the cast of British and American film stars and their crew descended on Havana.

On the surface the director found the Capri little altered since his recce with Greene a few months before. The casino had reopened, along with a few others not wrecked by the mob, after Fidel reversed his initial order to shut them down. He was still firmly opposed to the trade, both for moral reasons and because the casinos were a symbol of subjugation to the US, but there'd been a howl of protest about lost jobs and the revolution needed the tax revenue. The remaining casinos barely functioned, though, as if customers felt uncomfortable about visiting them in the new climate.

Soon after the revolution, Fidel had written an open letter assuring Americans they were welcome to come to 'a beautiful land of happy people'. But the new government wanted clean-living tourists drawn by the stunning scenery and history of Cuba, not gambling and a notorious nightlife, and visitor numbers would plummet. For Greene the changes to his good-time city were clear. A dozen brothels had already been shuttered and others informed they'd have to move beyond the city limits. They would eventually vanish altogether. When Norman Lewis returned in these first post-revolutionary months he caught a certain puritanism in the air, with drunks sent to detox and prostitutes re-educated. Teenage girls were practising military-style drills late at night in the streets with shouts of *Patria o Muerte!*

By then the Shanghai Theatre had shut up shop and Superman had vanished. The Sans Souci cabaret that once hosted the likes of Edith Piaf had also closed, no longer able to turn a profit after its slot machines were banned. At the opposite end of the scale, the hugely popular *bolita* and illegal numbers games that feature in *Our Man in Havana* were wiped off the streets as many of their operators were arrested. Greeneland was gradually being dismantled.

The *Our Man in Havana* crew was sharing the hotel with a peculiar mix of people. A photo in the *Havana Post* captures what it captions as a group of 'lovelies from New Orleans' posing in skimpy shorts and cowgirl boots in the lobby. The US majorettes were in Havana for the annual carnival. Along with the dancing girls, some two hundred rebel fighters had taken up unpaid residence in the Capri after riding into Havana with Fidel. Alec Guinness bumped into one of them loading a revolver in the hotel toilets, sending his bullets scattering into the urinals. The actor's wife, Merula, complained she couldn't get an appointment at the salon for all the revolutionaries having their hair permed and beards curled. They sat, she says, 'with sub-machine guns across their knees, being flattered and cosseted by adoring Cuban handmaidens'.

As we're booked into the hotel, my husband fancies a trim in the same salon as those bearded rebels. The place is empty, the ten-dollar cut probably the most perfunctory of his life and there's definitely no cosseting. We also discover that the hairdresser's has moved slightly during renovations. At the spot where the fighters were once tended to, tourists can now buy T-shirts printed with the image of the ultimate bearded icon, Che Guevara. The main hazard these days is not rebels with machine guns but *jineteros*, hustlers with bad chat. They hang around all Havana hotels offering anything from sex to cigars. One of them pounces as soon as I step into the street. 'Didn't I see you in the Capri?' he tries, unimaginatively, on the doorstep of that very hotel. 'Where are you from?' I tell him Moscow for a change and he says I don't look Russian, which I take as an insult. A little further along a woman tries the same line. 'Are you from the Capri?' 'Yes', I concede. When I tell her I'm English she just says 'fish and chips' and walks on.

* * *

The 'Liberty Carnival' opened on the film crew's first full day in Havana, and every weekend for a month a 'bevy of beautiful curved criollas' passed along the Malecon and up the Prado.

American marching bands paraded with the Cubans that year as usual, as well as an entire float from Miami. But alongside the sequin-clad dancers there were tractors and farm implements in celebration of Castro's agrarian reform. Banners proclaimed the latest revolutionary slogan *Consumiendo Productos Cubanos*, a new nationalist mission to choose Cuban produce over foreign alternatives. People had already stopped chewing gum. The revolutionary nationalism was also on display at the Capri casino where an all-Cuban cabaret act was named after the food campaign. The days when American musical giants serenaded Havana were numbered.

The Saturday before filming began, some of the *Our Man in Havana* cast attended a lunchtime press buffet at the Capri. Star-struck, the *Havana Post* society reporter Leta Wood swooned over her encounters with a 'modest' Sir Alec and 'gracious, charming' Noel Coward. As for Jo Morrow, the young American chosen to play Wormold's daughter Milly, the columnist was bowled over. 'She rides, swims, skis and skates,' Ms. Wood gushed. 'And one of her hobbies is BUYING HATS!' Greene himself felt that the coquettish teenager was of limited acting ability and sorely miscast.

Leta Wood's colleague Ted Scott didn't make the cocktail party. Later that week he informed readers that he was sorry he missed the 'tipple and tucker' as he'd been anxious to meet Sir Alec. He wanted to tell him that Cubans had hummed a tune from his film *The Bridge on the River Kwai* as they celebrated the fall of Batista. The tune was best known in Britain as 'Hitler has only got one ball'. After missing one chance to pass on this vital fact, Scott managed to corner the actor a few days later at a British embassy function. Pulled away from the guest of honour after just thirty seconds, the columnist turned his attentions instead to a 'lovely lady' from the Rovers Club. The men there, he informed the woman, found her 'the most exciting thing in shorts that they have ever seen – in shorts'.

As for the press buffet at the Capri, Scott felt he would have been an unpopular presence. The journalist was still bruised by his previous encounters with Greene. A big fish in the little pond of Cuba, Scott apparently felt snubbed by the famous visitor. Writing about the party, he referred scathingly to Greene's 'excruciating' fondness for the seedy Shanghai Theatre. He then warned that Alec Guinness would 'require all of his genius' to make *Our Man in Havana* a success. Parts of Greene's story, Scott wrote, 'appear to have been written in the substitute for secret ink recommended by the British agent to his sub-agent in the novel'. He meant bird shit.

* * *

It wasn't actually Greene who had kept Scott away from the press bash. The columnist had been held up at La Cabana, the old Havana fort, where an American man accused of plotting to kill Fidel Castro was due on trial. Scott had been following the case closely since Alan Nye's arrest and was trying to pull strings to get the NBC cameraman with him into court. The American was facing the death penalty.

Nye was a US Navy Reserve pilot who claimed he'd pretended to go along with an assassination plot in order to get close to Fidel and warn him of the danger. The case was making waves abroad where there was growing unease about the large number of prisoners detained without trial in Cuba and reports of summary executions. According to Ruby Phillips, some 475 prisoners had already faced the firing squads by that April. The *New York Times* reporter had attended one tribunal herself and found the whole procedure sickening. Even Alec Guinness saw farm carts covered with cages made of chicken wire in the streets, containing 'shocked and puzzled peasants on their way to be interrogated'.

Alan Nye got off lightly. It took the military judges just eight minutes to consider the evidence against him and he was pronounced guilty shortly before 4 a.m. With a court full of US reporters, the judges then suspended the death sentence on condition that the pilot left the country and never returned.

Had Nye been sent to the firing squads, the man in charge of dispatching him would have been a fellow American nick-named The Butcher. Herman Marks, a convicted rapist from Wisconsin, had been appointed to oversee the killings at La Cabana after fighting alongside Che Guevara in the Sierra Maestra. He appeared to have extraordinary relish for his task, personally leading prisoners out to a blood-soaked moat in the early hours of morning. After the riflemen had mowed their target down, lit by the headlights of jeeps, Marks would step forward with his pistol to shoot the victims in the head and finish the job.

Ted Scott knew the executioner well. Marks would occasion-ally drop by the office that Scott shared with Ruby Phillips, once joining him in target practice with an air pistol. It was one of Scott's favourite pastimes when he tired of writing, though reports of his shooting suggested he was no James Bond and Ruby said Marks was even worse. She doesn't record how she felt about having a man in her office who admitted to making cufflinks from the spent bullets of the execution squads. Scott's relationship with Marks assured him tip-offs on prisoners' fates and a chance to reach them at La Cabana for his stories.

One night while Greene's film crew were in town, the swaggering executioner dropped into the Floridita. The novelist wasn't there but the British theatre critic Kenneth Tynan and his wife were eating club sandwiches with Tennessee Williams and George Plimpton. While many tourists had stopped coming to Cuba, the island had become a big draw for writers anxious to soak up the heady atmosphere of revolution and try to meet Fidel himself.

That night Marks introduced himself to the group by announcing that he had so many people to kill he was flat out until 2 a.m. Diplomats and journalists were apparently falling over themselves to observe him on a night's work and he assumed that the daiquiri-sipping writers would also appreciate some execution tourism. Remarking that the evening would be particularly active, Marks invited the table to join him at 'the festivities'. He misjudged his audience. Incensed, Tynan declared Marks 'a frightful specimen' and yelled that he would come to the fortress and throw himself in front of the guns. With that, Tynan stormed out of the bar.

Away from the grim scenes at La Cabana a surreal, heady mood reigned in the city following what one *Havana Post* columnist called years of 'forced silence, blood and sorrow'. Alec Guinness noted that the American tourists had all but disappeared but among Cubans the city was full of 'excitement and chaos'. Men would stop him in the street, pull up a trouser leg and flash scars left by the torture of Batista's henchmen. They'd then laugh and shout 'Viva Fidel!' An American journalist saw paper 'Castro beards' for sale in a local supermarket. A newspaper advert in block capitals announced tours around Kukine, Batista's luxurious residence: one dollar per car to see the dictator's home 'just as he left it on December 31st', all proceeds to the city maternity hospital.

Maureen O'Hara, who played Beatrice, sensed a 'time of great hope' in a country setting out on a new way of life.

14

LOVE NOT MONEY

It took time to spot the coffin through the crowds in the Havana funeral parlour where everyone seemed to be talking at once and at top volume. But across the stark, functional hall, a queue moved slowly towards a side room where Cuba's most celebrated boxer was laid out. Inside, friends and fans filed past Teofilo Stevenson in his open casket, pausing to peer at the sporting legend beneath the glass. A pair of boxing gloves had been laid on a Cuban flag at his feet. In one corner a woman rocked gently as mourners stood alongside the coffin in a traditional honour guard. Cuba's latest generation of young boxers arrived in their team tracksuits to pay their respects just a few weeks before they would take to the ring at the London Olympics. Propped against the wall as a backdrop to it all was a wreath of white roses sent by Fidel Castro to the ultimate symbol of his sporting revolution.

'No other amateur boxer in history shone so brightly,' Fidel wrote in a short tribute that hailed both Stevenson's huge talent and his famous loyalty. Cuba's leader had banned

professional sport in 1962, insisting that the prize for revolutionary athletes was the pride and applause of their nation, not fabu-
lous wealth. Every Olympic medal won was to prove the suprem-
acy of socialism.

Stevenson was arguably the greatest in a parade of champi-
ons that followed. With his punishing right fist, this extraordinary athlete achieved the kind of international fame no other
amateur boxer could claim before or since. In Munich in 1972
he was one of three Cuban gold medal winners, the first since
the revolution, and he went on to take gold at the next two
Olympics in Montreal and Moscow. Most believe he would
have claimed a fourth title in 1984 if the Cubans hadn't joined
a Soviet boycott of the Los Angeles games. The small island
ranks a proud second only to the United States in the boxing
medal tables.

But Stevenson was also a national hero for what he didn't do. In 1976 the heavyweight refused millions of dollars to defect to the US and fight Muhammad Ali in a professional bout. It would have meant turning his back on his island for good and the boxer declared that he preferred the love of millions of Cubans. Stevenson, Fidel crowed in *Granma* on the boxer's funeral day, 'could not be bought for all the money in the world'.

'There were many attempts to buy him, but part of his greatness was that he resisted,' the president of the Boxing Federation told me at the funeral parlour. To him, America's constant attempts to lure athletes away were part of a bigger ideological battle, but they were also testimony to the achievements of Cuban sport. Felix Savon, the island's other three-time Olympic gold-medallist, told me Stevenson was his inspiration. He'd been crossing Havana on a bus when he heard the news and had to get off in tears.

As Stevenson's coffin was driven out in a car laden with flowers, fans filled the streets and broke into applause. Many escorted the cortege on foot all the way to Havana's colonial-era cemetery. When the casket was lowered into the ground there were shouts of 'Champion!' A woman broke into the national anthem and it caught on, rippling through the crowd.

Stevenson died just a few months after I arrived in Havana so I never got a chance to ask whether he regretted turning his back on a professional career and huge financial reward. If he did, he never admitted so publicly. There was no whisper either that day at the graveside of how the 60-year-old fighter had died a shadow of his once glorious self. It's an open secret that he'd turned to drink on leaving the ring. Perhaps that was a sign that he had regrets, I don't know, but the dilemma

Stevenson faced is one that Cuba's top athletes have wrangled with ever since the revolution. A combination of excellence and relative poverty has made Cuba's stars prime prey for sports agents whenever they compete abroad. Coaches say the pursuit is particularly relentless in the US where aggressive agents harass athletes as they leave the ring or pitch, prowl around them constantly and knock on their hotel doors. Many have been unable to resist.

After watching Cuba's current crop of boxers sweat in train-ing at their base, *La Finca*, I rooted especially hard for them at the 2012 Olympics. I'd seen them pushed to the limit long before breakfast: sprinting, skipping and shadow-boxing to the commands of their demanding coaches. I'd also heard how desperate the team was to bring home gold after disappointment in 2008. Cuba's best fighters had defected then shortly before the Beijing games and the team failed to win gold for the first time since 1972. One coach told me that they didn't count the silvers and he was only half joking.

During the London games, I'd get up very early to catch the fights live on Cuban television. I punched the air in my living room, urging on Ronny Iglesias and the others, and I'm sure I yelled as loudly as any of my neighbours when they did it: two gold medals and two bronze to erase the disappointment of Beijing. But I also knew that those triumphs and the romantic ideal masked an increasingly difficult reality. The sporting system was struggling to survive.

There were other signs that the revolutionary zeal of Stevenson's era was fading along with the inspirational slogans painted on gym walls. When I asked a member of the Olympic team at *La Finca* about his greatest ambition he joked that he wanted to be a barman at Varadero beach resort. 'You get good tips there,' the champion fighter laughed, away from his trainers and my camera. By contrast, athletes took home a basic state salary of around twenty dollars a month like any other state worker.

Maintaining free sports coaching from childhood was sacrosanct for the government, along with free universal healthcare and education. But Cuba was finding it increasingly difficult to fund its vast network of training facilities and sports schools. So the government began to experiment and in 2013 it allowed fighters to sign up for the semi-pro World Series of Boxing. Its backers had been courting Cuban participation since its launch in 2010. Now the athletes got the green light to join.

When I went back to *La Finca* ahead of the boxers' debut as semi-pros, the coaches told me the whole team had been reinvigorated. Boxers who competed could expect a decent salary as well as bonuses. They would fight without head protection for the first time and for five rounds instead of three, but they oozed confidence. No one would tell me much about the money side. The boxers had either been well drilled to keep quiet or were still in the dark, and the head of their federation was tight-lipped. 'We have a system of stimulation but the contract is confidential,' Alberto Puig told me firmly, as a fighter behind him jabbed and danced around a knotted rope. 'The World Series will contribute to recovering discipline,' Mr Puig said, which was Cuban code for 'boxers will be less tempted to flee the country.' When I persisted in asking about the money, the boxing boss announced that our interview was over and began to pull the microphone off his white shirt. I could only persuade him not to leave by dropping the thorny topic of pay.

It was an uncomfortable issue for a generation raised on the amateur ethos, proud that athletes put *patria* above personal ambition. The champion boxer was held up as a noble, pure ideal. But Cuba was having to adjust to a harsh new economic reality, and boxing was not the only sport being forced into radical change.

* * *

At the little ferry port for La Isla de la Juventud, baseball players and their trainers were spilling off a coach onto the jetty. My guide from Inder, Cuba's sports body, pointed out the star we'd come to meet, and following his finger I saw Michel Enriquez. The third baseman had captained Cuba's national team to gold at the 2004 Olympic Games in Athens, then silver in Beijing.

While boxing excites the nation every four years, baseball is Cuba's year-round passion. *Pelota* is the sport most children play in the streets and what men debate passionately on their doorsteps or beneath trees in Havana squares and parks. All too often, though, that talk would turn to the latest player to flee the country for a shot at the big time. Those who left were officially considered traitors and their departure was never reported in the official press. But by 2013 the government had decided to adopt a radical new policy that it hoped might stem the tidal wave of defections: it would allow some baseball players to compete for overseas teams for a season as paid professionals. The idea was that athletes would then be less tempted to defect.

There were catches. Players had to return to Cuba to play the season for their home club too, which could prove exhausting. Meanwhile, a state sports body would manage all the contracts.

That meant the state decided who could benefit from the system and the state controlled the cash. As far as I could establish, its cut was around twenty percent, but officials were coy when I tried to pin them down on the details. Their argument was that any money made would help to maintain Cuba's giant network of sports schools and keep providing training and facilities for free.

Michel Enriquez had just returned home from Mexico where he'd been part of this sporting experiment. I'd got permission to spend a day or so with him so we were travelling to La Isla to see his team in action. The rival team Cienfuegos was on the same ferry, crossing with us on the lower deck. After a couple of hours we all docked in Nueva Gerona, a sleepy little place with steep green hills and almost as many horses and carts as cars. The once-famous citrus groves no longer produce much and the island is now best known for its abandoned prison. The giant yellow cylindrical buildings are where Fidel and Raul were held in 1953 after their failed attempt to storm the Moncada Barracks.

As soon as we got off the boat it was clear that Michel was a local hero, hailed and greeted with kisses wherever we went in the appealing way Cubans have with their superstars. It was that unpretentious attitude that found me in Michel's kitchen the next day as he carefully helped wrap a hook-load of frozen fish in old copies of *Granma* for us to take back to Havana. Cubans have a habit of hunting for 'deficit' items whenever they're travelling and on La Isla my colleagues found good, cheap fish. As we stored our parcels in Michel's freezer until home time, I tried to imagine a similar scene with Ronaldo or Messi.

Michel's home was a simple bungalow behind a crazy paved wall. Inside, it was pristine clean, spacious and cool. He got it as a perk of the job when he began playing for the National Series, although his teammates said the waiting list had since become far longer. Raul's reform allowing Cuban emigres to sell their homes rather than abandon them to the state left fewer properties to reallocate to loyal athletes.

Leading the way to a back room, Michel showed me a glass cabinet full of balls, gloves and trophies marking his many triumphs. On a peach-coloured wall a picture of him with Messi caught my eye. 'That was 2008 in Beijing, when we bumped into him,' Michel explained. 'We asked permission for a photo and he was very nice!'

Barcelona football star Lionel Messi earned $43 million the year I met Michel. Michel told me that his own take-home pay was 560 Cuban pesos a month, or twenty-three dollars when converted. Baseball players got a whole three extra pesos for every game, though there were better bonuses for Olympic medals and the chance of a more generous 'stimulus' if a team won the national championship. But lucrative individual sponsorship deals are forbidden.

Michel was candid about how Cuba's 'pure' ideal translated into reality. 'You can't "resolve" everything with 560 pesos,' he told me, using a favourite Cuban verb. He admitted that fans would often treat players in cafes and restaurants. 'But if you work, you don't always want to have to be paid for, you want to be able to treat others too.'

Because of his success, Michel was better off than many athletes even before he was selected for the new experiment. As well as the house, he'd received a smart Peugeot 407 a couple of years earlier as reward for his long career in the national squad. Michel was one of forty athletes allocated a car that year, though they'd all had to wait a lot longer than usual as money was tight. 'It's not a present, we earned this,' Michel stressed, as we drove from his home to the stadium, a fluffy tiger and other trinkets swinging from his rear-view mirror. Like most Cubans he'd had to hitch rides to work before, or squeeze onto a packed *camello*, the enormous humpbacked truck-buses that have been phased out in Havana but still run on La Isla. 'I think it's right a Cuban athlete should know his society and know sacrifice,' Michel argued, manoeuvring his silver saloon slowly through the narrow streets to avoid all the bicycles, some with a passenger balanced on the handlebars. 'I think we should have to work for the stimulus. Just maybe not for so many years.'

In Mexico, Michel had been granted a taste of a very different sporting life. His season with Los Piratas de Campeche had been cut short by a knee injury but even so he said he'd been paid 'five or six thousand' dollars in one month. It was a staggering amount for Cuba, allowing him to buy furniture, air conditioning and kitchen equipment. 'We're moving away from the idea that the state has to look after us and we're taking charge of ourselves,' the athlete told me. The new system Cuba was trialling offered thousands of dollars, not millions like in the US, but it allowed players to return home instead of being disowned by their country. Michel told me he hoped his own experience would open up an alternative. 'I came back to Cuba with extra motivation. I see possibilities now, and that's the stimulus.'

The other players at La Isla were broadly positive about the new opening. Their own basic salary was being doubled to forty dollars a month, and the team told me openly that this would encourage them to perform better. There was also the spur of knowing that talent scouts from Mexico, Japan and beyond could watch players on the island. But the team pointed to one thing that threatened to undermine the whole scheme: the US trade embargo meant that Major League baseball remained off-limits to Cubans unless they defected and cut all ties with their country. The problem is, the US is where the best Cuban players are desperate to be.

'It's not just the money but the satisfaction of being at the top level of world baseball,' the director of La Isla, Armando Johnson, admitted as his team crunched one another's bones and stretched before the game. They'd lost another promising pitcher before the season started when Raisel Iglesias skipped the country. Six months after my visit to La Isla the 23-year-old signed a contract with the Cincinnati Reds worth close to $30 million. No wonder his old coach told me the enormous pull of the US would remain.

The reforms might slow the exodus of talent, Armando thought, but they wouldn't stop it.

As the start of the Cienfuegos game approached, the fans began arriving on bicycles which they left unlocked outside the ground. The early afternoon sun was fierce but La Isla were forced to play by daylight: a hurricane had knocked out the floodlights five years earlier and the club couldn't afford to replace them. When the teams filed onto the pitch, Cienfuegos were missing their star batter. Jose Abreu had defected a couple of months earlier and just signed a $68 million deal with the Chicago White Sox. 'We could never pay that much!' one of the La Isla fans sighed, when I asked what he made of the news. His friend did his best to sound hopeful that offering Cuban players higher salaries might help. 'Maybe it would be harder to steal them then,' he suggested, but even he sounded unconvinced that forty dollars a month would do the trick. No one I spoke to ever criticised the players who left; they understood. By then they could even follow their progress. After decades trying to scrub the defectors' faces from existence, state TV had begun screening some Major League matches.

Passion for the game remained strong and Cuba had young players emerging through the ranks to pin their hopes on. The sport was particularly important in La Isla, which was visibly worse off than much of the Cuba I'd seen, with very little tourist income and minimal sign of the new small businesses then transforming the mainland. Life was simple and baseball was still a cheap and popular pleasure.

Spread out over the open concrete stands to watch the game, the fans crunched home-made snacks from paper cones. Somewhere in their midst was a group with a drum and metal bowls that they'd bash energetically for every run. To the fans' delight, the home team snatched the game just before the sun dropped behind the hills, casting the baseball ground in shadow.

* * *

For Felix Savon, the changes in Cuban sport came too late. The boxer turned up for our interview in a boxy Lada he'd borrowed and somehow managed to squeeze his enormous frame into. His own car was partly disassembled in his garage, off the road for the perennial Cuban problem of a lack of parts. The vehicle and his bungalow in a quiet Havana suburb were reward for winning three Olympic gold medals. Savon is Cuba's most celebrated Olympian after Teofilo Stevenson.

I'd come to speak to him ahead of the 2012 games in London, having already filmed his teenage son sparring at the local academy. Felix Jr told me how he'd get up at 4:30 a.m. to train, driven by the goal of becoming the champion son of an Olympic champion. When I mentioned that I planned to interview his father, he informed me proudly that he wouldn't ask for cash 'like the others'.

That comment had slipped my mind by the time I arrived at the peach-painted family bungalow. Felix Sr began showing me round a mini museum to his own career. The shelves in the hot, airless room were crowded with trophies and plaques, squeezed alongside old boxing gloves, shiny cloaks and training shoes. Dangling from a slightly sinister-looking wooden bust of the fighter himself were two Olympic gold medals. Savon told me a relative had helped himself to the third one and sold it for some quick cash.

The boxer began pulling photographs from the wall one by one. The twenty-seven snaps of him with Fidel were his most prized possession. Sounding at times like a giant child and play-punching me periodically on the arm, the heavyweight champion recalled the days when Fidel would see off the Olympic squad in person at Havana airport and greet the athletes on their traditionally triumphant return home. Savon remembered the honour of being chosen by Fidel as Cuba's flag-carrier for his own final games at Sydney in 2000 and how the *Comandante* would send congratulations cards and a basket with rum and some money. 'But we don't need money to fight. We're millionaires in love here. That's love for our country, the flag and our homes.'

When we emerged shiny with sweat from the stuffy trophy room to begin setting up for our interview, Savon called my producer over. The two men began muttering, then stepped outside. The boxer was asking for payment. So much for Felix Jr's promise; love no longer paid all the bills.

Savon was born into poverty in Guantanamo, near the US military base at Cuba's southern tip. He played baseball in the yard of his barrack housing and enjoyed athletics at school. When his sister got a place at one of the free specialist sports schools known as Eide, Savon became determined to join her. It was when another child was expelled for indiscipline that the future champion got his chance. A teacher offered the young Felix a place for the only sport with a free slot: boxing. Tall and a hard puncher, the boy was soon impressing his coaches and by the age of thirteen he was competing, flooring a young opponent from Santiago on his debut. 'I thought I'd killed him!' Savon smiled as he recalled the bout, his long frame sprawled in his armchair. His opponent was unconscious for about fifteen minutes. 'People told me to calm down, but I couldn't. I was sure he was dead. Later I saw him in the canteen and had to apologise. But I was traumatised.' Savon's school friends nicknamed the first-time winner 'Fresh Meat'.

Teased as a child, Savon poured all his frustration into training. Proper binding had been hard to come by in those days and at fifteen Savon went into a fight with bare fists beneath his gloves. His broken bones never healed properly and Savon showed me his mangled right hand. 'Other boys had problems too,' he told me. 'But the ones who were operated on had to stop boxing and those who weren't went on. So I slept with ice on my fist and did physio and with a lot of work I could carry on.' He then pointed out the scars of all the other blows to his body over the years, including the peculiar way his shoulder bone now sat too high. 'I'm very pretty!' he chuckled, as I reacted.

Warming to his theme, Savon bounded across his living room to pull out a cardboard box full of VHS videos of old fights. We then sat on rocking chairs in front of his TV and watched as he scrolled back and forth, searching for one of the highlights. The picture was fuzzy and Savon couldn't recall the name of his opponent but he was definitely from the US. The boxer told me proudly that he'd never lost to an American.

Like Teofilo Stevenson, Savon had the chance to fight the greatest professional heavyweight of his generation. 'I was offered five million to fight Mike Tyson in 1993 and in 1997 it went up to ten million dollars,' Savon recalled, smiling. He admitted that such a fight would have been physically tough. The champion fancied his chances against any amateur over three rounds but long professional bouts were a different matter. Still, it wasn't fear of failure that stopped him. 'We fought for medals not the money. For an ideal. To defend our country and our flag.' Behind his professions of patriotism lay another brutal reality: fighting as a professional would have meant defecting, with no hope of return. 'You won't be happy without your family, not with all the money in the world,' Savon insisted. But he admitted that his decision had boiled down to one fact: 'I was not my own master.'

The boxer's admiration for the real master of Cuba ran deep. Savon told me that without Fidel he would have ended up in the fields cutting sugar cane. In the old Cuba, he said, sport was for the rich and the white. The boxer believes that the revolution gave poor black men like him opportunity. 'What he doesn't know, no one knows,' Savon told me of Fidel, still in awe. Then a thought struck him. 'I paint! I can show you some of them if you like?' he offered, and promptly disappeared to rummage in a side room. Savon had been given a desk job at the Boxing Federation after retiring at thirty-four but admitted to feeling useless there. Unsure what to do with his days outside the ring and struggling to stave off a sense of emptiness, the fighter had turned his smashed hand to art.

'How many do you want to see?' the boxer asked, thrusting the canvasses towards me. 'I have sixty-nine!' One had a tiny cut-out photo of his own face, looking down, with chaotic blobs and dribbles of blue, red and black paint running away from it. Another was mainly black with a thin white outline of Fidel's face. Savon had painted that one on the night the *Comandante* had announced he was too ill to continue in power. 'He's like a lighthouse,' the boxer said of his hero, holding up his own work of art which had a bright star shining in one corner. 'Fidel Castro lights up the world,' the boxer told me. 'Everything I've done, I did thinking of him. Of the people and of the country.'

15

ENEMIES AND ALLIES

I have to direct the taxi driver to Cuba's national football stadium because he has no idea where it is, or who's playing. In fact we're heading for a historic fixture: it's October 2016 and Cuba are playing the United States. As the pink convertible we flagged down draws closer to the Pedro Marrero stadium there's a decent stream of fans heading for the gate.

The concrete benches on one side of the ground are already full, including hordes of high-school children still in uniform and perhaps two hundred American fans. Somewhere among them is the US vice president's wife Jill Biden, in town as part of the latest bridge-building exercise since Cuba and the US restored diplomatic relations. There are a couple of huge Cuban flags hanging from the roof but the side fencing has been draped in the Dutch national tricolour. I guess the thaw in relations hasn't reached the point of mass-producing US flags and some-one thought the Dutch colours would do.

I ask Cuban fans to point out the ones to watch in their team but they can only shrug. 'There's no investment in football and we've lost a lot of our players,' one man explains. He's not exaggerating. I covered one story in 2012 when four of the national squad fled their training camp in Canada before they even made it to the match. Three years later another four stayed behind on a trip to the US.

We bump into a group of Americans looking for seats after failing to reach the section where fans in Stars and Stripes scarves are chanting: 'We are the US, mighty, mighty US.' One of the group tells me he'd contemplated offering a policewoman money to let him through. 'Do you think I should have?' he wonders, and I tell him I think that would have been a bad idea.

Most of the Cuban crowd are more enthusiastic than knowledgeable, gasping and roaring even when their striker fires miles wide of the goal. When the superior American team finally go one-nil up, the teenagers abandon all interest and go back to the games on their phones or flicking through music. The US section breaks out in cheers. 'You're not singing any more!' an overweight man wrapped in a flag hollers good-naturedly at the bemused Cubans, who hadn't actually been singing at all. A self-appointed Cuban animator blows frantically on his whistle and tries to rouse the crowd around him to respond, but after a couple of unconvincing bursts of *Si Se Puede!* they fizzle out.

Watching from the back of the stands are a handful of agricultural scientists from a US university who tell us the match is light relief from touring urban farms on their officially sanctioned academic visit. One man is a turf specialist and horrified by the bald and bumpy pitch which sends the ball skidding off at odd angles. When another learns that I'm a journalist, he starts talking politics. 'People here are just waiting for the historical leaders to die before everything changes,' he declares, and I squirm at his loud pronouncements after a couple of farm visits and half a football match.

The match ends 2–0 and as I'm heading for the exit a Cuban fan turns back to speak to me. 'Thank you for coming and for bringing your team,' he says very sincerely. He seems deeply disappointed to learn that I'm English.

* * *

The first public sign that decades of antagonism between the US and Cuba might be drawing to an end came while I was still working in Havana. In December 2013, at the funeral of Nelson Mandela – a close friend of Fidel – Barack Obama extended a hand for Raul Castro to shake. Smiling broadly, Cuba's president accepted. The leaders of two sworn ideological enemies then shared a few seconds of apparently friendly chat. It was a historic encounter, choreographed to look casual. The White House insisted that the men had exchanged mere pleasantries and that its Cuba policy was unchanged. But the symbolism of that gesture was unmistakable.

Shortly afterwards, Raul raised the issue of US relations at a rare meeting of parliament. He informed the country that Cuban and US officials had discussed various issues in recent months, from immigration to restarting a postal service. Cuba's political system was not up for negotiation, Raul cautioned. But he called for 'civilised' relations with the US, respecting one another's differences. 'That's the only way', he told the deputies. 'Otherwise, we are willing to continue in the same situation for another fifty-five years.'

In July 2015 the two countries officially restored diplomatic ties, and the following March Obama headed to Cuba with his wife and children. When I travel back to Havana in May 2016, the city is still buzzing from the recent visit. Friends tell me Obama had been greeted like a rock star. 'Police would close the streets, but people would run to the roadblocks and wait to get a glimpse of him passing,' one expat remembers. A colleague would see the crowds get animated as she drove down Fifth Avenue in her black car until they realised she wasn't part of the presidential cavalcade.

A Cuban friend found Obama fresh and inspiring. She particularly remembers him telling people he wasn't there to interfere, that it was up to the younger generation to shape and build their society. Obama's speeches stressed that it was time to 'bury the last remnant of the Cold War' and look forward as 'neighbours and as family'. Importantly, he said he'd urged Congress to lift the trade embargo as an unfair burden on the Cuban people. He even appeared on the popular comedy show *Panfilo* in a sketch which involved him uttering Cuban slang phrases like *No es facil!* and *Que bola?*, What's up? He praised Cuban food and music – 'Some of the best musicians in the world are right here in Cuba' – and played dominoes. The show's main character was left awestruck.

At a joint press conference, Obama's performance was measured and smooth. He even cited Cuba's independence hero Jose Marti on the 'human impulse to freedom'. But Raul was unused to such events. When the US press pack asked about human rights and political prisoners, as the Cuban side must surely have been expecting, Raul fumbled with his headphones for translation and stumbled over his words. He did recover later to defend Cuba's system of free healthcare, equal pay and universal education as valid human rights, but it made for an uncomfortable watch.

A week later, Fidel lashed back in print at 'Brother Obama'. Writing in *Granma* he warned that Cuba didn't need gifts from the 'empire'. He listed multiple examples of US aggression over the years and declared that Obama's 'syrupy' words about brotherhood were enough to give Cubans a heart attack. The following month Fidel made a rare appearance in person. In a royal-blue tracksuit top, voice occasionally trembling, he told the Seventh Communist Party Congress that he was nearly ninety and would soon be 'like all the others', meaning dead. But to fierce applause, Fidel vowed that his ideas would live on. It was to be his farewell speech to the nation.

All thought of accelerating the reform programme was quashed as Raul reiterated that changes would come 'without haste or improvisation'. Having announced previously that he would step down as president in 2018, just shy of eighty-seven, Raul clarified that he would remain First Secretary of the Communist Party, and so in ultimate control. 'It was like a slap in the face after the Obama visit,' one European resident in Havana tells me.

I take a tourist coach up to Varadero for a few days at the beach and pass proud wall murals declaring that 'Cuba's dead will never be forgotten' as well as handwritten 'For Sale' signs on private houses. 'We Cubans do smile a lot,' the guide informs passengers through her mic. 'But we smile more for a tip.' After answering a few questions from the tourists about daily life, she begins giving what I realise is now the official line on Obama's visit. 'The Americans want to change the regime here,' the woman goes on, into her squeaky mic. 'But we have our ways and our rights. If they don't respect that, we don't want them.'

* * *

Cuba was always keen to show that six decades of ideological war with the US had not deprived the island of allies. Hosting peace talks between the Colombian government and the Revolutionary Armed Forces of Colombia, the Farc, allowed it to do just that. The two sides had been meeting in secret in Havana for months to explore the scope for formal negotiations aimed at ending five decades of conflict. We journalists didn't hear a whisper until the peace talks were officially announced in August 2012.

Inspired by the Cuban revolution, the Farc emerged from an agricultural commune overrun by the Colombian military in 1964. The conflict that erupted killed and injured tens of thousands of Colombians and forcibly displaced millions from their land. It also turned the country into a byword for kidnap, as the guerrillas seized hostages for ransom to fund their fight. Drug trafficking and extortion were the other trademarks of the Farc, which was labelled a terrorist organisation by the US and the EU. Right-wing paramilitary groups which sprung up to resist it were guilty of brutal attacks themselves.

My own first encounter with the Farc was when one of its militants handed me a DVD of rebel rap. He'd come to my office with the man the group called their 'foreign minister'. The stand-out number on the disc was a riff on the peace process by four fighters performing a jerky dance somewhere in the Colombian mountains. The young Marxists switched outfits as fast as the beat, from military fatigues to Che Guevara T-shirts and berets, then back again. 'The bourgeois hunted us, but they couldn't defeat us,' they rapped, mocking Colombia's president for turning to communist Cuba for help. It was a decade since the last attempt to reach peace had collapsed. This time the two sides had agreed to meet outside the country and Havana was both relatively close and supremely discreet. The talks were mediated primarily by Norwegian diplomats, overseen by Chile and Venezuela as well as Cuba, all looking to end the longest-running conflict on the continent.

The venue was the Palacio de Convenciones, a 1970s convention centre that had hosted everything from the annual cigar festival with its tobacco-rolling contests to Communist Party congresses with their interminable speeches. Now I found myself there most mornings as the two Colombian delegations arrived at carefully spaced intervals. The government team never said a word as they passed our cameras but after years in the wilderness the Farc were keen to use their new-found public platform to the full. On good days they'd issue a statement directly linked to developments in the talks, but as the process became more sensitive and secretive I'd struggle in for the early-morning security check only to hear some 'statement of solidarity with the Palestinian people'.

The Farc had been airlifted out of the jungle specially for the talks so whenever there was a short break in proceedings they had to remain in Havana, tucked out of sight in a government guest house. When they held their first press conference, a large contingent of journalists flew in from Colombia and beyond for the chance to challenge senior commanders. After a few encounters, the novelty began to wear thin. The militants were unreconstructed Marxists, inclined to answer everything with long lectures on their theories of land reform and wealth redistribution. Cuba's reforms were at least a nod to twenty-first-century reality; Farc politics were stuck squarely in the 1960s.

The rebels hadn't been entirely isolated from the contemporary world, though. When I asked to see their press officer one day, he suggested the airy lobby of the Habana Libre. The hotel had been overrun by Fidel's own bearded revolutionaries in January 1959 and seemed a fitting location to meet a modern-day Marxist. Sipping our cups of Cubita coffee near a gallery of photographs from those days, I attempted some small talk before launching into my pitch listing the benefits of a one-on-one interview with the BBC. 'BBC? Wasn't Jimmy Savile at the BBC?' asked the man who'd just emerged from decades fighting in the Colombian jungle.

The person I was pursuing for interview intrigued all of us journalists. Tanja Nijmeijer was an attractive 34-year-old Dutchwoman who'd spent the past decade fighting with the Farc. A former English teacher in Colombia, when she joined the insurgency her parents had been flown over the jungle in a military helicopter, calling over a loudspeaker to try to persuade their daughter out. Now this intelligent middle-class European, mixed up in another country's war, had arrived in Havana for the peace talks. A couple of months into the process, I finally convinced the Farc to let me talk to her.

The Dutch guerrilla turned up for the interview with a light scarf draped over bare shoulders, long brown hair left loose. She was wearing dangling dragonfly earrings and a delicate necklace to match. As I watched her approach with two other women fighters, I thought perhaps she'd missed feminine clothes in her years in the mountains or that she was attempting to project a gentler image for the camera. Either way, the supposedly hardened fighter looked queasy. Unused to cars, she arrived complaining of travel sickness. After some water she was ready to talk but any idea that I'd be able to connect as a fellow European woman quickly vanished. The Tanja Nijmeijer I met that day in Havana was a zealot. Even as the Farc were in Cuba to put an end to their long and vicious fight, she was unbending in the rebels' cause.

In fluent English with a soft Colombian lilt, the Dutchwoman told me that she'd known nothing about the conflict when she first visited Bogota in 1998 as a student teacher. She learned of the insurgency while watching local television to improve her Spanish. It was a fellow teacher who then radicalised her, taking her to the slums and talking of 'social justice' before revealing that he was a militant for the Farc. 'I saw the poverty and I was really impressed [struck] by that,' Nijmeijer recalled, relaxed at first, on comfortable ground. 'I started to question the capitalist system, everything around me.' The young student went home to complete her university degree but returned four years later, unable to go on living the 'good life' knowing that others were in 'misery'. Back in Bogota she first made contact with the militia and eventually joined the Farc.

Nijmeijer has been indicted by a Colombian court for attacks on a police station, the Bogota bus network and warehouses. A court in the US was also demanding a prison sentence of up to sixty years for her alleged role in holding three of its citizens hostage in 2003 after their plane crashed in Farc-controlled territory. As soon as I questioned the guerrilla on her involvement in direct violence, her calm demeanour disappeared. 'We are an armed movement and with that I think I answer your question,' she flashed, eyes narrowing. 'I didn't choose to use violence, I chose to do politics in a country where doing politics implies violence.'

I did catch some glimpses of the former teacher when she laughed at her hesitations in English, or mentioned long phone calls to family she was able to make from Cuba. But the bloody conflict in Colombia has transformed the lives of millions and Nijmeijer admitted to no feelings of guilt for her part in it. 'I feel realised as a woman, as a revolutionary, fighting for something really worth it,' she told me, almost dreamily. The Dutchwoman also insisted on describing the Farc practice of kidnapping civilians, sometimes holding people for years on end, as 'economic retention'. When I wanted to know how she could possibly justify that, she demanded that I reformulate my question. As I pointed out that the Farc were widely condemned as terrorists for attacking civilians among other things, she bristled. 'I thought I came to an interview, not a trial?' she said slowly, her mouth breaking into an uncertain, unsettling smile.

Before interviewing Nijmeijer, I'd imagined she joined the talks hoping it would play well in any future discussion of her fate, that she was looking for a way out, perhaps an amnesty. After the camera was off, I wondered whether she'd drop her guard a little. I tried chatting about what she and the other women fighters turned negotiators did during the regular breaks in talks and she mumbled something about having lots of documents to study for the peace process. 'It must be nice to be back in civilisation for a bit, though?' I persisted, as a diplomat had told me that Europeans overseeing the peace process sometimes brought Nijmeijer packets of Edam cheese. I wondered whether her hope was to go back to Holland one day but standing looking over Havana from the terrace, the guerrilla shook her head. 'I would like to see my family and to talk Dutch,' she told me. 'But just for a couple of weeks.' It wasn't Holland that Nijmeijer missed, it was the Colombian jungle.

A couple of weeks later I was called to another press conference. Unusually, the venue was an outdoor restaurant in the woods and I arrived to find Rancho Palco full of tourists with a band playing the obligatory 'Guantanamera'. Eventually, the unsuspecting holidaymakers were bussed away and Farc fighters in green shirts began appearing through the trees. Smoking fat cigars, they looked very much at home and I wondered whether they might be dragging out the peace process deliberately. They'd already been ordered to keep a low profile in Havana after photographs taken during a break in talks showed them relaxing at sea on a yacht. The images of the Farc having fun had caused a scandal in the Colombian press.

Emerging into the restaurant clearing, the chief negotiator Ivan Marquez headed for a small stage, opening with a loud speech accusing the Colombian state of torturing prisoners. Then he switched tone completely to announce that it was international journalists' day and the rebels were treating all of us to cocktails. Waiters promptly appeared with trays of pre-mixed mojitos. I was driving so I ducked the rum but the Farc were persistent. 'Made an effort to engage Farc number two commander in conversation', my diary noted that day, as I'd attempted to discover the fate of three hostages just captured by the Farc in Colombia, the latest hitch in the peace talks. 'All he would say was "Come for mojitos!"' When I tried the Farc Foreign Minister Rodrigo Granda instead, he actually hurried away from me. I made one final attempt to corner Ivan Marquez. 'He said "mojito?" and shrugged me off,' I wrote. 'It's hopeless.'

It was then I noticed that the male photographers were ignoring the Farc leadership completely and buzzing around Tanja Nijmeijer. She seemed self-conscious, unsure whether to lap up the attention or keep up her guard. I wondered whether she'd seen our interview on TV and whether her family in Holland had caught it too. As I studied her, the Dutch guerrilla caught my eye and gazed back coolly. Four years of tough talks later, Nijmeijer's commander would ask 'sincere forgiveness' from the Farc's victims as he signed a historic peace deal. But if Tanja Nijmeijer did regret her youthful decision to join the militants, if her tough talk was just a facade, in all her time in Havana she never betrayed a hint of it.

* * *

Venezuela under President Hugo Chavez was Cuba's closest ally and greatest benefactor. But as the Colombian peace talks got under way in Havana, Chavez was seriously ill in a city hospital. The state of his health was another secret carefully guarded by Cuba.

In October 2012 the socialist firebrand had won a further six-year term in office, a victory achieved after he'd had cancer surgery in Cuba. Announcing himself cured, he thanked God, medical science, Fidel and Raul. But two months later Chavez was back in Havana for another urgent operation. We received precious little information from that moment on.

The Venezuelan embassy on Fifth Avenue was draped in a giant national flag and cars from the Venezuelan state oil firm PDVSA were daubed with good wishes for their leader. *Pa'lante, Comandante!* But Cubans were almost as worried as Venezuelans. Chavez was both a political prodigy and close friend of Fidel, but over the years the economic links between Havana and Caracas had become as significant as the personal ties. By 2012 Cuba was importing two thirds of its oil from Venezuela at a cut-down cost, met by sending some thirty thousand doctors to work in that country's toughest neighbourhoods. Venezuela paid an additional lump sum for the medics' service. But the opposition had vowed to cut the whole deal if Chavez died and they came to power.

Cubans were increasingly apprehensive, fearing the island would be thrown back to another economic crisis like the one that followed the loss of their previous state sponsor. 'We had power cuts in the 1990s that lasted for hours,' a cook in a state-run enterprise told me, remembering what Fidel had dubbed the Special Period after the collapse of the USSR. 'Things are bad here even with Chavez. If he goes it will be a disaster.'

State economists were worrying a little less, in public at least, pointing out that tourism was a much bigger source of income than it had been in the early 1990s. But trade with Venezuela still accounted for over a third of the island's GDP. So Cubans were wishing Chavez the kind of miraculous recovery Fidel himself made in 2006, when he survived intestinal surgery against all the odds.

*   *   *

Pavel had already been on a three-year mission to Venezuela when we met, one in the army of doctors Cuba sends around the world. It was a practice Fidel began in 1960 as a humanitarian, internationalist gesture. Hundreds of volunteers were dispatched to Haiti after the devastating earthquake in 2010 and dozens more to Sierra Leone to help fight the 2015 outbreak of Ebola.

Increasingly, though, the government was offering doctors for hire. The medics earned more abroad than they could at home, and the Cuban state earned more still from the countries contracting them. At the start of 2014 there were more than 44,000 Cuban medics deployed to sixty-six countries from Angola to Qatar, though the vast majority were in Venezuela.

This time Pavel was part of a large group heading for Brazil, and I found the young doctor in a vast lecture hall making a valiant effort to role-play in Portuguese with hundreds of other medics in white coats. 'I've always wanted to visit Brazil and we just want to help people in need,' he told me earnestly. The contract Cuba had signed was for more than eleven thousand doctors to be sent on a three-year assignment to remote, impoverished spots. 'There are so many people in Brazil that have never seen a doctor,' another man said. 'This is a very beautiful opportunity for us to help. And if we don't go then who will?' Others talked of the professional challenge, confronting problems they wouldn't see at home in Havana and improving their skills. Doctors I spoke to told me that while serving a 'mission' was not obligatory it was strongly encouraged. But there was another clear motive. Pavel and his colleagues would earn a salary over forty times higher than in Cuba: not $23 a month, but $1,000.

Some previous perks of the medics-for-hire system had been phased out, like the right to ship containers of goods back to the island, tax-free. Another quirk of the system meant that doctors were only paid a portion of their salary while they were abroad, with the rest placed in an account in Cuba. Their relatives could access just $50 a month until the medic returned home and the remaining funds were released in full.

A few months before I met Pavel, a furious row broke out over the Brazilian contract when a couple of Cuban doctors abandoned the mission, complaining they were being treated as 'slaves'. They claimed they'd been tricked over their pay deal, and were only getting a fraction of what Brazil was giving the Cuban government. Cuba had to revise the arrangement slightly, under an uncomfortable spotlight, but in Havana an official informed me that the doctors were slaves only to 'serving their patients and saving lives'. The mission continued.

I arranged to catch up with Pavel a few days after his Portuguese class to film him at work in Central Havana. The three-storey clinic had a large picture of Raul Castro pasted just inside the entrance and an air of dejection. It was as clean as it could be when everything I saw was old, cracked and battered. I'd asked to film Pavel carrying out a consultation. It was all officially approved – after eight months of requesting access – but the young doctor shook with nerves as he began examining a middle-aged woman complaining of a cold. We started filming as he placed a spatula in her mouth and asked her to say 'aah', but then he stopped. He decided he should be wearing disposable gloves so an assistant rushed off to find some. Once his hands were safely covered Pavel started again, then stopped and called the assistant back. 'The gloves are pointless without a face mask,' he told her. She produced one, the patient obligingly said 'aah' once again, and the camera rolled.

Pavel came from a family of doctors and told me he enjoyed being a GP. In Cuba medics live and work within the community they serve and will often call patients directly to ensure they turn up for all their vaccinations or treatments. For a long time, Cuba has boasted of one of the highest ratios of doctors to patients

in the world. 'Cuba's medical service is very social,' Pavel told
me. 'Patients come to my house all the time and I treat them
there, whatever the time, whatever the circumstances.' But
the system was expensive to maintain and while I was in
Havana the government launched an awareness campaign to
remind people that the service 'is free, but it costs'. The real
price of medical procedures was pasted up on clinic walls in
an attempt to persuade patients to think twice before dropping in to get their blood pressure checked just because they
were passing.

Cuba is acutely sensitive to criticism of its healthcare system.
The fact that it's state-funded and accessible to all is a matter of
pride and of principle. But like other countries it's struggling
with increasing demand and shrinking resources. After we
finished filming, Pavel threw his disposable face mask and gloves

in the waste basket. When the assistant came back, she was horrified. 'You can't just bin them!' she scolded. 'Have you forgotten you're in Cuba?'

Low-paid, like all state workers, doctors live off salaries supplemented by gifts from grateful patients. Those range from a bar of soap to cash, depending on the patient's means. I remember calling a friend when I first went to a GP in Havana wondering how much I should tip and when. Should it be before any examination or after? I worried that the doctor might be insulted. The island has showpiece hospitals and clinics, some world-leading research and a separate service developed for health tourists and foreigners with insurance. But local clinics are basic at best. On the other hand, the doctors' bedside manner is extraordinarily good. After my husband spent a couple of sleepless nights suffering with an inflamed eye, his doctor not only treated the infection but gave him a jab that had him flying and forgetting the pain for an entire day. He got a good tip.

* * *

The secluded hospital where Hugo Chavez was being treated was the best in Cuba. Just a few miles from our flat, tucked in an area of woodland, fields and giant plastic greenhouses, Cimeq attended to Cuba's own leaders. Chavez chose it both for the treatment and for its total privacy. When I drove up to the pink, low-rise hospital buildings I found two guards in military fatigues. Official statements on Chavez's condition were sporadic and there were no leaks at all by medical staff. Asked to do a radio interview one day during a long gap between statements, I couldn't tell the programme much more than they already knew: that Chavez was sick and in Cuba.

But mid-December 2012 brought an announcement that Venezuela's leader had suffered internal bleeding during surgery, followed by an infection. New Year street celebrations were cancelled in Caracas as the country was called on to pray for its president. In mid-February 2013 the government released smiling photographs of Chavez in his hospital bed and insisted he was fully capable of fulfilling his duties. Three weeks later came the announcement that he was dead, having been flown back from Havana in the middle of the night.

Across Cuba flags were lowered and bars ordered to turn off the music. The government praised Chavez as an honorary son of Cuba and a hero who had squared up to the United States. *Granma*, whose masthead was usually bright red, turned black in mourning. It took some days before Fidel himself issued a statement as reports circulated that he was devastated. Admitting that the news had dealt him a 'heavy blow', Fidel hailed Chavez as a fighter for social justice and 'the best friend the Cuban people have ever had'. Those Cuban people were mostly left worrying about what the loss of that friend meant for them and their struggling economy.

16

CUBA LIBRE

F ilming of *Our Man in Havana* got under way on 12 April 1959, but the government's assurances that the team needed no permissions didn't last long. On day two, with Noel Coward and Alec Guinness due on set, an Interior Ministry official demanded to see Greene's screenplay. The Labour Ministry had already been given a copy and granted work permits, but now the thirty-thousand-word script had to be translated into Spanish and checked again. Word had reached the government that the film took a flippant approach to the revolution. Greene's contention that he was only poking fun at the British Secret Services did not spare him.

Filming continued as negotiations began. A couple of days later an official minder was sent to ensure the film stuck to the approved text with nothing disparaging the new government. The first requirement was that American actor Ernie Kovacs should shave. Kovacs was playing the role modelled on President Batista's repressive police chief Esteban Ventura, but beards were firmly associated with Castro's rebels. Ted Scott seized on the chance to lecture Greene in his newspaper column, informing the novelist that the name of the police chief was spoken only in low tones in Havana and with a backwards glance. Ventura was 'a synonym for terror – the terror that comes by day or night', Scott warned, and Cubans wouldn't take kindly to him being presented as a romantic rogue.

The police chief character in Greene's film didn't alter but Carol Reed counted almost forty changes to the script. Instructed to insert more of the 'atmosphere of the fight against Batista', Greene added a few sirens. The team was permitted to bring back some former strippers for scenes in Havana nightclubs, but in keeping with Cuba's new puritanism the censor would leap up and object whenever too much flesh was exposed. Despite this, Reed was said to be 'simply amazed' at the authorities' cooperation as large parts of downtown Havana were cordoned off for filming. Fed up with all the roadblocks, Ted Scott chastised the police for falling over themselves to accommodate the film crew.

The arrival of Maureen O'Hara to begin shooting her scenes as Wormold's secretary and love interest, Beatrice, created a fresh stir. The Irish actress tucked into bacon and eggs as she chatted with the press in her hotel suite. Despite forty-eight hours without sleep she 'looked fresh and lovely', Leta Wood recorded in the *Havana Post*, clearly enamoured. The actress's suite at the Capri soon filled with flowers from admirers.

Reed needed extras for his film and drafted some from the local English-speaking community, including the society columnist. 'Quite a day – and they paid me for having fun! Imagine!' Wood gushed after eight hours on set. She and her friends laid on a pot roast for the English crew at the end of it.

When it came to filming street scenes the challenge was to keep bearded rebels from wandering into shot. Hundreds of locals would stand under the sun to watch the crew in action. At one point a couple of American tourists were spotted explaining that the story mocked the British, not the Cubans. Spectators would boo, hiss and even spit when extras wearing the powder-blue uniform of Batista's hated policemen appeared. When one such 'officer' began arguing with a bystander, the crowd turned on him. You can't do that any more, the *Havana Post* reported the next day. This is *Cuba Libre*.

* * *

In those first months of 1959 even Ruby Phillips agreed that the revolutionary government was wildly popular. Writing in the *New York Times*, she described how people welcomed the land reform, rent cuts and wage increases, as well as campaigns against corruption and vice. Meanwhile, for Havana's foreign residents life had reverted to something like normality, with the usual mix of bridge teas and charity functions. One report described the Americans 'sharpening their rackets' to take on the British at the annual Rovers Club tennis tournament.

But Ruby had begun to spot the shadows, reporting growing disquiet among middle-class Cubans who'd backed the revolution. As early as April 1959, she wrote of their concern at an 'extreme nationalistic spirit', the increasing influence of communists and a growing anti-American rhetoric. The journalist also recorded unease over the island's jam-packed prisons, as all trials other than military tribunals of suspected Batista-collaborators were halted.

A few days after Greene arrived in Havana, Fidel flew in the opposite direction on his first foreign tour. Setting out from Ciudad Libertad, Cuba's renamed military airport, he was on a mission to persuade America in particular that his revolution was nothing to fear. He wanted to reassure Cuba's neighbours that he was neither a communist nor a dictator. It was his chance, according to the *Washington Post*, to 'reveal something of his real self under his beard'.

Fidel's visit was ostensibly a private one at the invitation of the American Society of Newspaper Editors. President Eisenhower was famously too busy playing golf to meet him, but Fidel managed to make an impression on the American people. For ten days he preached that a free press was sacred and the greatest fear of dictators, that American property in Cuba would not be expropriated and that his revolution was not communist. Most of the 26th of July Movement members, he pointed out, were Catholic.

Fidel already had plenty of enemies in exile, some of whose relatives had been killed by his firing squads, and there were multiple death threats during his tour. But at Washington airport he was met by an enthusiastic crowd of Cubans whose cheers drowned out the student protesters. Still, questions over the arrest and execution of opponents dogged Fidel's trip. Back in January he'd invited dozens of American reporters to Havana to witness the start of the military trials, hoping to convince them of the justice of the proceedings. In the vast Ciudad Deportiva sports arena the journalists saw a baying mob yelling for the execution of Batista's henchmen. Answering his critics, Castro cited the thousands killed under Batista. The dead, he said, were shouting out for such justice. Several weeks later, as he arrived in

Washington, the execution of eighteen more Cubans made the front page of the *Havana Post*.

Fidel condemned international pressure over the firing squads as a campaign to discredit Cuba, marking the beginning of a habit for him. In the US he told a large audience gathered by the American Society of Newspaper Editors that those being executed were war criminals and not mere collaborators of Batista. The aim was to ensure that 'future tyrannies' would not torture and kill their enemies as Batista had. When he repeated that argument to a gathering of Harvard law students, he was met with boos and hisses.

But on the whole the charm offensive was effective, and crowds flocked to see the olive-green-clad revolutionary wherever he went. In New York that included an unscheduled stop at the zoo where he tucked into hot dogs and ice cream and patted a tiger through the bars of its cage. In Central Park a crowd of twenty thousand turned out to hear Fidel speak and ended up chanting his name.

* * *

The scene where a bemused Wormold is recruited by British intelligence takes place in the toilets of Sloppy Joe's. A thriving business before the revolution, the bar faltered after it was nationalised and eventually closed. But in 2013, as tourist numbers grew, the government restored and reopened the famous bar. Not long afterwards I got an email from the CPI inviting foreign correspondents there for a 'Social Friday' to promote the now state-run venue. Frustrated that the CPI wasn't getting me the news access I wanted, I didn't go to the drinks party but my silent protest passed unnoticed.

A few years later, I decide to head to Sloppy's to see what I've missed. Walking up Zulueta, I can read the bar's name from a distance. It's spelled out in large red letters on its pillars just as in the 1920s and early 1930s when Americans would stream here direct from their cruise ships. The prohibition years in the US made Cuba a prime getaway. Once seated at Sloppy Joe's famously long mahogany bar, many visitors would not stir again until sailing time. A 1941 guidebook described the place as a 'dubious shrine'. If you didn't take on a 'cargo of firewater', as Ted Scott remarked scathingly, 'you simply had not been to Havana'.

When I walk in early one afternoon in 2016 it is quiet, with air conditioning that brings immediate goosebumps. Faithfully recreated from old photographs, Sloppy Joe's is now an obligatory stop-off on the pre-revolution nostalgia tour. Its columns are pasted with photographs of the great and good who've drunk here in the past, including a snap of Noel Coward and Alec Guinness meeting Hemingway. The American novelist dropped in on the set as the two were filming the recruitment scene here, when the British agent Hawthorne informs Wormold, 'We must have our man in Havana.' The bar would have been glad of the business given the big slump in tourism after the revolution. According to Ted Scott the film crew brought in more people than Sloppy's had seen since prohibition.

There's still whisky behind the bar, though not the eighteen kinds of Scotch Hawthorne counted, and the glass cabinets all around are stuffed full of Havana Club rum. Greene had Wormold describe Sloppy Joe's as the 'rendezvous of tourists', not residents, and it remains that way. Only a few tables are occupied, but in state-run style none of the waiters rush to serve us and we eventually leave without ordering.

* * *

Soon after returning from his foreign tour, Fidel asked to see Greene and the stars of the film. Alec Guinness described the group waiting over ninety minutes in an apartment from which they could see Fidel through a cloud of cigar smoke, deep in conversation with other bearded members of his government. In the end Carol Reed declared it a 'bloody waste of time' and Greene agreed. The group gave up and left, to the distress of the lackey who'd summoned them.

It appears that Fidel didn't take offence. On 12 May, the last day of filming, he arrived on set unannounced bringing a crowd in his wake. He chatted to Maureen O'Hara who later had to deny reports that he'd asked her on a date. Fidel had spoken in such a whisper, O'Hara said, that she hadn't understood a word he'd said. Alec Guinness was eating bean soup in a nearby cafe when Fidel showed up, and he didn't rush. An anxious aide came twice to fetch him, telling him that Fidel was asking for the leading man. Sir Alec sipped a second coffee before wandering out. In his memoir he describes finding Fidel surrounded by boy-bodyguards, each with a dagger pointing outwards. The tips of those daggers touched Guinness in the chest, side and stomach as the actor and the revolutionary talked.

Fidel was a model of magnanimity, apologising for the problems with the censors. It was a mistake that only happened, he claimed, because he'd not been present. 'You are to make your film exactly as you please. Those are my orders.' But by this point filming was finished and the crew were packing up to head home. Greene had already left, flying back to the UK to attend the opening night of one his plays. *Our Man in Havana* premiered at the Odeon in Leicester Square on 30 December 1959, almost a year to the day since the revolution.

17

ATHENIAN FORUM

T he first May Day parade I went to was over in record time. The stream of workers took under two hours to cross the vast open space of the Plaza de la Revolucion. Cuba was on an efficiency drive and even Workers' Day, the great socialist celebration, had been cut back. Leading the crowd was a sea of medics in white coats. Waving mini Cuban flags, they marched past the pale marble podium where Raul Castro stood in a straw hat smiling at the masses down below. Many people had brought props to help them stand out. One woman paraded carrying a plastic window frame in front of her and a group of tobacco workers had a giant model cigar. Later I spotted a cage of live hens held aloft by scientists from a research institute.

For five decades since the revolution had expropriated all private businesses, May Day had been about state workers bussed in from factories and farms. But 2012 was different. The day before the parade I met the owner of a burger bar as he handed out bright red T-shirts and caps emblazoned with the company logo to staff. The march would be broadcast live to the nation

and Sergio was planning to use it to promote his business. 'Of course it's an advertisement; we want people to see we're present,' he told me. 'There are no TV adverts here, but we do what we can.' The next day I watched his staff parade past a giant poster on the square that vowed Cuba would never return to capitalism.

A choir in red neckerchiefs and matching sun hats sang revolutionary songs as the workers shouted their familiar chants, 'Down with imperialism!' and 'Long live Fidel and Raul!' The main slogan was the less catchy pledge to 'preserve and perfect socialism'. The crowd was cheerful, bursting into applause as they passed the main stage, but the choreographed march had a whiff of routine about it. The most genuine excitement seemed to be displayed by socialists visiting from Europe. Giddy with idealism, they mingled with the Cubans waving banners proclaiming 'Socialism or Death!' and took photographs of images of Lenin and Che Guevara.

I slightly regretted missing the grander parades of May Days past and the sight of Fidel himself up on the podium. He was an electric presence in the early years. Graham Greene heard him speak on this same square in 1963, standing among a 'cheerful Bank Holiday' crowd. The author felt there was 'a touch of Athens' about Fidel's style: accessible, close to the people, willing to discuss and debate. Greene used the Greek democracy analogy again three years later, likening Cuban politics to an Athenian Forum where the people are 'consulted, informed, confided in'. To the novelist this engagement was key to keeping the revolutionary flame alive.

By my time there was more ritual than experiment and excitement. Raul preferred to leave the May Day speech to the trades union boss whose main message in 2012 was one of efficiency and savings. After arriving before dawn for security checks, I was quite content to see the last happy worker file past by 9:15 a.m. before the heat of the Havana day kicked in.

* * *

In February 2013 Cuba held a general election, not that you'd have known it on the streets of its capital. There were no party flags or big billboards and no campaign buses or rallies. I had thought I might go door-to-door with one of the candidates to film them canvassing for votes, but there was no such practice. The only sign of the upcoming ballot was a series of A4 sheets of paper pasted to some shop fronts with the potted biographies and pictures of local candidates. There were 612 of them running for 612 seats in the National Assembly.

Fidel described the elections of Western democracies as 'a carnival, a farce – totally staged'. In Cuba candidates were nominated by the people, based solely on their revolutionary credentials. They were not obliged to be card-carrying members of the Communist Party, but the majority inevitably were. Alternative political parties were banned as Fidel argued that a multi-party system was impossible while the United States retained its 'aggressive' policies against the island. At the 2012 Communist Party conference, Raul stressed again that ending one-party rule would open the doors to the 'parties of imperialism'. It was an argument for maintaining tight control that played on a history of US intervention in Cuban politics stretching back long before the revolution.

Over my years as a journalist I've covered passionately contested elections in Turkey, Spain and even Russia, though the vote there is stacked against any real opposition. But before Cuba I'd never seen an election entirely stripped of any clash of ideas or interests. Antonio Castaneda, one of the candidates for the National Assembly, had no problem with that. He was a retired musician from the Tropicana cabaret and a high priest, or *babalao*, of Santeria. He believed deeply in Cuban socialism too. 'All those debates they have in other places like the United States, with their Republicans and Democrats, just bring fights and conflicts,' the Cuban politician told me firmly when we met. 'The fight here is to keep our country stable, and to keep the achievements of our revolution intact.' Antonio was confident that the revolution would thrive and prosper even after the Castros left power. 'We don't pay for funerals here,' he explained, choosing an unusual illustration of the benefits of socialism. 'Our education and health-care are free too, and no one wants to lose that.'

As the elections approached I attempted to interview voters, but getting people to say something meaningful on the record was difficult. I'd spent most of my first year in Havana learning to read between the lines and decipher hand gestures: a stroke of an imaginary beard for Fidel, or a two-finger tap on the shoulder to denote the military, and a lot of dramatic eye-rolling. It was all very well to understand what people thought but it didn't make for great quotes.

As my time in Havana went on, I began to notice that tongues were loosening a little. More Cubans were cutting their economic dependence on the state, and paying taxes for the first time, and some began to talk more freely about their struggles. A message came from the top that criticism 'within the revolution' would be tolerated. When I discussed the change with a friend she pointed out that it was quite common to complain openly in queues to strangers now. 'You never knew who was listening before, but people don't really care any more.'

The Cuban *glasnost* was strictly limited – criticising the country's leaders and questioning the political system was still taboo, particularly on camera – but it was nevertheless a change. Discussing the economic reform process became one of the safest topics for interview, given that improving the economy was an official goal. But Cubans were still wary of being interviewed about politics. When I emerged from speaking to musician, turned parliamentary candidate Antonio Castaneda, I found a man selling birds on the busy square. Introducing himself as Ronaldo, he said he'd set up his stall a year ago and although it was tough going, he got by. He was happy enough chatting about his business as the canaries chirped beside him into my microphone, but as soon as I asked about the elections and his hopes for the new parliament, Ronaldo clammed up. 'I don't have any opinions on politics,' the bird man declared, and turned his back.

On election day itself I visited several polling stations including one inside Havana railway station. Young pioneers in neckerchiefs stood guard over the ballot boxes against a backdrop of a huge Cuban flag. They would salute as each slip was dropped into an urn. Despite the lack of choice, voters entered a private booth to complete their ballot papers. All day long, state television hailed the vote as a great exercise in democracy and a display of support for the revolution. The TV set had been dressed in an effort to look modern, though someone had put a stationery kit complete with scissors beside the shiny laptop on the news anchor's desk.

The only surprise of the day was when Fidel turned up in person to vote. Stooped and looking every bit his advanced age, he was reported by state media to have spent an hour chatting to the crowds at the polling station. The cameras caught a little of it. Fidel's voice was weak but his message was strong as ever, praising the Cuban people for their revolutionary spirit and declaring that the United States hadn't 'defeated them in fifty years and they never will'. The foreign press were not invited to record the moment.

That night my Cuban producer called to tell me that TV had just declared the result. '7.8 million people have voted,' he informed me down the line. Momentarily thrown, I pointed out that was the turnout, not the result. 'Oh yes', William said. 'All 612 candidates were elected.'

*   *   *

Despite their peculiarly Cuban nature, the 2013 elections marked a key moment in the handover of power from Cuba's *historicos* to a new generation of revolutionaries. After the vote, Raul confirmed that his own second term as Cuba's president would be his last. He also promoted 52-year-old Miguel Diaz-Canel to be his first vice president, so marking him as his most likely successor.

Diaz-Canel was born in Villa Clara province, about 170 miles east of Havana. Its capital city, Santa Clara, is dominated by memories of Che Guevara, who led the last triumphant battle of the revolution there in 1958. Diaz-Canel is not a military man and was born after the revolution. He's no upstart, having spent thirty years rising through the Party ranks to join the Politburo in 2003. But before now few had paid much attention to the tall, broad man with a thick head of grey hair. Diaz-Canel was largely a mystery figure at home and abroad.

Driving into Santa Clara, I passed larger-than-life images of the Castro brothers in military fatigues as if to remind me who was still in charge. In the city itself, people I stopped appeared to have genuinely warm memories of Diaz-Canel. He was just thirty-three when he was appointed Communist Party boss in the province. 'He worked all hours and would go round seeing for himself how things were going, checking up,' an old neighbour and Party colleague, Ela Perez Montpellier, recalled. I heard a lot more about this habit of dropping in unannounced to factories, the hands-on approach. 'He had an official car, but didn't use it for personal things,' Ela added. 'He walked or took his bike. He was honest – that's why so many people here like him.'

Other neighbours told me that the politician came from 'humble' stock, that his mother was a retired teacher and his father an 'ordinary worker' at the local brewery. I hadn't pre-arranged this trip or sought permissions so I didn't manage to meet his parents or close Party comrades, but I did find the family home. A humble-looking place from the street, its exterior had long gone unpainted. It was Diaz-Canel's sister-in-law who opened the wooden front door, but she would only tell me that the family were 'very proud' of his promotion.

Diaz-Canel's political career took off during the first wave of economic liberalisation in the 1990s. There was some talk of the new vice president as a Gorbachev figure, perhaps prepared to countenance more radical change. But his true feelings on the reforms launched by Raul remained unclear, as did his views on Mikhail Gorbachev. After all, the Soviet leader's policies led to the collapse not only of a political project but of a whole empire.

There is one place in Santa Clara, though, that perhaps hints at a more liberal side to Diaz-Canel. The city is home to El Mejunje, Cuba's most famous gay club and a venue that welcomed nonconformists of all kinds at times when Cuba as a whole did not. When I met the manager late one afternoon an elderly couple were dancing slowly around a patio enclosed by brick walls covered in graffiti. Ramon Silverio told me that Diaz-Canel had always been an important supporter of El Mejunje, bringing his own children there for weekend art classes. 'He defended it against protests,' Ramon explained, at times when people 'didn't share' the club's ideas. 'I think this place is an example of his broad mind and forward thinking.'

* * *

It was about six months later that I spotted the first vice president himself, bopping his head at a concert on Havana's seafront. It was widely reported that Diaz-Canel was a Beatles fan in his youth, when Western rock music was banned as 'decadent'. The concert venue was the dramatically named Anti-Imperialist Platform, just in front of the American diplomatic mission, and the event marked fifteen years since the arrest of five Cuban intelligence agents in the US. Securing their release had become the chief national cause and there were faded or flaking images of the five plastered to billboards and painted on walls across the island. Cuba didn't dispute that *Los Cinco* were spies but it argued that they'd been sent to the US to infiltrate groups of extremist Cuban exiles who were plotting attacks on the island.

As foreign correspondents, we were regularly called to events dedicated to the national heroes and regularly wriggled out of them, but this concert was clearly important for the government. A slick 'Feed the World'-style video had been playing on television all week featuring big names singing 'Tie a Yellow Ribbon' in heavily accented English. Shots of local celebrities were intercut with images of the prisoners' relatives wandering through a wood, carrying yellow cloths to hang on a tree in a clearing. The message that Cuba wanted its agents back was meant to resonate across the Florida Straits. It also seemed intended to inject some energy into a flagging cause here at home, as young Cubans were forgetting the names of the five.

For four hours that night top artists took to the stage. Many in the crowd were college and high-school students still in uniform. They gave a huge roar as the reggaeton star El Yonki emerged sporting a yellow jacket as bright as his rainbow Mohican. Then came swoons and squeals for a muscly, tattooed Baby Lores in tight yellow T-shirt. Most of the artists declared 'Free the Five!' before leaving the stage, some with noticeably more gusto than others. Diaz-Canel was close to the front with a group of Party officials, standing like everyone else for the entire concert. Alongside him were the relatives and wives of the five, dressed or draped in yellow. As the younger crowd clambered on one another's shoulders and cheered at the TV cameras, those at the front waved condoms they'd inflated in place of balloons. An older woman was clutching one with a smart yellow bow tied round it.

That's how the party would have ended if it weren't for Robertico Carcasses. Some three hours into the concert and in the middle of one his best-known songs, the curly-haired musician stood up from the piano and began to ad-lib. 'We want our brothers to return home, but I want a lot more too,' Robertico began cautiously. 'I want free access to information, to form my own opinion,' the artist continued, his backing singers not missing a beat. 'I want to elect a president directly. We're not militants or dissidents, we're all Cubans.'

The singing protest was broadcast live to the nation and reaction was swift. The artist's music was banned from the airwaves and he was barred indefinitely from state-run venues. As there were no private venues, Carcasses found his livelihood suddenly cut. Summoned to the Culture Ministry, he was informed that his actions were out of line with the revolution and that his words would only benefit 'the enemy' in the US.

Robertico kept his silence for a couple of days before posting a defiant statement on Facebook. He insisted that change in Cuba was only possible if people had the courage to say what they thought. 'I don't think that electing a president directly would affect our system. It would give people a real chance to feel represented at the highest level.' When I called the singer to hear more, Robertico was suddenly cautious. He told me that he'd said all he wanted to. The Culture Ministry also ignored my requests for comment.

Robertico and his band usually performed each week in a packed basement of the Bertolt Brecht theatre. I'd seen them myself several times but now they were removed from the billing. On the street outside the venue one girl told me emphatically that the punishment was wrong. A few steps further on a man called Maykol was taping a sheet of plastic to the broken windscreen of his old Chevrolet. He answered me more quietly and cautiously than the girl but his feelings were clear. 'Robertico was only saying what we all think.'

As I talked to people near the theatre, I recalled a play I'd seen there some time before. It was an adaptation of one of Leonardo Padura's hugely popular detective novels. As usual in Cuba the production featured abundant nakedness and this one also had a drag queen. But the backstory to the murder plot was darkly political, exploring the repression of homosexuals in the 1970s. At one point a gay playwright character described being voted out of his job by writers afraid to support him, and then reassigned to work in a library. The fact the play was staged, and extremely popular, suggested that Cuban artists were experiencing more freedom. But Robertico had bulldozed his way over Cuba's invisible red lines and he and his band were paying the price.

Four days later the singer issued a surprise new statement. He announced that the sanctions against him had been lifted following a series of conversations with cultural officials. Robertico claimed to have 'learned a lot from the criticism' and he was duly allowed back on stage. The band's next concert was at a state-run cafe near my house and at the end I went up to ask Robertico what had happened. The musician looked at me in silence, then shook his head. He'd had enough trouble. He didn't want to comment.

* * *

Robertico's experience was the latest in a long history of Cuban musicians pushing boundaries. In the 1990s it was timba music, a more hardcore salsa, that caused controversy. As Cuba opened up to mass tourism, the influx of outsiders and their cash brought an explosion of consumerism, and the social tumult that provoked was captured in the lyrics of timba. The music was performed by classically trained artists but the message was demotic. *You think you're the best . . . because you take a tourist taxi through Buena Vista*, one controversial hit by NG La Banda began. 'La Bruja' was aimed at a Cuban woman who'd hooked up with a foreigner. *You swapped my love for cheap thrills . . . I compare you to a witch.* Such songs caused a furore in the Party press, highlighting uncomfortable truths including the return of the sex trade.

By my time, the scandal had moved on. Cuban salsa was still a major musical force but reggaeton had become the island's soundtrack, pounding from houses and cars in most streets. The brash style entered Cuba from Puerto Rico and Jamaica in the early 2000s with video clips full of fast cars, money and sexual imagery. Utterly disconnected from the values of the revolution, the songs were enormously popular with young Cubans. One of the biggest hits played on the double meaning of the Cuban word for lollipop – oral sex.

Concerned about the impact all this was having on Cuba's 'revolutionary' youth, earnest experts debated the topic at length on television. They highlighted the foreign origins of a genre which appeared to denigrate women and promote a cult of cash. Before long, officials were threatening a ban. The head of the Cuban Music Institute warned that artists who 'violated ethics' in their shows would be struck off its books, which meant no access to state facilities. He complained to *Granma* about the 'questionable' musical content of the genre given the excellent free education on the island. He also slammed the lyrics as aggressive and obscene, calling for a ban on reggaeton in public spaces.

Around the time of that debate I arranged an interview with another cultural chief, the head of the Writers' and Artists' Union. Miguel Barnet was a published author and as we sat down to talk in the converted Vedado mansion that housed his organisation he was jovial, discussing English weather and London landmarks. He also had ready answers to my questions about the proposed restrictions. 'Unfortunately, most reggaeton lyrics are dirty and stupid,' the writer told me. 'They are grotesque, even pornographic. We are not puritans but this is something that we have to attack.' Given that he'd already admitted that the genre 'hurt his feelings', I was interested in how exactly Miguel Barnet proposed dealing with this 'dirty' music form which was so popular. He insisted there would be no ban, acknowledging that attempting to repress it would make things worse. But the author did think the lyrics should be cleaned up. 'Let them enjoy reggaeton, but improve the words.'

As our cameraman packed up his kit, I continued with my theme. I wanted to know how obliging artists to change their lyrics was not censorship. I suppose I hoped my interviewee might be more candid off camera. The author was polite but defensive and a few moments later we left. As we did, he reported me to the Culture Ministry. The next day I found myself in front of the CPI. In future, I was instructed, I should stick to the topic. The Foreign Ministry official then produced a sheet of paper. It seems I had requested an interview with Miguel Barnet to discuss 'Cuban Culture as the Standard Bearer of the Revolution'. It was the first I'd heard of that.

18

SYMPATHETIC VISITOR

Graham Greene flew into Havana in late August 1966 wondering how the revolution could maintain its momentum. 'Heroism is easy,' he reflected in his journal, suspecting that the real challenge for Cuba's leaders seven years on would be combatting routine and boredom. The writer had been commissioned to report on Castro's Cuba for the *Daily Telegraph*, his second visit for the newspaper in three years. In 1963 he'd submitted his work along with a letter announcing that it was impossible to travel to the island and not feel in favour of the revolution.

The writer admitted that he was a 'sympathetic visitor'. What he neglected to tell his newspaper readers in 1966 was that he was in Cuba as a guest of its government. The authorities placed a Cadillac with a French-speaking chauffeur at his disposal and Raul Castro himself lent a military plane for one journey. Greene was offered a grand guest house in Havana, complete with servants, that was usually reserved for heads of state, but opted to stay in a hotel. He also had company. A writer, a poet and a photographer travelled with him for the entire trip. What remained of the country's own press had been reduced to mouth-pieces for the government and the days of free-roaming journal-ists, foreign or otherwise, were over.

Greene kept a detailed journal this time which describes a whistle-stop tour from Havana to Guantanamo and back, involving very little sleep and a lot of rum. There were dead-of-the-night summonses to meet officials, endless jeep rides through muddy mountains and a chase to cross paths with Fidel that ended up just missing him each time. The first stop, though, was the beach resort of Varadero.

When Greene visited Cuba in 1957 tourism had reached a peak with some 350,000 visitors, mostly from the US. By the mid-1960s the number had slumped to the low thousands and on this trip the traffic east from Havana was no longer made up of holidaymakers. Instead Greene saw Cubans heading into exile on the two daily flights from Varadero airport. He didn't spare those families much sympathy, even as they aban-doned their homes and almost all they owned. He described them in his newspaper article as voluntary exiles and declared their departure 'inevitable' in a clash of ideologies. In his diary he noted that there was even a free buffet laid on at the airport.

On the road Greene noticed that prices had risen and food was rationed but the shops were no longer empty. In 1963 the only thing filling window displays had been pictures of atrocities committed under Batista. Greene didn't have to worry about shortages though. His literary companions were also his 'fixers' for the trip and ensured that their illustrious guest was wined and dined all the way. His diary is filled with good food reports including one from Santa Clara that describes 'the best steak I can remember eating'.

Post-revolutionary hotels didn't make such a good impression. In Havana the luxury hotels the writer had known were filling up with state workers. Out in the provinces Greene complained of no room service, too few bed sheets and cold water. 'One can put up more easily with frank poverty but one is irritated by the failure to live up to the surface,' he wrote. In one hotel his sleep was interrupted by a dying frog that was eventually located beneath his bed.

It was in the eastern city of Holguin that Greene encountered comfort, Communist Party-style. The bedroom of an official guest house impressed him in particular. 'Never in a brothel such a fine assortment of 8 ft mirrors face [on] and sideways to two double beds', he noted in his diary. 'Wasted on me alone'. Meanwhile, he and his companions entertained themselves on their long journey with talk of sex. Greene recorded that the Cubans' favourite words in English were 'fucking and fornication'. One of the four revealed that he'd made blue movies before the revolution: as a good-looking boy growing up in an area of Havana full of brothels, he said it had been inevitable.

The tone of the group's daytime stops was more earnest, focusing heavily on education and the mass literacy campaign then in full flow which Greene judged to be 'incontestably right'. On the road to Varadero he'd seen waiters getting grammar lessons behind their restaurant. In the Escambray Mountains he visited a teacher training school where thousands of mostly female students were carrying out practical tasks like planting coffee as they learned. Greene's concerns about revolution-fatigue were banished as he felt a 'sense of happiness' and enthusiasm.

Elsewhere in rural Cuba he heard of grand plans to grow straw-berries and grapes, viewed prize cattle and new sports stadiums and visited a housing project to hear how rent would be abolished.

There were incidents on the way that momentarily checked his enthusiasm. In Santa Clara his diary recorded watching the education minister quiz children on their knowledge of Che Guevara. As they responded dutifully that Che was then 'fighting the revolution among our brothers', Greene wondered briefly about indoctrination before deciding he was witnessing 'honest, natural romanticism'.

At one camp, Greene met student teachers being drilled to spread revolutionary ideology among the masses, along with the alphabet.

<u>Cuban Government Literacy Manual, 1961</u>

The Alphabet

A

AP: Associated Press. American news agency serving the interests of Yankee imperialism

B

[Economic] Blockade: state of siege placed on the Cuban Revolution by Imperialism . . .

C

Censorship: interference by the Batista tyranny in public texts and communication in order to prevent people knowing the truth

Initially enthused by the students' vitality and commitment, Greene then wavered, reflecting that Cuban youth also wanted glamour, consumer goods and the Beatles. This literacy camp, he suggested in his journal, was an idealistic peak. 'I do not wish to live long enough to see this revolution middle-aged,' he jots down at one point.

The topic of freedom and communism must have been high in Greene's mind on this trip. Like many Western writers and intellectuals he had been deeply disturbed by the recent show trial of two writers in Moscow. In February 1966 Andrei Sinyavsky and Yuli Daniel were sentenced to hard labour after their satirical fiction was declared 'anti-Soviet'. Greene campaigned actively for the men's release and refused to travel to Moscow again until that happened. He also attempted to get the royalties from all of his books sold in the USSR diverted to the wives of the prisoners.

In Cuba, Fidel had instructed artists and writers on the limits of their freedom back in 1961. 'Within the revolution' everything would be acceptable; everything outside it was banned. But Greene believed there was 'small danger' of writers on the island being repressed like in the USSR with the world-renowned novelist Alejo Carpentier running Cuba's state publishing house. He met Carpentier himself in 1966 and also had drinks with the poet Heberto Padilla. A few years later Padilla would become as well known abroad as Sinyavsky and Daniel, when Cuba too turned on its writers.

Greene's most serious concern on this visit was the emergence of the UMAP forced labour camps, or what he referred to in his journal as 'poof persecution'. In one of his *Daily Telegraph* articles he warned that such places were a 'moral mistake' that risked endangering the revolution. Just three years earlier he'd praised Cuba for keeping its churches open. Now there was a network of military-run camps that housed religious believers along with homosexuals and hippies.

Greene's diary shows that he was discussing the UMAP repressions over dinner with the Vatican nuncio when he got word that Fidel was ready to meet. He'd seen the revolutionary leader in action at public events and been impressed by his engaging style and comic touches. But Greene had been waiting for a face-to-face encounter since 1957 when the interview he tried to arrange in the Sierra Maestra fell through. He finally met Fidel on 18 September 1966 and was beguiled. A few years later Greene admitted to reporters in Chile that he'd 'fallen' under Fidel's spell. Perhaps that's why there's no record of him raising his concerns about the UMAP directly. In an article Greene produced from this trip, he merely expressed the hope that the Cuban leader's recent criticism of slave labour would be applied to the camps.

Greene spent some three hours with Fidel that evening, describing him later admiringly as a Marxist heretic. He praised Fidel in private too, writing to Catherine Walston that he liked him 'enormously'. The meeting began with a forty-five-minute lecture on agriculture during which Greene barely said a word. After that, they talked. The writer found Fidel an idealist and experimenter who played communism by ear, 'not by books', and he fancied he could see his revolutionary brain whirring. Clinging to the hope that he'd found the human face of communism, it seems Greene dismissed the shadows, 'some of them perhaps imaginary, some of them real enough'.

The novelist returned home from Havana laden with gifts including a crocodile-skin briefcase from Haydee Santamaria, the woman he'd first met in hiding in Santiago in 1957. He also brought multiple paintings. One canvas was a signed present from Fidel himself.

* * *

Graham Greene, journal entry, 2 September 1966

What centuries of change seem to have passed since ... the Havana of Superman performing nightly to American tourists.

The sympathetic visitor didn't forget what had attracted him to Cuba in the days before literacy campaigns and work battalions. In print Greene now referred to Batista's Havana as the 'sad time', but in life he sought out his old haunts. One night on his 1966 visit to Cuba for the *Daily Telegraph*, he bailed out of the Santeria initiation ceremony on his official itinerary to head for the Tropicana cabaret with its beautiful *mulata* showgirls. He was also relieved to find his favourite Floridita stocked with limes again and back making its signature daiquiris. He was able to enjoy shrimp cocktail there followed by red snapper, not the 'tunny fish and eggs' he'd been served in 1963.

But the days of Greene's 'brothelley good-time city' thronging with tourists had passed. The old mafia-run hotels that once lured gamblers and cabaret crowds now stood empty 'like bourgeois tombs'. The main clubs and brothels had already been closed by his previous visit in 1963 when prostitutes were supposedly being retrained as taxi drivers and seamstresses. Still, in 1966 the writer noticed a few 'expensive tarts' outside the Hotel Nacional. His guides brushed that off, claiming that they were 'for the diplomats'.

For Greene, one character above all symbolised the corrupt Havana of the 1950s: the notorious showman known as Superman. Legends abound of the performer who would have sex with multiple women on the stage of the Shanghai Theatre, his manhood described by some sources as up to eighteen inches long. There are tales of Superman swinging on a trapeze, great attribute dangling, and the audience selecting who he should penetrate right in front of them. Much later, a character based on Superman would wow the crowds in Francis Ford Coppola's film *The Godfather Part II*. There is said to be one real black-and-white video of the performer in action during a private show for a Florida mafia boss. An American travel journalist who has viewed the grainy footage describes a sinewy Superman having joyless sex in multiple positions, 'naked except for black socks'. His penis, the author concedes, is large. 'Maybe not eighteen inches, but a good twelve.'

Considering how often Greene referred to Superman, his only account of the famous show at the Shanghai is brief and flat. The novelist took Catherine Walston there in late 1954 but Superman put on a display, Greene noted, as 'uninspiring as a dutiful husband's'. The disappointed couple came out seeking cocaine for stimulation instead, only to snort what they suspected was boracic powder supplied by their taxi driver.

When he went searching for Superman again in 1963, Greene found the Shanghai shut and mouldering. The writer wondered idly if the showman had left for Miami, but never found out. I decided to pick up the search.

Chinatown was a shady district of brothels, opium dens and strip clubs when Greene first visited the Shanghai. One account talks of dope addicts and drunken wrecks in the streets, nerves shot by cheap liquor. But the *Barrio Chino* also bustled with real Chinese life. The narrow streets were lined with groceries, laundries and restaurants run by and for a sizeable community that had settled in Havana a century before. The first Chinese were shipped to Cuba as 'coolies', a form of near-slavery. By the time of the 1872 census, Cuba was home to close on sixty thousand Chinese people.

The *Barrio Chino* really expanded after the coolie system was abolished in 1874 and a fresh wave of Chinese merchants and craftsmen arrived from the US. That's when Chinese banks, newspapers and theatres began to appear. A third surge of Chinese immigration followed an increase in demand for sugar during the First World War.

The shopkeepers and small businessmen left in droves after the revolution and the area today has barely a Chinese person left. What it does have is a giant portico, a gift from the government in Beijing as Cuba tried to recreate the idea of the *Barrio*

Chino to pull in tourists. Concrete-grey with a yellow-gold sloping roof, the outsize Asian arch straddles the road near a graveyard for rusting locomotives.

Through that arch on one hot summer visit back to Havana, I see no sign of people stoned or dead-drunk. But there's no immediate sign of the old Shanghai either. Walking down a dusty Calle Zanja, I find myself close to a martial arts club where I once filmed a Wushu champion in turquoise silk punching and slicing her way through the air. I'd wanted to profile an athlete for a story on the anniversary of the revolution and was looking for someone other than a boxing or baseball star. Meyling Wong Chiu was unmistakably Asian but with a thick Cuban accent. Both her grandfathers were Chinese who married local girls, a common occurrence as most Chinese migrants were men. She and her coach were working to keep traditions like Wushu alive.

There's no Meyling this morning, though, and no free Tai Chi on the patio for local pensioners. But I do see a couple of men outside the bright orange-painted building who look to be in their sixties so I ask for directions. A photo of Fidel hangs on one side of the club's entrance and a sign on the other reads *Abajo el bloqueo!*, Down with the blockade!, the Cubans' term for the US trade embargo. When I mention the Shanghai, the men immediately know what I mean.

Originally built for Chinese drama, by the 1930s the theatre was staging burlesque and by the 1950s it was thoroughly sleazy. Stories suggest the bill then included everything from live strip sketches to on-stage ejaculation. One writer described the frenzied action as like a 'nudist camp gone berserk'. The live acts were interspersed with pornographic films played on a drop-down screen. Hawkers would wander the aisles in the intervals offering dirty postcards to those still not satisfied. The theatre could seat more than seven hundred lustful spectators and the clientele was mainly male and local, but adventurous tourists would also find their way there. A repeat visitor to the Shanghai himself, Greene has his spy-hero Wormold and assistant Beatrice leave dry-lipped after watching just one blue film.

Following the directions from the men at the Wushu school, I round the corner to Zanja 205 and discover not a single brick of the Shanghai still standing. In place of the emporium of sex is a small park with a statue of a squat, robed Confucius. A quotation hand-painted onto the back wall reads: 'Everything has beauty but not everyone sees it.' As a woman passes, a group of men sitting in the shade of some trees shout something cheeky. 'Remember where you are!' she reproaches them, pointing to Confucius on his plinth, and they snort.

Surrounded by painted metal railings, the well-kept park stands out in the area. A large apartment block behind it has been gutted by fire and the Bar Pekin over the road doesn't look particularly inviting. Dodging bici-taxis, I cross the street and ask the first person I meet if he knows where the Shanghai was, just to be sure. 'It was there, a cinema and a theatre,' the man tells me immediately, pointing back towards the park. 'But it wasn't really a theatre. It was for prostitutes.'

The man's name is Ricardo and he tells me he was born in this neighbourhood. He's well into his seventies which would make him around twenty at the time of the revolution. His legs and arms are strangely puffy, perhaps with the heat or more likely with illness, and he's carrying a cardboard box full of empty cans that he's collecting to sell. Ricardo knew the Shanghai well and isn't shy about sharing his memories. 'Prostitutes would go in and for a peso they'd pull off the men in the audience,' he chuckles through his walrus moustache, gesturing with his hand in the street in case he hasn't been clear enough. 'It was really cheap so it was always full. It was very popular.'

Warming to his theme, Ricardo says there used to be lots of brothels round here once. 'That's all stopped now,' he says, almost wistful. Like the Shanghai, they were closed after the revolution. He doesn't remember when the theatre building was finally pulled down or collapsed. 'There was a transvestite who used to wear a dress, then start taking it off bit by bit,' Ricardo tells me, pointing to his chest to indicate where she'd start. 'Then she'd wiggle her bare bum at the audience, and suddenly turn around and flash her cock!' It turns out that this particular transvestite was not Superman, but Ricardo knows exactly who I mean. 'Oh yes, I knew La Reina,' he responds immediately, using another name commonly used for the performer and describing him as *mulato* or mixed race. Pointing to my husband, who's six foot three, he tells me the Cuban was even taller. 'He was gay,' Ricardo insists. 'And he was huge!' As I laugh self-consciously my husband gets straight to the point. 'Did you see him? How big was it?' and Ricardo gestures with his hands. The gap between them is about fifteen inches.

Nodding towards the empty space where the Shanghai once stood, I ask Ricardo if he knows what ever happened to Superman. 'He left, after the triumph of the revolution,' he tells me, mimicking a plane in the gesture every Cuban knows to depict flight for Miami or beyond. 'Everyone's gone, only us shit-eaters are left,' Ricardo adds, his mood suddenly shifting. When I raise an eyebrow in surprise, he is insistent. 'No, really', he says, before shuffling off slowly with his box of junk. 'We are eating shit here.'

19

THE CASE OF OSWALDO PAYA

The Damas de Blanco irritate the authorities immensely. The women who'd tried to get 'a minute' with Pope Benedict during his visit are the most prominent face of opposition to the revolutionary regime. The wives, sisters and mothers of seventy-five pro-democracy activists swept up in a wave of arrests in 2003 that became known as the Black Spring, the Damas continued to protest after the last of their relatives was released in 2011.

Over the years the Catholic Church has become the women's refuge. Many of the Black Spring detainees were activists for the Christian Liberation Movement, or MCL, founded by a devout Catholic dissident, Oswaldo Paya. While the Damas themselves are not all Catholic, they congregate each week at the church of St Rita in the smart neighbourhood of Miramar. 'We're in a neighbourhood full of foreign diplomats and press,' the parish priest Father Jose explained when we spoke one day after Mass. 'It's not that the Damas are safer here, but they get attention rather than protesting into a void.' The women's

choice has not been easy for the parish; other churchgoers have been frightened off at times when counter-protests have turned violent. But Father Jose told me that the women remained as welcome at St Rita's as anyone, 'including the intelligence officers'.

During Mass the Damas sit together towards the front of the airy church with sparrows flying through the big open doors. They then pray out loud to the patron saint of desperate causes before processing down Fifth Avenue dressed in white and holding bright pink gladioli in front of them. Some fifteen or twenty minutes later, back in front of St Rita's, they stop and shout *Libertad!*, Freedom!, at the top of their voices.

I watched the protest many times and if the women followed their normal route without deviation it generally went ahead unimpeded. Plain-clothed characters always kept an eye from nearby parks, often filming on handycams, and occasionally a bus full of police would be waiting in a side street. But whenever the government got nervous the Damas would be blocked in their homes or detained as they headed to church. Sometimes they'd be driven to the city limits and dumped.

In 2009 Fidel referred to 'so-called dissidents' as a 'virtual reality . . . run by the American Interests Office' and the Damas were regularly denounced as mercenaries. That label was reinforced after cables released by WikiLeaks confirmed that the women, whose political activism meant they struggled to get jobs, had received some US government funding. I once rounded a corner in Central Havana to witness what the government called an 'act of repudiation'. Supposedly a spontaneous denunciation of 'traitors', what I saw was an act of organised hysteria. Around 150 people were crowded outside the house the Damas use as their headquarters, yelling that the women inside were worms and enemies of the revolution. Some were dancing, waving their arms in the air and chanting Fidel's name, working themselves into a fury. Pushing towards the front of the baying mob, I found a chain of women police officers guarding the Damas' door. A wave of my giant laminated press card got me through. Inside, several of the activists were crammed into the small front room chanting *Libertad!* back at the crowd outside, just as ferociously. 'I think the Catholic Church should do more to defend all Cuban people, a lot more!' one of the group's leaders protested, as she saw me taking in the ugly scenes. Through the open door I spotted some younger Cubans looking more subdued on the edge of the crowd. They were university students, getting a practical lesson in battling dissent.

One Sunday, with a major international summit looming in Havana, I made for St Rita's. I wondered whether the Damas might stray beyond their usual route to make a point about the tight restrictions on human rights. Driving up the rutted road beside the church, I spotted one of the senior officials who kept an eye on the foreign press hovering outside. As I approached he leaned in to greet me Cuban-style, with a kiss to the cheek. Moments later the deputy leader of the Damas de Blanco saw me and did the same. I hoped that the state security cameras filming from the shadows captured both.

* * *

At 6 a.m. on 22 July 2012 Angel Carromero climbed into a navy-blue hire car outside the Hotel Sevilla. Aron Modig, a conservative Swedish youth politician who had travelled with the Spaniard from Madrid, was seated alongside. At an agreed meeting point, the Europeans picked up two passengers. One was the well-known opposition activist Oswaldo Paya and the second was 31-year-old Harold Cepero, described as his 'best disciple'. Paya paused to recite a prayer out loud and the four men then set out on their long drive.

The group were heading east to meet other members of the Christian Liberation Movement in Santiago. For Carromero the trip started as something of a romantic adventure. The 26-year-old was a member of the youth branch of Spain's conservative Popular Party and his trip to Cuba was arranged by a Swedish NGO. His own narrative of the trip, produced much later, talks excitedly of the clandestine nature of his mission to 'collaborate with the fighters for freedom'. On the road, Carromero says he talked politics with the Cubans. Modig spoke no Spanish and says he spent much of the journey napping in the passenger seat. The group stopped to snack at a service station and Paya bought a Beatles CD for the journey. At approximately 1:50 p.m., more than 430 miles from Havana, they crashed. Oswaldo Paya was reportedly killed on impact. Harold Cepero died shortly after reaching hospital. The two Europeans survived with minor injuries.

The first we journalists heard of Paya's death came from a tweet by the opposition blogger Yoani Sanchez, confirmed soon afterwards by Paya's own daughter, Rosa. A short official statement eventually followed which reported a 'regrettable traffic accident' in which the driver of a hire car had lost control and hit a tree. The statement said that two men had been killed, and gave their names, but made no mention of their status as prominent dissidents.

The Paya family quickly began to voice suspicions of foul play. Oswaldo's daughter said that she had information 'from the lads who were in the car' that another vehicle had been trying to force them off the road. Ofelia Acevedo, the dissident's widow, later revealed that someone had tried to do the same to her husband in Havana a month before. She believed the government wanted Oswaldo silenced. The family's accusation quickly flashed around the world.

It took the government five days to furnish its own, detailed account. On 27 July I received an email from the CPI containing a 1,200-word Interior Ministry report on the fatal crash including photographs of the wrecked car. The same statement was read out verbatim on Cuban television. According to calculations in this official account, Carromero had been driving at approximately seventy-five miles per hour when his car hit a

long stretch of unpaved road. The vehicle spun and skidded on the gravel surface, then smashed into a tree. The report said that neither of the passengers in the back was wearing a seat belt. It claimed that there had been clear warning signs of the upcoming roadworks, though Carromero didn't see any. The official account then cited three eyewitnesses who described the car moving at high speed before hitting a stretch of temporary road surface and crashing. The Interior Ministry concluded that blame for the fatal accident lay squarely on the shoulders of the Spanish driver, citing his 'failure to control the vehicle' as well as 'excessive speed' and an 'incorrect decision to apply the brakes abruptly on a skiddy surface'.

Paya had been an outspoken critic of the government from a young age. At just seventeen he'd been sent to the UMAP labour camp for three years as punishment for his political opposition.

He went on to study physics at university but had to leave because of his activism, eventually finding work repairing electronic medical equipment. But Paya's drive for democratic reform never stopped. That got him branded a traitor, with insults smeared on his family home. *Paya: CIA agent.*

It was in 2002, ten years before his death, that the activist became known to the wider world. Paya had mounted an extraordinary campaign for democratic reform, collecting thousands of signatures for a petition demanding a referendum. The ballot was to include freedom of speech, the release of political prisoners and free and fair elections. The project was named after Felix Varela, a nineteenth-century Cuban theologian and priest who advocated political and religious liberty.

On 10 May 2002 Paya gathered his petition together in cardboard boxes and delivered it in person to Cuba's parliament. Radically, the Varela Project used a mechanism available under Cuba's own laws: according to the constitution, parliamentary deputies are obliged to consider any proposal that has the support of ten thousand citizens. No one before Paya had ever dared try. But his initiative persuaded more than eleven thousand Cubans to sign their real names and ID numbers to what was the most significant peaceful challenge to the one-party state since the revolution. A further fourteen thousand supporters signed up later as the petition was passed door-to-door and through church networks.

The government denounced the project as an act of subversion backed by its enemies abroad. But Paya always insisted that his was a Cuban campaign, a non-violent demand for rights enshrined in the nation's constitution. He was also driven by deep Catholic conviction. 'We also have them [those rights] because we are human beings, sons of God,' Paya explained as he submitted his petition. That year he was awarded the Sakharov Prize for Freedom of Thought by the European Parliament.

The referendum call was rejected on a technicality: the signatures had not been verified by a notary as Paya had been unable to find one brave enough to oblige. But a few days later former US president Jimmy Carter ensured that all Cubans heard of the Varela Project. The most prominent American public figure to travel to Cuba since the revolution, Carter had been invited by Fidel in a display of openness. The American then referred to Paya's campaign in a live address to the nation. Given free rein by Fidel to meet anyone he liked on that landmark visit, one of Carter's choices was Paya.

The government's response to the challenge of the Varela Project was swift and crushing. First, Fidel led a huge crowd onto Havana's seafront. Waving Cuban flags, they marched on the US Interests Section. Next, tens of thousands of polling stations went up across the country to gather signatures for a counter-petition. Ninety-nine percent of voters duly signed a declaration that Cuban socialism was 'irrevocable', a position subsequently written into law.

It was less than a year later that several dozen of the Varela Project activists were arrested in the so-called Black Spring and handed draconian prison sentences. With American troops heading into Iraq and an openly hostile new head of the US Interests Section in Havana, Cuba's leaders were more nervous than usual about foreign-backed attempts to oust them. Paya himself remained free but his family reported that he was under constant surveillance, intimidated and threatened by State Security agents.

The activist's profile was much reduced and his room for manoeuvre severely restricted. US diplomatic cables dating back to 2009 and exposed by WikiLeaks described him and other dissidents as out of touch and riven by rivalries. Paya's most recent initiative had garnered just 1,200 signatures online. There appeared to be no obvious motive to remove him, especially in a crash with two European youth politicians in the car.

But as claims of foul play from the dissident's family grew louder, the government increased its own efforts to counter them. It tried to discredit Paya by focusing on the fact that he received money and support from abroad. Sweden's centre-right Christian Democrats party, which Aron Modig represented, told me it had been in contact with Paya's pro-democracy movement for many years. Such links are fairly common as sympathetic visitors deliver flash drives, mobile phones or cash to dissidents. The support is usually conducted quietly, but the car crash was public confirmation of the connections and the government used that to round on its critics. A few days after Paya's death, Raul Castro used an anniversary speech to warn that 'groups' backed by the US were attempting to provoke in Cuba 'what happened in Libya and what they are now trying to do in Syria'. Cuba, he vowed, would 'remain independent and free'.

A week after the fatal crash we journalists were bussed to a mystery press conference at a ranch run by the Interior Ministry. Inside, the CPI chief read out a new statement which accused the Europeans of attempting to supply counter-revolutionary groups with cash and organise them for subversive activities. Now, we heard, the young Swedish politician had agreed to participate in an 'exchange' with the press.

First though, we were to watch a video. When the screen flickered to life, Carromero appeared seated in front of a wall covered in a patterned sheet with the frond of a giant pot plant curling in from one corner. Speaking directly to the camera, he confirmed that he had been driving the hire car and lost control after breaking sharply to avoid a bad patch of road. 'No car hit us from behind,' the Spaniard stated. 'It was just a pothole.' The video then cut to Modig. 'It's possible I was sleeping just before the accident,' he told the camera, before adding that the first memory he had was of the vehicle heading for a tree. After that 'everything went blank.'

As the video ended, a side door opened and the Swedish youth politician himself was led into the room to a flash of cameras. Tall and blonde, dressed in navy-blue shirt and shorts, he was shown to a table loaded with press microphones. The head of the CPI took the chair next to him to field questions. Looking subdued but calm, the Swede began with a prepared statement in which he issued a short apology for 'doing illegal activities'. He admitted that he'd been to the island before, delivering funding and equipment to dissidents. This time he came specifically to help Paya.

Watching Modig, I supposed his appearance was part of an agreed prelude to returning home. The Swede hadn't been driving the car and the accusation that he'd been helping dissidents seemed more likely to end in deportation than prison. If Modig had seen something suspicious about the crash, he was patently unlikely to say so while still in custody and with a government official by his side.

Even so, once the Swede finished his apology I called out to ask whether any other car was involved in the crash. Modig had 'no memory' of any other vehicle and declined my request to elaborate. In the circumstances, it felt uncomfortable pushing him. Asked if he was speaking under pressure and whether he would change his story once he left Cuba, Modig stressed that his apology had been honest. To a muddled question about SMS messages he'd reportedly sent after the crash claiming that the car had been forced off the road, Modig said his only messages were to assure friends he was fine. Very quickly he signalled to the CPI chief that he'd had enough and he was led out of the room.

Modig flew home the next day without facing charges. In later interviews he described his extreme anxiety while in Cuba and his fear of being rearrested right up to the moment he got out. Speaking to me later from Sweden, he did retract one of his comments from that press conference. He forwarded a screen shot of a text message he'd sent from Cuba shortly after the crash. Written in Swedish, it reads: 'Angel says someone tried to force us off the road.' Modig told me that was the first thing the Spaniard said to him when the two met in hospital after the crash. But he repeated that he hadn't personally seen any car trailing them, and had been sleeping at the time of the crash 'and some time before'. He only came round in the ambulance. It was frustrating, Modig said, but 'I don't know what happened and I have accepted that fact.'

* * *

On 5 October 2012, in a freshly painted courtroom in Bayamo, Angel Carromero was put on trial for involuntary manslaughter. State prosecutors were demanding a seven-year sentence. Spanish diplomats had been hard at work behind the scenes, but the case was straining relations with Madrid. In the dock, Carromero expressed 'deep sorrow' for the deaths but insisted that he had been neither speeding nor driving carelessly when he crashed. Ten days later he was found guilty and given four years behind bars. It was a sentence short enough to make him eligible for repatriation to serve out the remainder of his term in Spain. In December 2012, five months after the fatal crash, Carromero flew back to Madrid.

It wasn't until March 2013, two months after emerging from custody in Spain, that he began to present his own version of events. Carromero complained that his lawyers had not had access to the evidence against him and that no independent forensic report was allowed. He asserted that his initial video confession had been taped with threatening-looking military men in the room and said he'd deliberately used Cuban expressions in order to alert Spaniards to the fact he was reading a prepared text.

Carromero was also adamant that he had not been speeding. He pointed out that Cuba's motorway ends abruptly just over two hundred miles from Havana, at which point the main highway narrows to one lane in each direction. That road then becomes crowded with farm vehicles, bicycles and pedestrians. Also slowing the traffic are potholes, unmarked and difficult to detect until you plunge into them. In such conditions, the Spaniard argued, it was physically impossible to travel 'even at a moderate speed'.

The route certainly is hazardous and getting stuck behind a tractor or horse and cart is unavoidable. But I've also seen plenty of frustrated drivers accelerate as soon as they reach a clear stretch, convinced they can spot any hazard before they hit it. On one occasion my own hire car was a near write-off when we smashed into an uneven section of road very close to where Paya died. The surface had melted in the sun and then been mashed up by heavy farm vehicles. The danger was invisible until we were on top of it. The driver somehow managed to keep control and steer us towards a sugar cane field and we emerged with nothing worse than shock and sore heads from bumping into the roof, but we were lucky.

The Paya family continued to voice profound suspicions about the investigation. The eyewitnesses claimed in court that they'd seen Carromero's car passing at high speed. But Paya's family say that in the immediate aftermath of the crash a local police officer recorded the same witnesses describing a red Lada at the scene. Those travelling in the Lada supposedly pulled the men from the wreck and called an ambulance. The family maintains that these were State Security agents, assigned to trail the dissidents. Carromero frequently mentions being heavily sedated after the accident and suffering from 'long lapses of memory'. But he also says that a red Lada followed their hire car 'for a considerable stretch' on the way to Santiago. Whoever was in the vehicle, if indeed it existed, has not been traced.

The Spaniard went on to claim that just prior to the crash another car appeared with the licence plates of a state-owned vehicle. In his first interview after leaving prison, Carromero stated this was the vehicle that had forced them off the road. Fiercely denying responsibility for the two deaths, he argued that he'd been made the scapegoat for a killing. 'I am not only innocent, I am another victim who could have been dead now.'

* * *

Those who'd known Oswaldo Paya personally talked of an irreparable loss. The day after the fatal crash, the bells of the small stone church of San Salvador in Havana rang for hours calling people to a memorial service. The crowd grew until every pew and all the aisles were filled with Paya's friends and family. Dotted among them were fellow dissidents and many Western diplomats. The activist's friends were still in shock. 'More than eleven thousand Cubans calling for democratic change, that's his legacy', Dagoberto Valdes, another Catholic activist, told me quietly. A younger man called Luis Fernandez described Paya as one of the most important figures in Cuba's struggling civil society. 'I think a new generation will continue his legacy,' he said, trying to remain hopeful. 'That is what we are fighting for.'

As the crowd gathered, I wandered round the side of the church and found Paya's son waiting for his father's coffin. The 24-year-old, also Oswaldo, talked of a man without hatred or violence who had tried to fight for Cubans' rights. Oswaldo was convinced that his father had been killed, describing multiple threats by State Security agents over the years. The pressure intensified, he remembered, after his father submitted the Varela Project petition. 'That's when the government felt the strongest, most direct pressure in fifty years,' he said. 'People were demanding their rights. The threats then increased, until today.'

As the young Oswaldo returned to his mother's side, I returned to the front of a church that by then was full to overflowing. When Paya's simple grey-painted coffin was finally carried through the door, laden with lilies and pink and white roses, someone shouted out 'Long live the Varela Project!' and the crowd burst into emotional applause that didn't stop for eight minutes. I'd never seen such fierce, open defiance in Cuba. When the service ended, the passions of Paya's friends spilled over again. First they broke into the national anthem and then I watched as all around me people raised one hand with their forefinger and thumb forming an L shape and chanted the word 'Libertad'.

When the chants finally died down, the crowd began to file quietly past Paya's coffin. His widow and daughter sat alongside dressed in black, their faces raw from tears. The family kept vigil until Cuba's cardinal arrived to say a funeral Mass early the next morning. Once again, the small parish church was packed. This time, police and security officers in plain clothes lined the streets. Addressing the congregation, Cardinal Ortega remembered Paya as a man with a 'clear political vocation' inspired by his deep faith. He read out a message of condolence from Pope

Benedict. In her own address, Paya's daughter Rosa vowed to seek justice.

As the service ended, several dozen funeral-goers spilled out onto the street chanting anti-government slogans, and police moved quickly to detain them. Government bloggers denounced the protestors as 'shameless', accusing them of blocking the funeral cortege and creating a scene meant to impress their backers abroad. But for Cuba's small dissident community, usually weak and divided, it was a rare united outburst. The death of Oswaldo Paya had deprived them of a man whom they all recognised as a moral authority. Unsatisfied with the official explanations of his death, their calls for an international investigation go on.

20

EXILE

PHILLIPS, Mrs. Ruby Hart (Amer.). Staff Correspondent, N.Y. Times, Refugio 106 (altos). Tel. 6-2723.

Res. Ave. 7-A No. 9805, Miramar, Mar. Tel. 2-4863.

I get quite a start when I find Ruby Phillip's home address in the 1958 phone directory and discover that this other 'woman in Havana' had lived on my own street in Miramar. Calle 7A stretches a fair distance, but when I go looking for Ruby's family house in May 2017 I start outside my own old apartment.

It's a warm walk past the cracked tennis courts I used to play on, then up through the typical Miramar mix of angular low-rise houses from the 1950s and smaller makeshift dwellings now wedged in between. *If gossip were flowers, my yard would be a botanical garden*, someone has painted on their metal gate. Next to it is a battered basketball ring daubed with the letters 'NBA'. Past a hotchpotch of neat lawns and upturned rubbish bins, I eventually hit the intersection of 7A and 98.

On the corner there's a small vegetable stall and a privately run car wash with a snack bar that's doing a brisk trade. Number 9805 is just a few metres further up. The house is not as grand as I'd imagined, certainly not the smartest in the street. One of the upstairs windows has smashed glass but the garden is neat and there's a woman in a flowery dress mopping the front step as I approach. I tell her I'm interested in an American who used to live here and she tenses. I quickly reassure her that Ruby is long dead and in no position to reclaim the house that was seized when she had to leave Cuba. I also assure her that I'm no long-lost relative eyeing the place up for myself.

Relaxing, the woman tells me her name is Carmen and that four families now share Ruby's old home. Carmen was born here in 1962, the year after Ruby became the last of her family to leave Cuba. Ruby's daughter, a dancer, was already abroad. 'People started taking over houses when people left and dividing them up,' Carmen says, referring to the exodus first of Batista allies in the early 1960s, then foreign businesspeople and eventually most foreigners. 'The bit we live in now is the old garage,' she adds, pointing to the bottom left-hand section of the building which has been painted pale blue on the outside.

Ruby and her husband Phil had initially made their home in Vedado, closer to the historic centre of the city. Her parents also moved from the US to Havana in 1935. After Phil died in a car crash, Ruby and her daughter moved to Miramar and eventually lived at the big house on Calle 7A which doubled as a base for various family enterprises. Her sister Irma ran a dance studio there whilst Irma's husband, Gene, had an odd-job shop. He'd abandoned work as a news photographer for NBC when the censorship under Batista became too restrictive.

A few days later I return to the house hoping to find someone older who might know something of the former owners. This time I find Anna and her 18-year-old daughter Karla sitting in the doorway, and a pensioner inside called Josefina. 'The house was totally empty when we got here,' Josefina says, explaining that her own room at the front of the building was once the dance school reception. A Spanish man who had worked for Ruby's husband was still living in a flat at the back but died soon after Josefina moved in. 'There used to be a figure of a dancer on the door,' Anna chips in, the husks of the seeds she's chewing sprinkled around her mouth. 'She speaks English you know,' she then adds, nodding towards her daughter. Karla dutifully gives it a go. 'What can you tell me about England?' she asks me. 'The weather is cloudy, no? London? Big Ben?' Karla's mother looks proud of the teenager's efforts. 'See? She studies hard!'

By now the women have called me in to sit with them, as curious about me as I am about them and their home. Karla is a medical student who enrolled because her father was a surgeon. She now fancies becoming a forensic pathologist. 'The United Kingdom is leaving the European Union, isn't it?' she suddenly recalls, speaking Spanish now. 'I think it's bad you have to pay to leave. That's not fair.' The women ask me about English weather, television and food. Anna wants to know if life in the UK is 'atomic' and frenetic like she's heard it is in the United States. 'It's better to take things slowly, like here,' she advises.

'Do you use Wikipedia for your sources?' Karla jumps in at one point. She says they don't really have access to the Internet at her medical school. 'But it's OK. We get all the information from our teachers and our text books.'

At her mother's suggestion, Karla takes me to see her bedroom in the back of Ruby's old family garage. The entrance is round the side of the house where I see that the whole building has been extended out into the garden. Inside Karla's room a small radio on the floor is playing *son* music and she has hung a tourist calendar and carrier bags on the wall as decoration. The teenager plumps onto her bed behind a handmade partition and pulls out the album from her fifteenth birthday party. 'These things are so expensive,' she tells me. 'It cost 120 CUC. My Mum started saving for it when I was five.'

Girls' fifteenth birthdays are big business in Cuba, involving elaborate photo shoots and parties. A teenager once asked to borrow my tennis racket, then struck a sporty pose with it for the camera before wrapping herself round a tree trunk for her next shot. Some photos are very sexual given that the girls are just fifteen, but Karla's album is tasteful. In one picture she's in a long white gown, coming down a spiral staircase like a bride; in another she is more childish, dressed up as a pirate. As we flick through the pages Karla's little cousin slides back a plank of wood and pops through from the next room. 'That's Karla, Karla and Karla . . .' she says, poking at the album to show me her favourites. When we near the end, Karla's mum comes in and wonders if I want some black beans to take away with me as I'd mentioned that I liked them. 'We have lots!' Anna insists. I thank her and promise to return, but I have another stop to make in my search for Ruby Phillips.

* * *

The Colon cemetery is one of the most peaceful, elegant sites in Havana. It's late spring when I visit and the central avenue through the grand archway is lined with trees covered in pink blossom. Christopher Columbus Avenue runs up through a vast expanse of graves dating back almost 150 years and spread over some 140 acres of land. Some are marked with elaborately carved headstones and religious statues; others stand smashed and battered, unvisited by relatives for decades. Dotted among the individual tombs are art deco family crypts like mini houses, Freemasons' mausoleums and monuments to fallen heroes of the 1959 revolution. Somewhere in the midst of it all is the grave of Ruby's parents.

John Edward Hart died in April 1960, two years after Ruby's mother, Martha. The *Havana Post*'s Ted Scott, clearly very fond of Hart, reported that Ruby's father had been buried in the American Legion Mausoleum alongside his wife. Formed primarily for veterans, the Legion's Havana members had mostly served in the Spanish-American war. After wandering the cemetery alleys for some time in the midday sun, I eventually give up trying to locate the spot on my own and tire of the attentions of gravediggers who *pssst!* as I pass. Instead, I head for a small queue at a window near the entrance where two women are bemoaning the chaotic state of the cemetery archive which has failed to locate the graves they are looking for.

'You need to label all those boxes clearly,' one of them advises the girl lighting a cigarette on the other side of the glass. She is surrounded by small cardboard boxes heaped on top of one another at random, each filled with hundreds of scraps of paper filled in by hand. 'No, you need to burn them and get a computer,' the second one snorts, before complaining that 'the other skinny girl' who normally works here is much better. The archivist informs them that this is only her second day in the job and the whole group then begins a detailed discussion of her monthly salary and related benefits. 'Is lunch included in that? Is there a canteen you can use?' one of them demands to know, on learning that the woman takes home around five hundred Cuban pesos or just over twenty dollars a month. 'I wouldn't eat here if there's no toilet though!' the older of the two women retorts and the other one laughs as she catches me smiling. 'She understands,' she tells her friend, who looks me up and down before declaring that impossible for a foreigner. 'They can never understand Cuba. This place is a soap opera.'

Now I can get a word in, I tell the archivist what I'm looking for and she sends me round to a side door. An older woman in bright blue leggings so thin I can see her underwear takes one look at the names on the piece of paper I hold out and shakes her head, suggesting little hope of finding them. Then she strides outside. '*Oye, negro! Ven aca!*' the woman, black herself, shouts to a thin man on a bike. 'Do you know where the Americans are buried?'

The cemetery worker directs me down the long central avenue and I follow his directions, dodging a sudden swarm of bees. There are two funeral cars loaded with flowers outside the domed central church and just beyond that I reach a mausoleum for the Revolutionary Armed Forces. Meticulously tended, this one has a Cuban flag raised outside and the shape of a bearded rebel to decorate the front. Beside the white marble monument is a more modest plot that is clearly marked 'Anglo-American Association'. I spot a Violet Watts, Frances Butler and Wallace Johnston among the names engraved on a central stone but the list stops in 1953. 'I can't see the people I'm looking for,' I tell my guide, disappointed, when he eventually cycles up. He shrugs and suggests the names probably weren't updated after that year, already getting back on his bike to leave. As he pedals off he waves towards a dark head-stone across the way. 'There's more Americans over there.'

Across the path and one block further up, I find the second grave. In front of the dark granite tomb the words 'American Legion' are spelled out in capital letters on the path. The head-piece is decorated with a sinister-looking eagle, wings spread. The American Legion became infamous here in 1961 when its Havana president, Howard Anderson, was accused of helping to smuggle weapons to an anti-Castro group and executed. His trial was held during the CIA-led invasion of the Bay of Pigs when anti-US feeling was running sky-high. In court the prosecutor had launched a tirade against the US, at one point climbing onto a table to point at the accused and yell, 'Death to the American.'

I scour the tombstone for names but none are etched on it so I can't confirm whether John and Martha Hart were indeed buried here. The underpaid archivist and her chaotic cardboard boxes clearly wouldn't be much help and the American Legion itself, when I enquire, has no information. But this quiet corner of Colon cemetery seems as close as I'll get to Ruby's family in Havana, the city that they thought of as home.

* * *

It was soon after her father's death that life became increasingly difficult in Havana for Ruby. In one of her books she recalled how her father had foreseen the trouble, calling her to his bedside in 1960 and warning that everything she owned in Cuba would be lost. 'He was certain that Castro was taking Cuba straight into the communist orbit,' Ruby wrote.

In June 1960, just two months after John Hart's funeral, Ruby's great friend Ted Scott was detained and then expelled. The charges against him were never revealed, though Norman Lewis hinted later that Scott's spy cover had been blown. Graham Greene's friend Nicolas Mendoza wrote almost straight away to inform the novelist that 'Ed Scott, Your Man in Havana Post, suddenly departed' and no one in town knew why. Greene declared himself 'delighted' at the news. Later that year the *Havana Post* was shut down for good.

That September, Ruby removed the *New York Times* sign from her office door after a group of youths attempted to storm the building, fired up by anti-American speeches outside the Presidential Palace. Fearful, Ruby's friends began leaving Cuba. Writing to her foreign editor on 4 September 1960, the journalist described her position as 'extremely difficult', with every phone conversation recorded and constant criticism in the government press. But at that point she was still defiant. Ruby told her editor that she might be arrested 'but I have been here through many administrations and I expect to stay here through this one.'

Ruby's sister Irma and husband Gene were less hopeful. As the takeover of foreign businesses increased, they decided to shut up shop and leave. Their clients for dance classes and odd jobs had first dwindled, then disappeared, as the expat community shrank and thousands of Cubans streamed out for a life of exile. Angry at having to go, some vandalised their own homes to make it harder for others to move in, pulling out the plumbing and electrics. The airport was full of crying crowds as those staying behind saw off those heading out. The government would eventually ban send-off parties at the terminal as bad for revolutionary morale. Irma and Gene became guardians of a young Cuban girl who they took with them to America. That left Ruby to rattle around the big family house in Miramar with 'two servants, three cats and a puppy' which someone had given Gene before they departed.

Ruby carried on working for as long as possible but in April 1961 the failed US-backed invasion of the Bay of Pigs tarred all foreigners by association. The journalist's home phone was flooded with threatening calls. Two days after the attack began, Cuban soldiers pounded at Ruby's door demanding to search her house. Her colleagues Sarita and Raul had already been arrested and now disappeared for two weeks with no trace. Thousands of Cubans were being rounded up as suspected counter-revolution-aries across the island and foreign correspondents were seeking refuge in embassies to avoid the same fate.

Ruby was not arrested, something she later put down to the quick-thinking efforts of Sarita. Her loyal assistant had warned the police that Ruby was too sick with a stomach ulcer to go to prison and surprisingly they left her alone. But the *New York Times* office was seized. The journalist was permitted to clear out her clothes and rescue Mickey the parrot and the cats. Overnight the place was then stripped of everything else, from the television set to the scissors.

A series of cables between Ruby's head office and Havana eventually established that she was 'okay' though unable to talk much about 'the situation'. A reporter for the American network NBC who had fled to the Italian embassy could only add that things were 'very hot' for correspondents. Scott had cabled the *New York Times* from New Zealand to ask after his friend's safety and on 20 April her editor cabled him back with reassurance: 'GLAD REPORT RUBY OKAY CHEERIO.' The following day the correspondent told her bosses that she hoped a 'rather serious problem' was now over.

But Ruby realised that life as she knew it on the island had ended. Her office was sealed and out of bounds, at least temporarily, and her staff were in custody. She was prohibited from filing copy and had to call New York each day just to confirm that she was safe. Reluctantly, the correspondent put her name on the list for evacuation. Her reporting work now impossible, she began to give away a lifetime of belongings. 'I might as well leave because I would no longer be able to send the truth of the situation out of there.'

Plans to get Ruby out were under way by 4 May 1961, although the theft of her passport and other documents during the raid on her office delayed her departure. But on 19 May Ruby's editor received a telegram: 'Mrs. Phillips left at five o'clock for Miami.' She'd been flown out of Cuba with a handful of other American reporters. After some thirty years on the island Ruby left carrying just the thirty-six pounds of clothing she was permitted, abandoning everything else including her home. The never-failing Sarita was there to the very end, handing Ruby a glass of milk through the bars of a window at the airport to calm her ulcer as she waited for the flight.

The office at Refugio 106 would eventually be returned to the *New York Times* stripped of its valuables, and Sarita and Raul would continue to work there for a while with the office pets. But the couple would spend another spell in police custody before Ruby arranged for them to be evacuated too in 1963. Sarita told Ruby she'd left a 'land of queues' and shortages. 'Laughter [had] disappeared from the island.'

On landing in Miami herself in 1961, Ruby wrote a bitter farewell to the Cuba she had been forced to leave, 'a beautiful tropical island filled with fear and hate'. The Havana Yacht Club was lined with anti-aircraft guns and the Malecon equipped with sandbags. As Ruby went, she reported that hundreds of Americans and thousands of Cubans were also preparing for exile.

It's only much later that I find a picture of the woman whose ghost I've been chasing across Havana. In 1955 the *New York Times* promotions department had written to Ruby's bosses describing the pictures they had of the correspondent as 'somewhat dated and not particularly attractive'. They requested something new and 'I should hope ... better' for future use. Ruby's editor softened the message, telling her he needed a 'recent photo' for future promotions. Finally, in Moscow in 2017, I click on an image from the *New York Times* archive and meet Ruby Phillips face to face.

21

LET'S DANCE

We didn't get a seat right at the front in the Tropicana; they were too expensive. But Cuba's Paradise Under the Stars is spectacular even from a distance. I had treated my father to tickets and it looked like every seat in the world-famous cabaret was full. Male tourists smoked fat cigars and snapped photos as gorgeous showgirls sashayed past in sequinned bikinis, balancing extraordinary headdresses in the shape of chandeliers. Up on a main stage glowing with multicoloured lights, dozens more dancers performed to a live orchestra. At one point the music slowed and the lights lifted to reveal a wall of women on multiple levels before us, swirling brightly coloured capes like birds.

The Tropicana still had a hint of the glamour of the golden years when Graham Greene would visit. It was then among the most opulent clubs in the world, with Nat King Cole and Carmen Miranda among the international stars to take to its stage. There was even a 'Tropicana Special' flight that jetted passengers in from Miami for dinner, a show and one night in Havana before heading home. In his 1954 journal, Greene declared the cabaret 'fantastic'.

Like all the city's big clubs, the Tropicana was once a place where the roulette tables spun and champagne flowed. On our visit there was the more egalitarian Havana Club rum on the tables and a pot of peanuts included in the entry price. The cabaret still attracts occasional celebrity visitors: Beyonce and Jay-Z came on their 2013 wedding anniversary trip to Havana. But that same year almost the entire audience I saw were older tourists from Latin America.

The famously voluptuous showgirls have given way to a skinnier model over the years, partly down to fashion and partly economics. Indian silk costumes have been replaced by synthetics and many dancers wore flesh-coloured bodices beneath their pointed golden bras to protect their modesty. At the end the glittering cabaret was followed by a compere calling the audience up for limbo competitions and Latin line dances. 'Is there anyone here from Canada? From England?' he shouted into his mic like any other hotel animator, and rum-fuelled enthusiasts scrambled to join him.

Even so, the audience on our Tropicana night was enraptured. The main show included a journey through Cuban history told through all the dance traditions the small island has invented and exported to the world. Cuba's influence on popular culture was at its peak when Greene first visited and the styles of his day were on display. In 1954 the craze was for mambo; by 1957 when he came again it was cha-cha-cha. But the tall, slightly stooped Englishman was very much an observer, not a participant. He'd been terrified of dance since childhood, a trait he transferred to Wormold. On Milly's birthday, Beatrice approaches the sales-man at the Tropicana with an invitation: 'Let's dance.' Wormold protests feebly that he's 'not very good' before shuffling awkwardly around her on the floor.

Unlike the English, Cubans are natural dancers. You can see it in the way some girls walk, gliding with rotating hips. I once watched a young couple dance salsa on their balcony, oblivious to the world; fathers and daughters would twirl each other at birthday gatherings in their backyards. Dancing, like music, is part of island life. Like Wormold, though, I needed help. One day I mustered up the courage to drop into a building on the Malecon that was advertising salsa classes, but when the man in the gloomy upstairs flat mentioned massage I left in a hurry. In the end it was Cuban music that made me swallow my self-consciousness. I'd begun discovering live concerts and couldn't bear to spend another one clutching my drink, too nervous to move in case I looked stupid. That's how I found myself one evening on the patio of the British ambassador's residence with other journalists, diplomats and their spouses, all taking our first tentative steps of Cuban salsa. Giant fans whirled to keep us cool as a line of teachers demonstrated the basics and a voice on an instructional tape kept time. *Uno, dos, tres, cinco, seis, siete.*

* * *

'Welcome to the heart of the Caribbean!' Jose 'La Figura' pronounced the English words slowly, hand on heart and with a slight bow. Slim and dark-haired, he was wearing slightly pointed shoes and a black shirt with flame-red trim unbuttoned low over his shaven chest. The outfit and his extravagant dance moves made Jose the stand-out figure that evening at the Armando Mestre Workers' Social Club.

'He's gay, but he's a good dancer, one of the best,' our host Angel informed me bluntly as he beckoned Jose over to the small plastic table we were sitting at. It was covered in portions of boiled pink meat on polystyrene trays. The food was part of the all-inclusive package at the open-air social club where aficionados of casino, a Cuban dance that started in the 1950s, came every couple of weeks. Most were in their sixties, some older, and during a trip back to Havana in 2016 we'd been invited to join in.

'What do you like? Disco? Tango?' Jose wanted to know. I protested that I was bad at all of it but within minutes he had me spinning around the floor. I struggled to keep up with his lively style, salsa with extra bounce, and as soon as the song came to an end I lurched back towards the safety of our table laughing with relief. But Jose grabbed me back. 'You are beauuuutiful dancer', he crooned. 'I want to dance again!'

The social club was right on the seafront in Miramar, on a street mainly occupied by state firms and large houses with salt-water swimming pools. There were a few privately run cafes and *paladares* as well as a pricey nightclub. But there were still some spots for ordinary people along the way, including this place. By day it was a modest beach-club for locals and the evenings were given over to social activities. The night was cheap, simple and fun. No *jineteros*, no hidden agenda. Just music, rum and dance.

The tables were set to one side and the slightly broken dance floor which opened straight onto the sea never emptied. It was still early evening and warm when we arrived and dancing was thirsty work. As well as the meat, the tiny entrance fee covered two plastic cups of beer each and a bottle of rum with no mixers. With nothing else at all for sale after that, we sweated on.

'He's blind,' Angel told us, pointing out a man in his seventies in bright orange Hawaiian shirt and flat cap dancing Cuban rumba in one corner. In front of us a slim elderly man in black-and-white shoes, white belt and fedora was performing pelvic thrusts with a lady clad entirely in red as the crowd at their table cheered. Angel was head of security at a children's hospital and Alicia, his wife of almost thirty years, was a nurse. We'd met at a club further down the coast that was a favourite with salsa tourists. Many were middle-aged white women who'd spent all winter learning steps in Manchester or Moscow, then headed to Havana for dancing and maybe some romance. 'I'm escaping my shitty life back home,' one woman admitted drunkenly to my husband, telling him she'd abandoned her partner and a mother with dementia to spend two weeks in fantasy-land Havana. She'd already picked up a young black Cuban and barely let him catch a breath between songs.

Angel was there with his casino-dancing older friends and we admired his classic, understated style and struck up conversation. He'd offered to show us a real Cuban night, somewhere he described as being full of 'sincere, decent people'. At the social club, as we chatted and watched the other dancers, I pointed out their age. But Angel wasn't as worried as some that his beloved casino was being overtaken by new trends like reggaeton. There were still plenty of young people dancing, he assured me. They were bringing all sorts of new moves from different dance styles but Angel was happy that it was still distinctively casino.

The music suddenly switched to Kool and the Gang. Unfazed, the dancers immediately began stepping in line, clapping and following the leader. 'Celebrate good times, come on!' they sang, before the DJ faded up another Cuban number and Jose 'La Figura' shimmied back over to our table. 'I want one more dance but I'm out of *gasolina*,' he wailed, pointing coyly at the bottle of rum. Top-up secured, he bounced off back to the dance floor.

The night was short and as the music faded at 9 p.m. the crowd disappeared with it, all smiles and cheek kisses. As we left, my husband asked the lady in red for her top tip on how to improve. 'Just dance!' she told him, surprised by the question. 'You just have to dance.'

Angel had a smashed-up 1980s Moskvich car parked opposite that he'd borrowed from a relative. 'It still goes,' he assured us as we squeezed in. Just as I began hailing the durability of Soviet technology, the car bunny-hopped a couple of metres down the road and cut out.

* * *

Email to friend, 4 April 2012

It's a strange place. The other night I went to some club . . . there was a man in a silver suit jacket with a hairy chest on stage singing along to the music.

Think I need to find some better places to go out.

It took me a while to find the best Cuban music. The jazz is excellent, with regular concerts by the likes of Roberto Fonseca. But the venues have had all the Havana-life sucked out of them, full of tourists, over-lit and painfully air-conditioned. One place had adverts for cubed ham and cheese on sticks set on a distracting video loop near the stage. I tried approaching musicians after their concerts to ask where else they performed, hoping to discover some dark and smoky underground jazz clubs full of Cubans, but there seemed to be no such places.

The salsa venues when I found them were far better. 1830 was an outdoor club on the patio of a mansion where Graham Greene once dined in 1966, set right by the sea. But the best live shows were at the Casa de la Musica and the best time to go was the early evening matinee. The night shows tended to draw more tourists and with them the *jineteros* and hangers-on. At one concert we could barely move because the girls had spread out one per metal table, to sit and hope to be noticed. They didn't bother with the matinee. That's where a mostly local crowd would turn up, buy a bottle of rum and a few colas, stock up on cheese toasties and enjoy the show. There'd be groups of state workers who'd got a free table as some kind of perk and families celebrating the birthday of an elderly relative. The lively audience knew all the words and sang along loudly with the band.

There's no place for English reserve at the Casa de la Musica. At one concert the singer called people onto the stage to dance with him and a large lady rolled herself on from below to start gyrating. A skinny girl in jeans and cropped top then leapt up beside her and they began a dance-off. The bigger woman flung herself towards the floor in the splits then crawled across the stage to rub up against the speaker. The small one came back at her with some wild hip shaking. Finally, a woman in her sixties climbed onstage to top them all, dirty dancing with the singer. The afternoon crowd exploded in applause.

*   *   *

The Tropical sounded like the Tropicana, but that's where the similarity ended. The famous cabaret was high-end glitz, out of reach for most people; the Tropical was a no-frills venue where Cubans could see top bands at low cost. Before the revolution it was where poor black Cubans went to dance when whites-only social clubs would bar them. Racial discrimination was rife, despite its prohibition by the 1940 constitution: law and everyday reality were far apart. Cuban society remained segregated with many public places and institutions off limits to blacks, even parts of parks and beaches. There were dances for blacks and others for whites. Great black artists like Arsenio Rodriguez were excluded from the best clubs even as their records were increasingly popular with white audiences. Rodriguez never made the Tropicana, but in the 1940s nothing could stop him from performing at the Tropical, where the audience was demanding and the dancing the best.

That's where I head in May 2016 to see Havana D'Primera, one of Cuba's top salsa bands. Just past Havana's retro football stadium, stick-thin policemen stand in line patting down concert-goers for knives. They're not interested in us foreigners and wave us on. It's just two CUC today for the main open-air space down by the stage, and ten for the raised 'VIP' section at the back. We choose the expensive option for once, get tagged with armbands and slip through. The Tropical is one of Havana's best venues but it's edgy. Cuban friends suck air through their teeth in warning when we say we're going there. 'It's a bit dangerous,' they caution. One of them, Alexander, is direct. 'It's full of blacks, watch out for the fights!' he tells us, and his *mulata* wife doesn't bat an eyelid.

It's still early but our area is already filling up. This is VIP communist-style: there are no frills apart from tables and chairs and easier access to the bar. Sitting up here is mostly a chance to stay out of the fray. In front of me a woman in her late forties is with a man I imagine to be her son before the pair start kissing and canoodling. A couple of tables along a girl tugs an entire roll of toilet paper from her smart handbag then totters off to the loo. It's an improvement on a previous concert when we'd ventured down below for one CUC. There, when two women couldn't wait any longer for a cubicle, they'd squatted on the bathroom floor and gone on chatting cheerfully throughout. Havana D'Primera were so late on stage that day that the bar ran out of both beer and water. Most of the crowd had been pouring back one-CUC cartons of rough rum for far too long in the sunshine. When the fights broke out we watched from the relative safety of some steps. A brawling pair sent the crowd surging first one way, then the next, in a kind of manic Mexican wave. After some time a group of police dived reluctantly into the melee as the musicians played on. There were a few final surges before the men were successfully scooped up and hauled out through a side door.

The event this time is more sanitised, part of a music festival in collaboration with the US. It's a product of the brief glow of neighbourly friendship that has followed Barack Obama's visit. Someone has brought a couple of American DJs over and a group of their supporters are near us on the balcony. The man on stage is playing trance music and the tattooed Americans dance, jerkily. The Cuban crowd perk up as soon as a reggaeton act replaces the DJ. At one point the pair on stage break off from singing about their sex organs to shout 'Where are all the women? Happy Mother's Day!' and the women in the audience wave their arms wildly in celebration.

Eventually I hear the first beats of a Havana D'Primera song and we head downstairs. The view from VIP land is all very well, but we want to be closer to the action. The crowd is calm compared to the rum-in-the-sun day but we still pick our way across a carpet of crushed beer cans towards the centre of the floor. On stage Alexander Abreu has brought his trumpet. The frontman started out in jazz and he's classically trained, like many in Cuban salsa orchestras. As he plays one long hit after another, young couples grind their hips together and older ones dance salsa steps on the spot. Girls hanging from the railings around us sing along to every chorus.

Seeing what look like a couple of pickpockets heading our way, I slide my phone down the front of my trousers. I've already stopped a couple of light fingers in action. An older man in a white suit and trilby then clocks us and makes a beeline. He offers his wife to my husband for a dance, although she's carrying her shoes in one hand and a bottle in the other. The man then informs us that we should invite them for a night out. Slowly we retreat to the back and from the balcony of the Tropical I stand and watch an elderly woman moving alone to the music down below, dancing brilliantly and utterly uninhibited.

22

THE END OF THE AFFAIR

Cubans call it 'The Sword', and the stone tower of the old Soviet embassy did look like a giant dagger, thrust into the heart of Havana. Visible all over Miramar, it was a useful landmark if I ever got lost on the way home. But for many Cubans the imposing building was a reminder of a distant but powerful comrade, an ally as different as you could imagine from their colourful, noisy island in the Caribbean.

The embassy tower was built in the 1980s when Cuba's relationship with Soviet Russia was most productive. The novelist Pedro Juan Gutierrez described it as a 'gained' decade, rather than a lost one, and it was this Cuba that Greene would encounter on his final visit in January 1983. The USSR had stepped in to break the US trade embargo and as it bought up all Cuba's sugar, and Cuba bought food from the Soviet bloc, memories of hunger and shortages had receded. With the Americans long gone, holidaymakers were mainly solidarity tourists, 'red-faced Soviets' and North Koreans sporting lapel pins of their Great Leader. The travel writer Pico Iyer described tinned peaches for

breakfast at his tropical-island hotel in 1987, eaten primarily by 'pasty-faced Bulgarians'.

Greene would see little of Havana on this trip but the colourful accounts of two high-profile visitors around the same time paint a vivid picture of the changes. Martha Gellhorn was returning to her former home for the first time in forty years and spotted clear signs of progress. She reported more racial mixing, low crime and streets full of babble and laughter. People were 'remarkably cheerful' and better dressed than she recalled. On the grand Prado avenue, where Greene had once swerved pimps and admired prostitutes, Gellhorn saw elderly women knitting and gossiping and children romping, 'healthy, merry and clean as if emerged from a washing machine'. The food, while 'ghastly', was at least plentiful. She found people 'much better nourished' than when she had lived in Havana; in fact, she now thought the women 'much too fat'.

In 1985 the feminist author Germaine Greer joined a women's congress in Havana for two weeks and found a society that was 'healthy, busy and quietly self-confident'. She was struck by the progress towards equality. Cuba was a country where women could take any job, study any topic and get free access to both contraceptives and abortion. It was also a place where 'women who have been trained to kill will be wearing pearlised nail polish,' probably chipped because polish-remover was in short supply. Greer was even impressed by the style of Cuban politics. At the women's congress she watched the famously talkative Fidel Castro sit and listen for two days. When he eventually interjected, delegates felt free to disagree noisily and even boo. From Greer's description, it seemed something of the Athenian Forum Greene identified had survived.

There were shadows in the women's otherwise positive reports: the CDRs on constant watch – the committees 'defending' the revolution – and the political prisoners. Martha Gellhorn called the fact that some hundred men were behind bars after secret trials 'the undeniable shame of the Cuban government'. She concluded that Cuba was actually 'no place for a self-willed, opinionated loner' like her.

But there were plenty of self-willed Cubans too and it was in 1980 that huge crowds of them took a rare opportunity to get out. That March a bus drove into the Embassy of Peru full of passengers seeking asylum. Fidel withdrew state security from outside the compound and within two days thousands of would-be exiles had flooded in. Among them were homosexuals and dissident writers. Labelled 'undesirables', they were seizing their chance to leave. To be cleared for departure, gay men had to prove their sexuality. Those who did so report having to parade before an adjudicating panel as ostentatiously as possible, wearing the most flamboyant clothing they could find. Fidel claimed the US was performing a 'tremendous sanitary service' by removing the 'scum' of the island.

It was also in 1980 that the poet Heberto Padilla was finally allowed to leave Cuba for the United States. Padilla had been arrested in March 1971 when his work was condemned as counter-revolutionary, then forced to beg for his freedom. He'd been scraping a living as a translator ever since. Spotted on the street in Miramar one day by a fellow writer, Reinaldo Arenas, Padilla seemed 'wan, puffy and lost, the very image of defeat'. Stripped of his writing and his dignity, the poet looked to Arenas like a ghost.

Padilla was imprisoned for a month. In his memoir, written in exile, he describes a series of brutal interrogations and beatings, ending in a forced 'confession'. He was then made to appear before fellow writers to repent of his entire life's work. At this sinister gathering he had to denounce others, including his own wife, for harbouring subversive views. Padilla made a long speech citing 'psychological' problems and declaring that while in detention he had come to realise the 'beauty of the revolution'. He also signed a four-thousand-word confession branding himself a coward and a traitor. Each one of the 'counter-revolutionary' writers Padilla denounced was made to approach the microphone themselves and accept that they were unworthy. Among them was Pablo Fernandez, a poet whom Graham Greene called his friend and one of the group who had accompanied him on his 1966 tour of the island. According to Arenas, Fernandez went further even than Padilla in grovelling self-denunciation.

The Padilla affair caused uproar abroad as some sixty left-leaning intellectuals signed an open letter of protest to Fidel Castro. Famous names such as Jean-Paul Sartre and Simone de Beauvoir, once sympathetic to revolutionary Cuba, likened the case to the most sordid moments of Stalinism. Fidel dismissed them as 'miserable' and 'agents of imperialism'. But for the foreigners it marked the end of the utopia. For Cubans it was the start of what they referred to as the *Quinquenio Gris*, the Grey Five Years of tight restrictions and censorship which lasted in fact until the 1980s. It also heralded a fresh purge of gay men from cultural organisations and universities in a crushing drive for conformity.

A decade earlier, Greene had been an ardent defender of Soviet writers who were repressed. But despite having met Padilla on his 1966 trip to Cuba, he did not sign up to fight the poet's cause. Writing in exile in London in 1982, Guillermo Cabrera Infante accused Greene of displaying deep lack of judgement when it came to Castro. Initially an enthusiastic supporter of the revolution himself, Cabrera Infante left Cuba in the early 1960s after a battle over a short film directed by his brother. Now he accused Greene of closing his eyes to the firing squads, 'large labour camps for homosexuals' and what he saw as 'rampant, blind and total' censorship.

Greene himself had once suggested that the repression of a writer was at least a sign that his work was considered important and powerful 'even if his days are numbered'. Easily claimed from the comfort of Capri or Antibes where the Englishman had homes, it's impossible to see how Heberto Padilla could have agreed. In 1980 Fidel summoned him to a meeting where he lectured the broken poet for failing to support the 'social aspect' of the revolution and accused him of caring only for his personal freedom. Warning Padilla that he would be unhappy in exile, Fidel then informed him he could leave the country. 'When you want to come back, give me a call.'

Writing from New York a year later, the poet described life under the revolution as a series of frightening social experiments that always ended in tyranny. 'It is difficult to ask anyone born into freedom to realise exactly what she or he possesses.'

* * *

Graham Greene's final trip to Havana came in January 1983. Eighteen months after his friend and president of Panama Omar Torrijos had died in a plane crash, Greene was asked to deliver a message first to Nicaragua and then Cuba that the General's ideas were still alive. The *Time* correspondent Bernard Diederich told me Greene felt 'kind of pushed' over the trip and the writer himself acknowledged that he was being used. But he returned to Cuba.

He was met by Lisandro Otero who'd been his official chaperone in 1966. This time Greene spent just twenty hours in Havana, delivered to a VIP guest house on the outskirts of the city. He didn't get so much as a glimpse of the Malecon. Instead he invited old friends to drop by, including Gabriel Garcia Marquez who was then in the city. In 1971, the Colombian had added his signature to the letter in support of Padilla only to retract it, so remaining in favour with the revolution.

Greene gives a brief account of this last visit in *Getting to Know the General*, his homage to Omar Torrijos. Garcia Marquez told his own story at the time to the Spanish newspaper *El Pais*. He reported that Greene barely ate a thing during his brief stay, but got through a bottle of good Spanish wine and six bottles of whisky with his friends as they caught up.

Fidel showed up as usual in the small hours and Greene noted that he seemed 'younger, thinner and more carefree' than at their last encounter in 1966. Enchanted by Castro then, he had since described him in an interview as authoritarian. Now, face to face, the conversation remained decidedly light. Once Greene had delivered his message from Panama, the chat turned to discussion of the writer's Russian roulette games in his youth. On hearing how Greene would attempt to jolt himself from aching boredom by pulling the trigger of a loaded gun against his head, Fidel declared that he should be dead. Greene's explanation of the laws of probability was dismissed as Fidel made his own 'abstruse calculations'.

Both Garcia Marquez and Greene recalled that Fidel was keen to know what 'regime' the Englishman kept to be looking young and healthy at seventy-nine. Fidel himself was then fifty-six and according to Garcia Marquez did several hours of exercise a day, attributing his mental strength to physical fitness. It must have amused Greene to tell Fidel he did nothing. 'I eat what I like and drink what I like,' he replied, taking the fitness fanatic by surprise. After seeming to ponder the point of his own efforts, Fidel decided that Greene was 'an admirable exception', Garcia Marquez noted. 'But only an exception.'

Greene would not return to Cuba. After over thirty years, this whisky-soaked visit marked the end of his commitment. But his last recorded memory was not of Fidel. In the bathroom of the official guest house he began urinating onto what he thought was a scrap of paper in the toilet bowl, only for the scrap to leap six feet out of the toilet and land above Greene's head. He'd disturbed a frog.

*   *   *

Greene might have been done with Cuba, but I'm not quite done with him. I've come to meet Pedro Juan Gutierrez who I first interviewed at the 2013 book fair. The dirty realist, I now realise, has also chased Greene's traces through this city for his own novel, *Our GG in Havana*.

Gutierrez tells me the lift in his building has broken down so he's suggested we find somewhere other than his flat to talk. I've read somewhere about him getting trapped in that lift once and almost tearing his arm off, so I'm quietly pleased to avoid it. It also means we're meeting at the Hotel Inglaterra, which seems a fitting place to discuss Greene. The Inglaterra features briefly in *Our Man in Havana* as the hotel where Wormold's spy-secretary Beatrice first stays. It's also where the title character in *Our GG in Havana* checks into a room with a view of the park.

Directly opposite that park, the hotel terrace today is noisy with a band bashing out Cuban songs for the guests. The inside patio is quiet and cool, though, with Spanish-style coloured tiles and giant pot plants hanging like chandeliers from the ceiling. The Inglaterra was once the smartest hotel in town, where a young Winston Churchill stopped in 1895 on his way to observe Spanish forces in Cuba's war for independence. Its grandeur has faded slightly with time. A young couple in the patio cafe are sharing a can of fizzy drink, hooked up to the Wi-Fi and staring at their phone screen. The waitress brings me a can, too, and I sit with my notebook and wait.

The Inglaterra is just a few blocks from the home in Central Havana where Gutierrez has lived for thirty years, and whose grimy streets and stories of poverty and passion feed the dirty realism of his novels. When he walks into the bar no one gives him a second glance. It could be the baseball cap he's wearing, but it's more likely the anonymity he's cultivated deliberately over the years. As a writer who draws his fiction from the lives unfolding around him, rather like Greene, he likes to stand back and observe.

'So you want to discuss Graham Greene?' Gutierrez asks. Now sixty-eight, his tufty eyebrows are grey and he seems slightly shrunken since we last met. He's just back from Tenerife where he retreats to the hills for several months each year to escape the extreme heat. He admits it gets harder to readjust to Havana every time he returns. Not to the climate, but the mentality and the hardship. I offer him a drink but we start talking and the waitress never reappears. The power cuts out for a moment and I'm reminded of the dark bar scenes in *Our Man in Havana*. In 1958 the blackouts were a result of sabotage and political instability. Today it's a combination of rotting infrastructure and fuel shortages, since Cuba's supply from Venezuela has shrunk.

Hearing that I live in Russia, the writer entertains me with a tale of his adventures at the heart of the Soviet space programme in the mid-1980s. He'd amused himself as a journalist on assignment in Moscow – which he recalls as grey and full of alcoholics, and where he was trailed constantly by the KGB – by grilling a senior space official on whether the USSR was working on creating a time machine 'like the Americans'. He then enquired whether Soviet cosmonauts had ever sighted extraterrestrials.

The flustered director had to rush out of the room each time to consult his superiors on the politically correct response to this straight-faced but mischievous visitor from Cuba.

It was a little later in the 1980s that Greene met his own Soviet spaceman. The jolly Georgy Grechko had taken a copy of *Our Man in Havana* into orbit where he'd learned the novel by heart and improved his English. Back on earth and visiting Havana, he'd used the book as his guide. When Grechko met Greene in Moscow in 1986, he handed him his dog-eared copy as a present from outer space. I'd planned to talk to Grechko about their encounter and the cosmonaut told me by phone that he'd be delighted to share his memories. He died a couple of weeks later, before we could meet.

I explain to Gutierrez that I'm here from Moscow hunting for Greene in Havana. Given that he wrote a whole novel about 'GG', I'd like to know more about his own relationship to the author and whether he has more insight into his Havana days. Gutierrez warns me straight away that he won't be much help. The idea for *Our GG in Havana* had come from his publisher in Brazil who'd been looking for hundred-page detective novels revolving around famous writers. Gutierrez plumped for Greene whose novels he says he loves.

As research, Gutierrez spent eighteen months re-immersed in Greene's fiction and seeking out published interviews with the author. His resulting plot is a fantastical tale of espionage, murder and mistaken identity played out in 1950s Havana with details from Greene's biography mixed in. Gutierrez describes the book as his 'entertainment', using the same word Greene chose for his more commercial novels. The Cuban author tells me it took just two intense months to write *Our GG in Havana*, having sketched

out all the chapters on giant pages first. 'It's a fun novel and I enjoyed myself a lot.'

There are other connections between Gutierrez and Greene. Both trained as journalists and prefer their writing pared back to the minimum. Gutierrez is a diarist, too, who describes writing as an addiction, and both men share a pull towards the risky, sexual and darker side of life, though that's not what drew Gutierrez to Greene. 'I was interested in how he could be such a great sinner and a womaniser and be Catholic at the same time,' he tells me. 'I think he must have been very cynical.'

For all his talk of Havana's vice and sexuality, Greene doesn't describe any of it on the pages of his novel. He dismissed what he called pornographic writing, telling an interviewer that you don't 'advance the story by giving details of . . . favourite positions'. The one blue film Wormold and his secretary watch at the

Shanghai involves 'a great deal of flicker and fog' and the famous Superman gets only a passing reference.

Depicting the same venue and character forty years later, Gutierrez holds nothing back. In his 1998 *Dirty Havana Trilogy* he imagines the Shanghai showman close to eighty and minus his legendary penis. He reveals that it was amputated along with his legs and testicles when they became infected with gangrene. Gutierrez returned to Superman a few years later. In *Our GG in Havana* the performer is still at the height of his powers, an alluring black transvestite blessed with a 'beast of exaggerated proportions'. Gutierrez describes a show at the Shanghai in great detail, ending with Superman ejaculating 'like a bull' over the audience.

Though a fan of Greene's work, Gutierrez dismisses *Our Man in Havana*. 'For me it's a very boring novel, very schematic. It's like he wrote it for money and nothing more. And the film is terrible.' Taken aback, I wonder if he thinks Greene managed to capture anything of the essence of 1950s Havana, but the writer calls it a 'very superficial impression'. By contrast, he feels Hemingway portrayed the Cuban psychology 'perfectly' in *The Old Man and the Sea*. The American, who once sneered at Greene's cheek for writing about Havana after only days in the city and then getting all the names wrong, would have enjoyed that.

Gutierrez can't shed any further light on Greene's actual time in Havana but like me he'd asked around about the Shanghai. A saxophonist who once played in the orchestra there had told him more about the shows. One he described involved women dressed up as different nationalities, then stripping to reveal their different colours: black, white, Chinese and *mulata*. An elderly man who sold honey on the writer's street gave him another detail. 'I asked if maybe he knew the Shanghai and he shushed me and told me not to tell his family. Then he described how young girls would go into the theatre with a roll of toilet paper under their arms.' I look puzzled, so Gutierrez goes on. 'They were offering to masturbate men for ten cents. The toilet paper was the sign.' The author only managed to discuss the topic with the honey seller once. 'He told me all he could, then three or four days later he died.'

But the writer saves his most graphic tale for last, describing how a man had approached him at the Writers' Union after the official presentation of *Our GG in Havana*. 'This man's uncle was a taxi driver at the Hotel Nacional and he told me that one day he'd taken Ava Gardner to the Shanghai,' Gutierrez begins, reminding me that the American actress was a good friend of Hemingway in the 1950s. 'She picked up Superman and took him back to the hotel and they spent three or four hours there. Anyway, in the early hours this man's uncle had to take her to the hospital because she was bleeding,' Gutierrez grins, wondering if I can even include this part because it's too dirty. 'I told him he was making it up but he insisted she was pouring with blood and his uncle had to take her for treatment.'

The young Cuban couple are still glued to their phone screen, the famous author still hasn't been served a drink, and there are now reggaeton videos playing on a TV screen above the bar. In our corner, Gutierrez goes on with his story. When the Shanghai closed, Superman supposedly found work as a gardener at the School of Medicine in Miramar. He lived there in a hut he built himself until he died. 'According to this man, and I don't know who he was, the medical students then took him to the morgue and confirmed that he really did have a phenomenal thing,' Gutierrez continues. 'But they didn't want to use it for their anatomy classes so they stored it in a tank of formaldehyde like a phallic monument.'

The writer smiles, and shrugs. 'I repeat, I haven't checked this out. You'd have to go to the medicine school to see whether it's true or whether the phallic monument to Superman is a myth.'

* * *

Gutierrez leaves me laughing to myself and scribbling what he's said into my notebook. When I'm done, I head past the hotel *son* band and mojito-sippers towards the street. Weaving my way through rows of communal taxis, packed with passengers, I'm still surprised by how damning the author is of *Our Man in Havana*. In a 1979 interview Greene, who'd once dismissed it as a hack job, conceded that he'd written a 'good comic novel'. I suspect he knew perfectly well that the brothel-filled street off Prado was Virtudes not Virdudes. I think he was playing with us, blurring fairy story and reality, just like Wormold did in his spy reports. Cuba was only ever intended as the backdrop to his drama, but to me it was vividly painted and a scenery still recognisable, in parts, today.

Outside the Inglaterra a woman is trying to beg from tourists on the terrace, a baby clutching at her bare breast. Two tall and skinny policemen come to move her on, but the tone is light and they're smiling. As soon as the police pass, she will go back. I head on towards the Prado with its elaborate lamp posts and lions, my search for Greene in Havana now over. As I stretch out my arm to catch a shared taxi, trying to recall the correct hand-signal for my route, I realise I've ended up just a block from the Wonder Bar.

At the end of *Our Man in Havana* Greene's hero Wormold is forced to leave Cuba when his fantasy spy story implodes around him and he realises that nothing ties him to the ruins of this tropical city any longer. It is time, Wormold concludes, to return to the land of grey skies, 'Boots and Woolworths and cafeterias' that he dreads. Havana had its own Woolworths, though, at least three of them. I expect Graham Greene knew that all along.

23

NICE GIRL FROM VEDADO

The girl in the yearbook photograph is sixteen, head leaning slightly to one side, hair neatly brushed and a faint smile on her lips. Beside the picture a list of character traits describes the young Liana de Armas as a daydreamer who loves to dance and could never be without a phone. On the eve of her high school graduation she admits that her 'suppressed desire' is to own a house with a pool.

High School Yearbook, 1953–54

Although she is the baby of the class (sweet sixteen) Liana looks and acts like a girl of eighteen, or perhaps a little less. She is shy and sensitive and feels sad if she hurts other people's feelings. Since she is persistent in attaining that on which her heart is set we have no doubt that she will attain her most cherished ambitions.

When I met Liana she was in her seventies, a retired English teacher living in the downmarket neighbourhood of Cerro. Her flat was a few streets back from the Plaza de la Revolucion but she didn't feel at home there even after thirty years. Liana talked often of the once-smart streets of Vedado where she'd grown up. In the 1990s she'd swapped a flat there for two smaller places to allow her son a home of his own and she'd been dreaming of returning to Vedado ever since.

I got to know Liana during my years in Havana over many cups of coffee and mango juice. She'd laugh in the early days and tell me she was taught to think that all foreign journalists were spies. In Graham Greene's time, I'd laugh back, she wouldn't have been wrong. But gradually Liana shared her memories and her thoughts. She had preserved snippets of her personal history in newspaper clippings and photographs, all stored in a wooden cupboard rammed full of papers and books at the back of her flat. Flicking through Liana's albums and talking together for hours, I learned the story of a white middle-class girl whose world had been transformed by Fidel Castro. It was the story of a 'nice girl from Vedado' and the revolution.

*　*　*

The pale-yellow building of what was once St George's school has seen better days, but the lookout tower and mosaic-covered cupola still hint at its old grandeur, as does an elaborate wrought-iron gate at the front. The school that Liana graduated from is now named after a young revolutionary who took part in the 1957 assault on Batista's palace. Fructuoso Rodriguez and three other rebels were then hunted down and shot by police, their corpses dragged into the streets of Vedado. On the morning that I pass Fructuoso Rodriguez High School, 'The Time of My Life' is playing in the yard and two children are mimicking the routine

from *Dirty Dancing* as their classmates kick a tattered brown leather football around them.

In Liana's day the school was fee-paying and run by two elderly British women who she remembers as Miss Hannan and Mrs Butcher. Mr Daley, also British, was supposed to take Chemistry and English but spent most lessons telling war stories instead. 'I don't know what he was doing in Havana. Maybe running away from his ghosts.'

Liana came to St George's from a Catholic convent school. Her parents had sent her to the exclusive Merici Academy, hoping the nuns would turn their tomboy into a lady. As Wormold noted in *Our Man in Havana*, Catholic schools were praised for 'teaching deportment'. But Liana didn't think much of the teaching at the Merici. She remembers richer classmates winning all the academic prizes because the school relied on donations from their parents, who included sugar barons. So after a couple of years having her manners polished, Liana persuaded her parents to transfer her. The religious aspect of her education clearly hadn't sunk very deep, as she remembers there was only one reason she went to confession. 'The priest was so handsome everyone was in love with him,' Liana laughs during one of our long rambles through her memories. 'It was a closed confessional but you could still see him.'

Liana's father was a dermatologist and she describes her background as middle class, rather than rich. 'My mother had to budget,' as she always puts it. But as she grew up in the 1940s the family were clearly comfortable, with a cook and a nanny, like all Liana's Vedado friends. When her father was promoted, he acquired a chauffeur from the Health Ministry who would drive her to school.

The family were not members of the exclusive Country Club, but they did join a club for professionals in Miramar. Like all social clubs, it barred entry to blacks and Liana's childhood was lived out almost entirely among whites. There were no black children at school and she doesn't remember seeing black people at the beach or cinema. Before the revolution the only black Cubans she knew were employed by her parents. On my wanderings I once passed her family's old club, a faded building behind a row of palm trees. A black teenager coming out told me it's now a children's swimming club open to all.

On a meander through Vedado one day, Liana pauses on one of the grand avenues that sweep towards the sea. We're beside a mansion where she tells me a 'very rich' friend used to live. They'd had a butler and Liana remembers roller-skating on the terrace. As we stand in the shade, she recalls how the Ringling Brothers would bring their American circus to Havana each year. The main activity in what passes for winter in Cuba was ice skating on an artificial rink that would appear on the Malecon. Liana remembers being so smitten by skating in the tropics that she got her parents to buy her boots of her own. 'I loved them,' she remembers. 'My brother and I could not stop skating.'

Back at the flat, cooled by an old fan on high speed, Liana pulls out an image from when she was eight years old. It was New Year's Eve 1946 and her parents were celebrating at the Sans Souci open-air cabaret. The men around the table laden with food and wine wear jackets and ties and some have party hats. The women are elegant, hair swept back. 'I remember when my mother bought that,' Liana says, studying her mother's outfit with an embroidered front. 'It was the first evening dress I ever saw her in.' I recall the adverts I'd seen for fur coats in old Havana newspapers and how I'd laughed at the concept in the Caribbean. But Liana's mother owned a fox fur stole, complete with head, which Liana used to be terrified of.

In 1954 her graduation party was held at the Tropicana, a society event that made a full-page spread in the *Diario de la Marina*. She still has the clipping with pictures of all the girls in long, white ball dresses and photographs of the US ambassador and papal nuncio among the guests. But it's another visit to the Tropicana Liana remembers more clearly. An aircraft carrier from the US had docked in Havana and she and her school friends were invited to accompany the sailors to the nightclub as they spoke English and were 'nice Vedado girls' who could dance. 'I remember that mine was called Mike; he was really

handsome and told me he was an extra in Hollywood,' Liana tells me one day. But it seems the young Cuban was unimpressed, snapping at Mike after he dared put his hands on her waist. 'Those Americans were a bit fresh! Maybe that was normal in the US when you meet a man for the first time. But here? No way!'

Those were the days when affordable and frequent flights from the US were bringing large numbers of Americans to Havana. Anyone who ventured beyond the cabarets and casinos would have discovered plenty that was familiar. Havana's cinemas screened American films and the hit parade was full of American songs released in Cuba at the same time as the US. Liana and her family would fly the other way, to the US, for holidays. The shopping there was slightly cheaper, but everything Liana saw in New York was available in Havana. That memory is backed up by her school yearbook. Alongside black-and-white portraits and cutesy character descriptions are adverts for big American firms like General Electric and Coca-Cola. There were good restaurants in the neighbourhood then as well as stylish stores. 'We would eat duck à l'orange in Potin, here in Vedado,' Liana recalls. 'We could get all the most exquisite, exciting dishes.'

It wasn't long after Liana's graduation that an idyllic childhood gave way to tense times as the political violence in Havana intensified. 'There came a point when you didn't go out too much at night,' she remembers. But on 27 October 1956, Liana and her boyfriend made an exception. It was a Saturday night and they were going to one of the city's big three clubs. The Montmartre in downtown Vedado was renowned for a stage show that would 'set male audience members on fire'. It had a casino and was spread over the third floor of a building that covered a whole block. Run by American gangster Meyer Lansky, the club was popular with big spenders from the US and Batista government members alike.

Liana was chaperoned that night by her mother. Either she or Liana's grandmother would accompany the couple whenever they went out, right up until their church wedding over a year later. Liana and her boyfriend spent the evening dancing, her mother mostly sitting on the sidelines, and when the first show finished long after midnight they got ready to leave. In the foyer Liana remembers greeting an old friend but he was brusque, repeatedly demanding to know when they'd be leaving. 'He kept telling us to go, go, go!' Liana recalls, shocked then by his uncharacteristic rudeness. That was until she learned what happened next.

It was the night that a group of young revolutionaries assassinated Colonel Antonio Blanco Rico, the head of Cuba's feared military intelligence service. According to a *New York Times* report, the 36-year-old intelligence chief was hit by thirteen bullets as he left the club at about 4 a.m. Three other people were seriously wounded. The English-language *Havana Post* said Blanco Rico was shot in the back in what it called a 'diabolical' attack and the 'picture of savagery'. The very next day the chief of Cuba's National Police was also fatally wounded and ten other people killed in a gun battle at the Haitian embassy where it was claimed the assassins of Blanco Rico had taken refuge.

The glitzy Montmartre was closed down not long after. The building is just across the road from the CPI, but there's only a blackened facade left standing with the odd bit of vegetation sprouting from its window-holes. Gutted by fire some years ago, the former club was never repaired.

After the two murders of October 1956 the hunt for revolutionaries by Batista's regime intensified. 'Once, my dad turned his car into a dead-end street and the police were just there, aiming their guns at us,' Liana remembers. She and her father talked their way out of the situation but towards the end of 1958 it was her first husband who ran into serious trouble. 'I was six months pregnant with my daughter and we were having lunch in the apartment in Vedado. Then the police suddenly thrust a machine gun through the living room window blinds and began pounding on the door.' They took her husband away without explanation, leaving Liana frantic. 'The local police station was a centre for torture. It's where they took suspected revolutionaries and people sent there rarely came out.' The station was run by

Esteban Ventura, the notoriously brutal police chief portrayed in *Our Man in Havana*. Liana called her father-in-law, who used his substantial influence to secure his son's release some hours later. His car had simply been confused with another, but they were dangerous hours. 'We had to get to him, before they did anything. Suspects could just be killed then, for nothing.' Tipped off just in time, the police chief managed to flee Cuba after the revolution and lived out his days undisturbed in Miami.

Though Liana never knew it until much later, her own father was in fact helping the revolutionaries in the mountains, sending medication through couriers whenever he could. Given that the family was relatively well-off and well connected, I wondered why he was sympathetic to the Castros' cause. 'Batista was a dictator who was killing people all over the place,' Liana put it bluntly. She remembers her family criticising the president fiercely at home as she grew up, calling him an assassin, though she knew never to voice such opinions in the street. Support for the rebels was growing outside Havana too. Liana's current husband grew up in central Cuba, where his father owned a small cigar factory, and he remembers that businesses there would buy bonds which allowed funds to be transferred to the rebels. 'If you got caught you would be in big trouble, but it was very well organised.'

Almost all the faces in Liana's yearbook left Cuba after the 1959 revolution and the girls lost touch. It was partly the practicalities of writing as relations with the US deteriorated and the direct postal service was eventually cut, but it was mainly ideological. 'We were believers and we really thought we should not make contact,' Liana admits. 'I am very emotional and I was a revolutionary and that was that.'

Most of Liana's family stayed in Castro's Cuba out of choice. She had just turned twenty-one when Fidel took power, and she grew to believe profoundly in the social programme of the revolution. 'We could have gone to the US and made a better life, economically. But we wanted to take part in the revolution. We thought Batista was horrible and the new social programme was good and we lived believing in that for a long time.'

In the early days Liana supported the changes from a slight distance, mostly preoccupied with a new baby born just three months into the revolution. But around the time of the 1962 Cuban Missile Crisis, when the USSR shipped nuclear missiles to Cuba ostensibly to protect the island from US invasion, she remembers a surge of revolutionary fervour. Entranced by Fidel railing against America, she is sure that the vast majority of Cubans had no idea of the real danger. Liana had taken first aid classes at the local hospital in order to be ready to help in case of an attack. 'Of course it wouldn't have helped if they'd actually dropped a nuclear bomb.' She only realised how close to nuclear disaster they'd come as she watched a Hollywood film on the crisis much later. She emerged from the cinema horrified and in floods of tears.

The deadly stand-off began when a US spy plane snapped aerial images of one of the Soviet launch sites in rural Cuba, a scene that Graham Greene had predicted some four years earlier in *Our Man in Havana* with a far-sightedness he put down to sheer fluke. On the fiftieth anniversary of the crisis, I travelled to visit one of those sites on a cart pulled by oxen. The cheerful man driving was called Stalin because his grandmother had 'liked the name'. At the foot of the hills, not far from Havana, I found arched fragments of the old missile silos that were brought in for the nuclear warheads. A local family was using several chunks as the base of a storm shelter covered with palm tree leaves. The rest were heaped up and covered in overgrowth in the woods.

When the missile crisis was unfolding, Liana's current husband was in Santa Clara. He remembers how he and others in the militia had to round up several hundred suspected 'counter-revolutionaries' and herd them onto the university basketball court. They were kept there throughout the stand-off with the US, surrounded by the young men wielding ancient rifles. Back then he never questioned that it was the right thing to do.

The situation had been tense for a long time. The missile crisis came eighteen months after the CIA-backed invasion to topple Fidel at the Bay of Pigs and Liana remembers anti-aircraft positions in the gardens of the Hotel Nacional and US aircraft carriers that you could see from the Malecon. One Sunday she took her children to a park on the seafront where she bumped into Raul Castro and his wife, doing the same. 'We were sitting on benches next to each other, and started to chat. That was what it was like then. Maybe there were bodyguards, but I couldn't see them.' Worried by the American ships on the horizon, Liana pointed them out to Raul who assured her that everything was in hand.

In that climate the rhetoric of the revolution was highly infectious and for Liana a patriotic instinct kicked in. 'Fidel said if we have to disappear, we will, but we won't make a pact with the Americans. We were in a situation of war. When that happens, you have to choose whether you are for or against. There's no middle ground.'

The first economic crisis she recalls came later in the 1960s as the US embargo took hold, businesses were nationalised, and everyday items like milk ran out. There were other hardships and restrictions to adjust to. The annual family holidays to Miami and New York came to an abrupt end, the smart department stores emptied of fancy goods, and Liana had to get used to calling everyone *companero*, comrade. Life improved later economically, although the family had to adapt to canned meat from fellow socialist countries rather than dining out. A fan of Hollywood, Liana couldn't warm to Soviet cinema. She also remembers listening to Beatles albums, despite the ban.

But looking back to those days, Liana tells me that she never questioned her commitment to Fidel or his revolution. 'I think I was so young and idealistic and it was like discovering the other face of the moon,' she ventures, and a little of what I imagine to be her old revolutionary fervour kicks back in. She talks of signing up to the ideal of social equality, to education and health policies that helped the poor, and the national literacy campaign in particular.

The revolutionary government described illiteracy as a 'powerful enemy, which must be beaten' and in 1961 set a goal of eradicating it. A tattered khaki-coloured copy of the original teaching manual I found has the slogan on the back: 'To be Educated is to be Free'. Inside, on torn and age-stained pages, those drafted in for the campaign were instructed that it would require 'sacrifices' on all sides. The manual makes clear that as they taught fellow Cubans to read and write, they were also to spread the ideology of the revolution.

<u>Teaching manual, Cuban Literacy Campaign, 1961</u>

Topic II. Fidel Is Our Leader

We Cubans respect and love the leader who raised a people in arms against tyranny and foreign domination. We respect and love those who guide us in the fight to make Cuba a free and prosperous country in which we will live, educated and happy.

Swept along by a social programme she saw as defined by a lot of 'human kindness', Liana now thinks she either ignored or explained away any uncomfortable aspects of the new system. 'If I couldn't travel abroad then the reason was the country didn't have enough money, or it was the US embargo. It looks ridiculous now, but those explanations really worked. I really believed.' Events that caused a scandal overseas, including the repression of writers like Heberto Padilla, were not reported in Cuba's Party-controlled press and Liana didn't learn of the case until many years later. Thinking of all the people I've met in post-Soviet Russia who once listened to the BBC on shortwave under their bedcovers or circulated illicit samizdat literature, I wonder why Liana never sought alternative views and information in a similar way. 'I wasn't interested. I believed we were right and I didn't want to know what the Americans would say because it would be lies, so I never tried.'

For many years Liana taught English at university. She talks of devoting long hours to the task, creating entire new text books. She would try not to mention the fact she had children, anxious that no one should think her less than fully committed to the cause. 'I did what I really thought I had to do,' she says, though she now somewhat regrets her priorities.

In 1994, when Liana's husband was sent on a research place-
ment to Australia, she was able to go with him. It was the height
of the economic crisis and the country was hungry and suffering. Early in our friendship, Liana told me that she had collapsed
one day cycling to work during the Special Period, as the crisis
was known. With little or no fuel and no public transport,
Cubans took to bicycles to get around, many of them imported
specially from China. Liana had been trying to survive as a
'good revolutionary', eating only what was available with her
state ration book. But she was giving much of her meat alloca-
tion to her grandchildren and getting nowhere near enough
nutrition. In hospital she got a life lesson along with a medical
warning. 'The doctor told me I had to eat, and he had to say it
three times before I understood what he meant: the ration card
would never cover it.' By then almost everyone else was shopping on the black market. 'I didn't even know how to do it. I
had to ask. Then I told the people in the building to send the
sellers to my door.'

The year 1994 brought the summer of the *balseros*, when huge
numbers of Cubans fled the island on rafts for America. Anyone
who could get out was going. But despite everything, when their
six months in Australia were up, Liana and her husband returned
home. 'Everyone thought we were mad, but we never thought of
staying and getting the family out. Australia was so far away it
didn't even pass through our heads.'

The economic shock of the 1990s persisted and began to
have a profound impact on many Cubans' faith in the revolution. Fidel Castro's great social project had been dependent on
one ally and without the USSR as its backbone, the Cuban
economy had collapsed. Disillusion did not set in overnight;

Liana describes her own belief being chipped away gradually. 'All the blows accumulated until I realised that it was over,' she tells me. She'd been finding it increasingly hard to justify the cause. 'Usually when people criticised things I'd have an answer for them. Then one day I had nothing to come back with.'

After Fidel stepped down in 2006, Liana tells me she began to speak more openly about aspects of the system that she disagreed with. Raul had begun to encourage constructive criticism and Liana took him at his word. She remembers addressing a meeting of the CDR in her street. 'I said it was wrong that people were paid in one currency and had to buy real food like meat and oil in other,' Liana remembers. 'I said that policy was condemning them to undernourishment.' Her other chief concern came from a life spent in higher education around young Cubans. 'I said that even if young people studied they had no chance of prospering, getting a car or house, and that we were losing a generation, which was very sad.' She told the CDR they could quote her and use her name. 'People clapped. That's all they could do.'

She reminds me that she hadn't supported the revolution for herself. Liana, the 'nice girl from Vedado', thought it would improve life for those who were poorer and less privileged. 'I can't see the results,' she tells me one day, surrounded by cut-out memories of her past. 'This is no longer the revolution we believed in.'

* * *

Over the years we talk at length about Liana's fading faith as well as about her life, family and ambitions. I ask for permission to include her story here, using her name and pictures, and she thinks for a while before telling me emphatically to go ahead. 'I'm eighty,' she says. 'I'm just telling the truth.'

We turn back to her scrapbooks full of pictures from the society pages of newspapers and snapshots from holidays to America in the early 1950s. I see photos from Miami Beach and New York, the Miami Ritz where Liana stayed with her mother and a visit to the Empire State Building. And there is that picture from her yearbook, where her teachers have no doubt that the young Liana will achieve her greatest ambition.

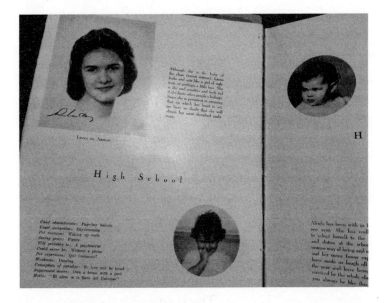

'Well, I never got the house with a pool,' she jokes, when I point to the list of descriptions and desires next to her photograph. But she had managed to move back to Vedado. A few months after we left Havana, Liana wrote to tell me she had finally returned to the neighbourhood she'd grown up in and where she's most happy. That's where we visit her these days, in a large block with warren-like passageways that put her in mind of a kasbah. It's not the house with a pool, the 'suppressed desire' from her school yearbook. But for Liana it is one long-held dream that has now come true.

24

SIERRA MAESTRA

Now it was my turn to leave the ruins of Havana. After three years in Cuba, I was heading for a new posting to Moscow but there was time for one last long trip. Ever since I'd arrived on the island I'd been getting regular emails from London asking me to update the obituaries we kept on file for Fidel Castro. Before I left I decided to take an extended journey east to do just that, by visiting some of the key sites of the revolution. I'd resisted such a history tour before as I searched for news, but now the trip had a purpose. It also took me to some of the most beautiful spots I'd seen in Cuba.

I started off, though, with a detour. As I was heading so far east I decided to visit Guantanamo Bay to see how two ideological enemies had lived cheek by jowl for so long. The US has occupied a chunk of Cuban land in Guantanamo for over a century and still has a military base there as well as the notorious detention centre. On the Cuban side of the bay residents of Caimanera are so close they sometimes hear soldiers singing the American national anthem in the mornings.

You need a special pass to visit Caimanera and there's a Cuban checkpoint as you drive up along the road. Beyond it is a little town frozen in time with minimal tourism, outside influence or cash. The only hotel appeared empty when I visited and the only sign of private entrepreneurship was a couple of men on a pavement threading wilting flowers into small bunches to sell. The Soviet-style housing blocks behind them were daubed with revolutionary slogans in sun-faded paint.

Even by Cuban standards Caimanera is a slow-moving place, but as we climbed out of the car I heard music coming from the building opposite. Inside pensioners were dancing energetically to *son* and changui, the music of the region, pumped through loudspeakers. They'd dressed up for the occasion; the men in hats and the women in their summer best and sandals. Those taking a breather sat around the edges beside walls covered in brightly coloured cartoons. 'We are the first line of defence against imperialism!' one of the women declared as her partner twirled her past me. It's the slogan the town has lived by for decades.

Some of the facilities on the US base, including the perimeter fence and a large hospital building, are clearly visible across the water from the town. The Americans first leased the land in Guantanamo Bay in 1903, but after the revolution Fidel denounced their presence as illegal and refused to accept the annual rent cheque. The original treaty, though, can only be revoked if both signatory countries agree.

Caimanera residents get extra meat and milk rations to compensate for the restrictions they face and to keep them loyal. But the bay was once a magnet for less 'revolutionary' Cubans trying to flee by raft. In theory, the American-controlled

territory was a lot easier to reach than Florida, which lay across ninety shark-infested miles of sea. But in 1995 the government completed a barrier to block the route across the bay and the boss of the local fish company told me that nobody tried any more.

Some legal traffic between the two sides did continue. Thousands of Cubans were employed on the US base over the years as well as workers, especially Jamaicans, who came to Cuba in the late 1930s. Many settled in Guantanamo as they had done in sugar towns like Baragua. The US stopped hiring new staff after the revolution, but many Cubans went on working at the base and earned substantial US pensions on retirement. I met one of them, Rodi Rodriguez, on the porch of his house in the nearby town of Guantanamo. The 83-year-old showed me original employment documents from his time as a 'Shop Material Controller' all stamped by the US Defense Department. Rodi remembers relations being good before the revolution, so much so that he named his daughter after an American.

When he retired, Rodi became the designated courier to pick up the Cubans' pensions from the base. 'I'd go to the gate to collect the money and bring it to Guantanamo,' Rodi explained in English with a West Indian lilt picked up from all the years working with Jamaicans. 'The officer and the girl who brought the pensions greeted me with warmth and affection. I would have liked us to have better relations.'

That evening I went for a walk in Guantanamo and put my head round the door of what looked to be the busiest spot in town. Inside was a karaoke club with lads in tight T-shirts queuing to sing reggaeton on a small stage. Before the revolution, Americans from the base would socialise on these streets and its expansion in the 1930s brought a big boom for local businesses. The city was once full of clubs, hotels and bars to cater for the foreigners. 'There was the Hotel Washington, the Roosevelt, the Arizona,' the official city historian Jose Sanchez told me. 'You'd have the impression you were in America, not Cuba.'

Jose believed there were more English speakers in Guantanamo than anywhere in Cuba at that time, but he was more than happy they'd gone. 'This was the biggest brothel in the Caribbean,' Jose declared, as he took me on a mini walking-tour of the former red-light district which he insisted was the 'most horrible area' in those years. Now it's just another poor city *barrio*. Jose pointed to ramshackle wooden houses that were once divided up for hourly use by US marines and Guantanamo girls. He'd calculated that there were around a hundred brothels in Guantanamo itself and as many as thirty in Caimanera. 'The marines would come by train or by bus to seek their pleasures.' There were even translators laid on to help. After the revolution, Jose said, the Americans' day passes were cancelled.

The fact that the Americans are still in Guantanamo Bay, even confined to their base, is an irritant to some. 'We're spending a lot of money protecting our border that we could use to improve life here,' the fishing boss in Caimanera argued, in an over-chilled office with a picture of Raul Castro on the wall and a poster nearby advertising a week of sexual diversity in cinema. The fisherman's chief concern was that the Americans controlled access to the best fishing zones; the Cubans had stopped venturing into deeper waters a long time back, after a man was shot.

There was no such drama any longer. On the shore I watched a wooden boat glide towards the pier; a woman in the shade of a tree sat reading *Granma* and a spaniel slid into the sea and paddled out towards a group of boys playing in the water, the sound of their laughter carrying across the bay in my direction. As we left Caimanera I spotted a sign referring to the Americans: 'They will never have Cuba.'

* * *

My obituary tour began on another shore, west of Guantanamo, where in December 1956 Fidel landed a boat full of rebels to launch the fight to topple Batista. The mission almost failed before it started, and when I reached the spot where the boat ran aground I could see why. 'They hit bad weather, a man fell overboard, and the motor wasn't powerful enough,' a local historian told me, listing a catalogue of near disasters that befell the rebels as they crossed from Mexico. The combination of bad luck and bad planning was not helped by the fact that the boat Fidel had bought, the *Granma*, was designed for just twenty people. He had four times that number crammed on board.

The plan was to land at Las Coloradas beach where a group of supporters would be waiting. But bad weather and miscalculation threw the boat two days behind schedule and several miles off course. When Batista's troops got wind of the arrival, the revolutionaries waiting on land were forced to withdraw. The *Granma* finally ran out of fuel on the edge of a swamp in what Che Guevara is said to have described as less of a landing and more of a shipwreck.

There's now a concrete path through the mangrove plants to allow visitors to reach the spot. The day we walked down, the place was deserted bar a few seagulls. To get an idea of what the rebels had faced I stepped off the path and into the sludge which immediately gave way with a loud squelch. Walking at all was a struggle, even on the edge, and the forest of bleached branches was thick and sharp. I tried to imagine the rebels struggling through here, loaded with kit and exhausted after a week at sea. It took them some five tough hours to reach solid ground. I gave up and headed back to the concrete after just a few steps.

Santiago Perez was nine at the time of the landing. He cycled towards me in a big straw hat to share his memories of the day the rebels came knocking at his door. His family gave the men food and drink: yucca, honey and water. Santiago told me he remembered the rebels lying in the shade, looking exhausted. His older brother eventually went on with them as a guide but the family paid heavily later for their actions. In 1958 their house was burned down and Santiago's father and brother were killed. I wondered how he felt now about the revolutionary cause and although he spoke in slogans he was passionate. 'Fidel gave me my freedom, education and work,' Santiago told me. 'There were no schools in this area before and now there's six – and I've had two operations for free.'

As we sheltered from a downpour beside a life-size replica of the *Granma* boat, the guide explained how the rebels were ambushed on their way from here to the mountains. They spent three days trapped in sugar cane fields, strafed by Batista's warplanes. Fewer than two dozen of the eighty-two men who boarded the boat for Cuba ever made it to the safety of the Sierra Maestra. Fidel and Raul Castro were among them, reunited more than two weeks after the landing. 'Fidel asked Raul how many guns he had,' the guide told me, relating the legend that every Cuban schoolchild knows. 'Raul answered five and Fidel had two, which made seven. Now, Fidel told his brother, we will win this war.'

At the home where Fidel was born in Biran I found some early hints to what drove him. The estate is set among woodland dotted with grazing goats. Most striking as we approached was its sheer size. Fidel's father, Angel Castro, first came to Cuba from Spain as a labourer but he soon began acquiring land and the family became wealthy. Their home was a large ranch-like building on wooden stilts in the style of Angel's native Galicia. Fidel's mother, Lina, was originally employed as a maid, before she caught the eye of her older employer.

Among the black-and-white photos on display was an image of a young Fidel dressed up in shorts and matching jacket like a little gentleman, hair carefully combed over to one side. But the guide who showed me round wanted to underline his acute sense of social justice. 'Fidel had plenty of everything, he didn't need to leave all this and fight for the poor,' insisted Helen Vargas, a die-hard fan whose eyes gleamed with passion when she spoke of him. 'Fidel would always give away his things to those in greater need.' In Biran, like the *Granma* landing site, history and hagiography were tightly knit.

In another building, Helen pointed out exhibits including the machete Fidel used in 1970 after he'd ordered a ten-million-tonne sugar harvest. The whole nation was mobilised as their leader declared that 'failure would be shameful,' but the target Fidel set was impossible to meet. In the same room I spotted a basketball up on a cupboard and the guide told me it came from a university competition Fidel had lost. 'He didn't like losing anything so he spent the whole night practising and he shot 104 baskets.' The number was written on the leather ball in marker pen. The highlight of this journey into Fidel's past for me, though, was the climb through the mountains to his command point. We drove as far as we could, and then a wiry old man called Luis Angel led us on foot up a narrow, stony trail through the trees. This was how Fidel's guerrilla army moved as they launched attacks on Batista's forces before retreating to the cover of the mountains. It was the most peaceful place I'd ever been in Cuba, a land where people live at high volume in houses whose windows have no glass. The loudest sound up in the Sierra Maestra came from red-bellied tocororos warbling in the trees.

After a steep climb we reached the concealed wooden hut that had been Fidel's base, its roof camouflaged with moss and foliage. There's not much left inside besides a big electric fridge with a fist-sized hole blasted in the side. A government plane had spotted the bright white shape as it was hauled up the

mountainside, and taken a shot. 'It didn't stop working though,' Luis Angel, another Fidel fan, informed me brightly. 'I think the revolution succeeded because there was a project for the poor, for people whose rights had been trampled on for many years,' he suggested, as we caught our breath beside the wooden shack. 'It was about bringing justice and dignity and I think at that stage the goal that Fidel set was achieved.'

Thinking back to that climb now, I remember the clearing we'd emerged into close to the top, with soft grass and dappled light. We paused there for a rest and to take in the view across the deep green valley to more distant peaks of the Sierra Maestra. It was somewhere in this magical setting that in 1957, less than two months after the near-disaster of the *Granma* landing, Herbert Matthews had sat and listened to Fidel. Captivated, the journalist produced his famous articles for the *New York Times* that fixed the romantic, heroic image of the revolutionary for years to come.

* * *

It is the film from my own journey into the Sierra Maestra that I see on TV the day that Fidel died. Havana correspondents had always been advised to watch for possible signs of his passing: a sudden military mobilisation; whispers on the street; a communications blackout. In the event Raul Castro simply appeared on state television to inform the nation of his brother's death, his shoulders hunched over a single sheet of white paper and voice cracking as he read. Clearly anxious to get word out before a hostile Miami did, Raul hadn't waited for the nightly bulletin and many in Cuba missed the announcement entirely. As news gradually filtered through, bars and clubs in Friday-night Havana quietly closed their doors and the crowds cleared the streets and headed home.

The first and loudest reaction came from Miami where Cuban-Americans took to the streets in unbridled celebration. They were the families of those who'd fled political persecution or the seizure of their livelihoods. 'I feel great, I'm happy he died,' I saw one man gloat to a TV camera, as the crowd around him banged drums and blew whistles. To such exiles, the world was well rid of a tyrant.

When the news spread to further-flung time zones, words of condolence and praise began to balance the Miami cheers. The pope sent a telegram and other world leaders past and present hailed a giant of history and a powerful symbol of defiance to the mighty United States. Fidel Castro had outlasted ten US presidents in power.

It was a little later that I began to hear from my own Cuban friends both on and off the island and a range of complex feelings poured out. Several talked of their regret at Fidel's death and their anger at those dancing on his grave. These were not brainwashed ideologues but young Cubans who had grown up with Fidel's revolution and spoken openly to me before about its failings. But when he died they were genuinely moved.

A former state journalist told me that people around her had been taken aback despite having years to prepare. 'People are experiencing their personal pain with a silence which surprises, moves and saddens me,' she wrote from Havana, describing Fidel's death as the news she'd never want to report, 'despite everything'. Another friend, Anailin, admitted that she'd cried when she heard, even though she was messaging me from Europe. She thought the reaction in Miami was 'monstrous'. Anailin recalled her grandmother who'd idolised Fidel for lifting her out of poverty and illiteracy. 'When he came to power', my friend wrote, 'everything changed.' This woman, who had been so anxious to leave Cuba for a better life, said she felt 'bad, unprotected and sad' at the death of the man whose revolution had shaped almost every aspect of her existence.

Later, a former Party militant in Havana would tell me how he experienced a sense of relief. He remembered having been bowled over by Fidel's energy and plans in the early years. 'I remember they said on TV that we'd produce so much milk we'd have pipes for it instead of water.' His enthusiasm gradually soured. 'Fidel made so many mistakes,' the man admitted quietly a few months after Castro's death.

For many people, Fidel's death rekindled memories of the heady first years when a handful of young, idealistic revolutionaries had toppled a tyrannous and corrupt regime to hail a socialist utopia free from the 'imperialist yoke'. It was that rebellious spirit that Graham Greene himself inhaled, as his own engagement with Cuba shifted and he began meeting and even helping the rebels. But that romantic peak had been reached six decades ago. In the Havana I grew to know, many Cubans had come to see Fidel as a brake on progress, as a rigid ideologue who'd stalled the change their country urgently needed. With the death of the father of their revolution, some dared hope that Cuba's transition – to something as yet new and unknown – might finally accelerate.

SLOW EROSION

If Graham Greene's *Our Man in Havana* were being filmed today the opening scene would not be at the Capri. It would more likely be on the roof of the brand new Hotel Manzana Kempinski, the camera rising from the infinity pool over the swaying palm trees to the grand dome of the Capitolio across the park. In the square down below the shot would pick out the statue of Jose Marti, recently scrubbed white-clean, flower beds replanted and trees trimmed. It's all part of a grand clean-up around the vast, expensive hotel that covers an entire block.

But in December 2017 the chaises longues on the Manzana's decked terrace are not filled with the affluent Americans this place was primarily aimed at. Instead there's a group of brash young Australian men, bare feet on the table, discussing the international age of consent. A family ride up in the lift to snap pictures of the skyline as dusk falls and leave without buying a drink. Bringing me a daiquiri like those that numbed Wormold's sinuses, a waiter agrees business is slow.

It's over two years since Havana was brimming with expectation following the restoration of relations with the US. Now Donald Trump is in the White House and he's been back-pedalling on some of Obama's initiatives, calling them 'misguided'. Trump has talked of the Castros' 'brutal regime' and depicted Cuba as a security threat. I suspect Fidel would have been delighted.

Landing back this time into the glare of a Havana morning, I see fewer girls in patterned tights at passport control and more men in sand-coloured uniforms; less *mi amor* and *mi hija*, more business-like. We drive into town past a new billboard showing a young black schoolgirl beside the slogan: 'They made the ideal of emancipation our reality.' Other signs announce a 'genuine demonstration of democracy' and I'm reminded that the next elections, the moment when Raul has said he'll step down, are drawing close.

That first night, still groggy from the long flight, we head to Don Cangrejo, an open-air club with a giant red crab statue in its car park. Havana D'Primera are playing and men work the short queue charging five CUC to get people in faster. About a third of those lining up are girls in figure-tight dresses and high heels never meant for dancing salsa. Once inside, the one ahead of me buys a beer then makes for a corner to look beautiful and wait.

We stand at the back near the sea, as ever too early for the band who won't appear until way past midnight. A group of women from Seattle hover chatting nearby until one staggers into our table, sending the drinks flying. Her friend apologises: they're on a short break to celebrate their fortieth birthdays and it's their first time away without children. They booked the trip before Trump made it harder to visit again, including barring Americans from hotels run by Cuba's military. He stopped short of blacklisting the island altogether and grounding flights, but for traditionally travel-wary Americans the fear factor is back. 'It's so sad, but at least we made it!' one of the women tells me. The group were persuaded to visit by two air-stewardess friends who began flying to Cuba when direct routes resumed from the US. Their enthusiasm was infectious.

As the first notes of the band sound, my husband invites one of the Americans to dance. Seeing them, her friend then demands a turn. He mentions that I'm writing about Cuba and the woman tells me to make sure to include her. 'Rocio, in a black dress with a red embroidered trim, was an amazing dancer,' she dictates between figures. 'That's R-O-C-I-O.'

It doesn't take long to catch up on the main news from friends: economic reforms and investment have stalled, relations with the US are down, prices are up. I'd seen reports of a toilet paper deficit so we've come well stocked, but that particular shortage doesn't last. On the other hand, eggs are only available on the ration book or on the street. *Pssst, huevos quiere?* the men outside the market now hiss when I pass, instead of pushing *papas*, or potatoes. The 'mule' system is still in force and a new goods route to Moscow is booming despite the distance, as Cubans don't need Russian visas.

While there are fewer Americans about, I do see more Cubans with money in Havana's new fashionable cafes and bars. A few years back most would have been the guests of relatives from Miami or foreign friends. Now private business is generating new Cuban wealth. One club has introduced face control and foreigners no longer get ushered automatically to the front. A long-time foreign resident laughs that he'd been to another new bar where the 'hot young Cubans' had shown no interest in him at all. 'It's the new Cuba!'

Many tourist spots seem quiet given the time of year. Rows of gleaming 1950s classic cars in every colour of the rainbow stand idling by the Capitolio. Sloppy Joe's, so carefully restored for a rush of returning Americans, is all but empty each time I look in. And after hiking up hotel prices the government hasn't dropped its rates. 'Some places are now asking more than a night at the Dorchester,' a British travel agent friend says, and the number of complaints he has to deal with has soared. 'One couple paid $360 for the best suite at a place in Old Havana but when they filled up the Jacuzzi the water was cold. Reception just shrugged and said "This is Cuba." But that excuse doesn't cut it any more.'

Every other house in Vedado, where we're staying, has a sticker indicating rooms to rent. Prices at the *casas* have remained steady, unlike the hotels. Perhaps that's why the government recently stopped handing out new licences: to cut the competition. Or perhaps there's too many people getting rich on the rentals. *Paladar* licences have been frozen too, and several popular, established ones shut down. There's fear the government's planning to backtrack more broadly on reforms again, like in the 1990s, though that might not be accepted so quietly now.

It's not just changes to US tourism policy that have slowed the surge of visitors. In an episode that smacks of one of Wormold's more fanciful inventions, some two dozen American embassy workers complained of health problems including temporary deafness and dizziness. Some reported strange noises at extreme volumes, producing claims that they'd come under some kind of sonic attack. The Cuban government dismissed the reports as hysteria and no high-tech weapon was ever detected, but the mysterious incident has badly damaged relations.

Officially the US termed it a 'health incident', not an attack, but a State Department travel warning pronounced the island dangerous for all Americans. After years of tiny but historic steps towards reconciliation, many US diplomats were ordered home by their own government. Washington then began expelling Cuban diplomats for their country's failure to protect Americans on the island. The US embassy on the Malecon remains open, but the number of staff has shrunk dramatically. 'The Americans were really annoyed, they didn't want to go,' a well-connected friend tells me, though it did mean a bonanza sale of food and electronic goods to expats as the diplomats left in a rush.

One of the theories circulating in Havana suggests that the Trump administration is exaggerating the 'acoustic attacks' as an excuse to reduce the rapprochement with Havana. Another suggestion blames renegade factions within the Cuban government, who supposedly fear growing American influence cutting into their position and privilege. But if there is such a dramatic struggle for power, it is carefully concealed. Meanwhile, many people question how such attacks could only target diplomats. 'Do they have different DNA from everyone else?' a Cuban friend wonders. She suspects the mysterious symptoms are psychosomatic.

* * *

We're staying a block from the former convent I believe Greene used as a model for Milly's school. The giant head of Maximo Gomez has disappeared from its pedestal since my last visit, knocked off perhaps by the hurricane. This is no longer the rich white neighbourhood that Greene described and that my friend Liana grew up in. Opposite my balcony I can see shanty homes built on the flat roofs of battered mansions which multiple families now share. But Vedado is still a place of wide, tree-lined streets and parks, and the telltale signs of wealth are reappearing. Many of the new bars, cafes and rooms to rent are in freshly painted houses. There's also stone cladding, higher fences and burglar alarms.

Workmen are digging up the roads to lay pipes and at night someone places a ceramic toilet beside a large hole to mark the hazard. Someone jokes that they're installing fibre-optic cable for the Internet. Getting online at home is still a long way off though, and the *paquete* of downloaded TV series, games and films remains big business. But there are more Wi-Fi points around the city and a friend shows me an ingenious, though utterly illicit, phone app that hooks you up to hotel networks at a discount. The local 'navigation salons' are cheapest of all, but the queues are long. Inside the one I use, a man sits viewing graphic gay porn and doesn't bother to click away when people walk past.

One morning I'm woken early by a loudspeaker and school-children lined up in the park below. 'Fidel is not dead, he lives on in our blood and in our hearts,' a young girl shouts into the mic, a Cuban flag knotted to the lamp post behind her. 'He is our brother and our father. *Hasta la victoria, siempre!*' Proud speeches over, the salsa and pop kick in. When there's more of the same at the weekend we wander down to street level to watch. It's UN Human Rights Day and at the party in the park a teacher in a tracksuit announces a dance therapy session. Children try to follow her steps, only to crash into one another a lot and giggle. A passing woman stops to dance rumba for a while, then picks up her shopping bags again and walks on.

This trip isn't quite the break from the Moscow winter I'd planned. A few days into my stay I wake to howling wind and rain pounding the windows. The water starts to seep through and soak the floor. With every short pause in the downpour the shouts of street sellers drift upwards. It's just a December cold snap and everyone assures me the rain will only last one day. But the chill lingers and Cubans dig out hats and scarves, even coats.

The storm is heavy but nothing like the category five hurri-cane that devastated Cuba just three months before. It's some-times hard to tell what's recent damage and what was crumbling before the edge of Hurricane Irma swept through. The waves crashed over the Malecon wall then, flooding homes and busi-nesses for several blocks. As sea and city merged, men played draughts in streets that looked like rivers and children turned a

344 — OUR WOMAN IN HAVANA

flooded tunnel into a diving pool. Extra police were sent to stop them but their deployment wasn't only for child safety; it was to prevent disorder and looting. Three months later many of the patrols are still in place. Most are young, skinny and quite relaxed but I've never seen so many police, moving in threes at a minimum. My regular taxi driver tells me the government is nervous. 'They were afraid the storm damage would bring people out in protest.' But most Cubans are too busy 'resolving' the issues of their everyday lives. This is a nation occupied with just staying afloat.

One day I head back to Calle Lamparilla and a new cafe I like nearby. A girl passes in a tight T-shirt marked 'Health is better than Wealth.' I've managed to find a copy of a Pedro Juan Gutierrez novel hidden at the back of a bookshop and as I begin flicking through the pages, a man sharing the table recognises the author and strikes up a conversation. Grinding salt into his hand, then sprinkling it into his lemonade, he tells me he's a former airline pilot from Ireland now living in Havana, on and off, with a Cuban girlfriend. He looks to be in his seventies and has dropped in to the cafe on his way home from a neighbourhood gym. The Irishman tells me he ended up working for Cuba's national airline after he retired, flying patients from Venezuela to Havana for free eye treatment. That contract was cut short when someone tried to hijack a flight at Havana airport and the plane took a couple of bullets on the tarmac. I don't dare ask how old his girlfriend is but he's trying to get her a visa to leave. 'How can a country run like this?' the pensioner protests. 'No one can make plans or have ambitions.' Swallowing his last salty sip of lemonade he heads off, trousers belted just a little too high, and I turn back to my copy of Gutierrez.

After a surge of major news, the foreign press pack and diplomats have returned to a pre-Obama slump. I remember the drinks party, not long after I arrived, when an ambassador had asked what I did all day. She was struggling to find anything to file in her reports. Now Raul has confirmed he's stepping down in 2018 but there's no 'end of an era' feeling. The words I hear most from both Cubans and expats are 'frozen' and 'paralysis'. 'There are no new business licences and none of the reforms they promised are being enacted,' a former colleague tells me. He thinks Obama's visit, with his easy confidence and his message of change, was too much for Cuba's rulers, too attractive. 'Everything is now on hold.'

It is perhaps telling that the whole time the US and Cuba were negotiating to restore relations, Cuban State Intelligence was working on a high-tech new monument to enmity and confrontation. The Memorial de la Denuncia opened in August 2017 on what would have been Fidel's ninety-first birthday. Right on Fifth Avenue, among foreign embassies and trade missions, the bright white museum is filled with touchscreen displays detailing CIA assassination attempts. There's information on counter-revolutionary plots and the US trade embargo. Looking at all this, imagining the money spent, I fear the detente is dead.

'When the Cuban revolution triumphed in 1959, our enemies in the north were not happy,' one brand new display declares, as a close-up image of an eye with a nasty case of conjunctivitis is beamed onto another wall. The text details infections and pestilences allegedly inflicted on Cuba over the decades by its neighbour. The floor in the next room is coated with spent bullet cases several layers thick beneath glass. Walking across them you reach a wall display of weapons which the signs say were captured from people attempting to kill Fidel. An interactive screen shows how each gun is assembled.

Moving on, I find smiling pictures of Obama and Raul behind a wall of barbed wire. The text notes that 17 December 2014 had marked a 'new chapter' for Cuba and the US as the decision to restore relations was taken. But, it regrets, the 'economic war continues'. Finally comes a whole section on how Cubans have fled the island over the years, including a real-life raft made of metal drums. 'How terrible', the Cuban friend I've dropped in with murmurs, as she inspects the display. When I ask if she herself knows anyone who left by raft, she snorts. *Un monton!* Loads! One neighbour tried four times to cross but she says he's now in America 'doing really well'.

Just before the exit a visitors' book is filling up with signatures and comments. Staff from the Tobacco Research Institute were the latest to leave a note: 'Many congratulations on this majestic place, which proves the resistance of the Cuban people.'

* * *

On my final night in Havana, at the 1830 club on the seafront, elderly veterans of Cuban casino dance in a circle as a younger crowd film on their phones. There's no sign of Jose 'La Figura' bouncing around but the man calling the moves is dressed in the brightest red suit I've seen, with all-white shoes and a bow tie. Watching from the sidelines, I realise the dancers are moving to the same rhythms as sixty years ago when Graham Greene passed through Havana, and when this revolution was in its infancy. The music, taken up by a new generation and re-energised, still resonates but the revolution, now elderly, is battling to stay relevant.

Leaning against the sea wall I soak up the scene: the genuine smiles and the gentle hustles, the all-Cuban couples dancing with passion and flair and a European woman in leopard-skin leggings clinging tight to her partner and her fairy tale. As they all move to the sound of salsa, the slogan on the top of a building across the water glows dimly as it has for years, proclaiming *Viva Fidel!* to the Havana night sky.

ACKNOWLEDGEMENTS

As a broadcast journalist I'm used to working in a team. Writing a book can sometimes feel like a solitary affair in comparison. In fact, many people have helped me along the way and I am extremely grateful to all of them.

Our Woman in Havana is partly based on my reporting on Cuba for the BBC, but it's also the result of many other conversations with contacts, friends and complete strangers. I have changed some of their names in my text and left others anonymous, but am grateful to all for their candour and their trust.

Thanks for bringing this book to publication must go to my editor Sam Carter, assistant Jonathan Bentley-Smith and all the team at Oneworld. I also thank my agent Matthew Hamilton. I'm grateful to my bosses at the BBC who deployed me to Havana from Madrid in the first place and then encouraged me to write this book.

I consulted several archives in the US in the process and would like to thank all those who helped, emailing copies of Greene's scrawled handwritten diaries, letters and other documents to

Moscow for me to try to decipher. Special thanks go to the Georgetown University Library Booth Family Center for Special Collections and to the John J. Burns Library at Boston College. The Foreign Desk records of the *New York Times* were also invaluable in reconstructing the life and work of Ruby Phillips, and I am hugely grateful to Dariya Merkusheva for the hours she spent at New York Public Library going through the files of the journalist who tried to be the 'firstest with the mostest' and whose character fascinated us both.

I'd like to thank my Cuban colleagues William and Alberto (Nanito) and their families for their help and friendship over the years, Eleanor whose mule services and knowledge of Kool and the Gang lyrics are unrivalled, Dom for his help with the maps, Marcus for his photo of the Russian embassy 'sword' and Emma and Little for their encouragement.

I'd especially like to thank all our Cuban friends for their warmth and generosity, particularly Liana who shared so much, and our foreign friends in Havana for their hospitality and kindness. Special thanks go to Michael and Tuen for putting us up and to Jeff and Elena.

Big thanks to my brother Jonathan for the 'author's photograph', to Ellie and Chris, Daniel and all my family for their love and support over the years, especially Dad. And to Mum, who I wish was here to share this and so many moments.

Finally, very special thanks to Kester, the best writer I know, without whose great help and endless enthusiasm for Havana this book would never have happened. This is for you.

NOTES

ENDINGS

Graham Greene's impressions of Batista's Havana are described in Graham Greene, *Ways of Escape* (Harmondsworth: Penguin, 1981), pp. 184–92.

References to *Our Man in Havana* in this book (abbreviated as *OMIH*) are from the Vintage edition: Graham Greene, *Our Man in Havana* (London: Vintage, 2004).

1: WITHOUT HASTE

Raul Castro's reform process is charted in Marc Frank, *Cuban Revelations: Behind the Scenes in Havana* (Gainesville: University of Florida Press, 2013).

2: THE RUINS OF HAVANA

The title of this chapter is taken from *OMIH*, p. 189.

On the architecture and fabric of Havana I was helped by Alfredo Jose Estrada, *Havana: Autobiography of a City* (New York: Palgrave Macmillan, 2008).

'Wedding cakes turned to stone': Norman Lewis, *The World, the World* (Basingstoke and Oxford: Picador, 1997), p. 157.

3: CONFESSIONS OF A MARTINI DRINKER

Graham Greene's list of prostitutes can be seen in Norman Sherry, *The Life of Graham Greene Volume Three: 1955–1991* (New York: Penguin, 2004), appendix 2.

The Cuban passion for the latest American household appliances, including vacuum cleaners, is discussed in Louis A. Perez, *On Becoming Cuban: Identity, Nationality, and Culture* (Chapel Hill: University of North Carolina Press, 1999), pp. 325–31.

Greer complained of being beckoned 'as if I had been a dog' in Germaine Greer, 'Women and Power in Cuba', in Ian Jack (ed.), *The Granta Book of Reportage* (London: Granta, 2006), p. 124.

The 'chattering, cajoling women' were noted in *Stag*, Vol. 1, No. 5 (November 1950).

Cited correspondence between Greene and his lover Catherine Walston is held at Georgetown University Library, Booth Family Center for Special Collections, Graham Greene papers, Correspondence: Greene to Walston, Box 18 Folder 8; Box 24 Folder 22; Box 26 Folder 9; Box 26 Folder 11; Box 27 Folder 13.

On Greene's idea of the 'entertainment', see Marie-Francoise Allain, *The Other Man: Conversations with Graham Greene* (London: Bodley Head, 1983), pp. 148–9.

The diaries and journals of Greene I refer to are held at Georgetown University Library, Booth Family Center for Special Collections, Graham Greene papers, Box 1 Folder 5 (1954); Box 1 Folder 8 (1957); Box 1 Folder 9 (1966).

Greene admitted to his taste for shady places in an interview with Allain, *Other Man*, p. 176.

'Drugs, women or goats': ibid., p. 59.

The Floridita and other venues are profiled in Consuelo Hermer and Marjorie May, *Havana Mañana: A Guide to Cuba and the Cubans* (New York: Random House, 1941).

For expat society life in 1957, I consulted the *Havana Post* of the day, microfilm copies of which are held at the British Library.

Greene's piercing eyes are noted in V. S. Pritchett's conversation with the author, published in Henry J. Donaghy (ed.), *Conversations with Graham Greene* (Jackson and London: University of Mississippi Press, 1992), p. 111.

4: CONSUMPTION ANXIETY

On Havana's reputation for fine restaurants, see W. Adolphe Roberts, *Havana: The Portrait of a City* (New York: Coward-McCann, 1953), p. 245.

6: THE SLEEPING FAITH

For Fidel Castro's defence of his treatment of Cuba's Catholics and the clergy, see Ignacio Ramonet (ed.), *Fidel Castro: My Life* (London: Penguin, 2008), p. 236.

7: RED LINES

Leonardo Padura tackles the repression of gay men in his novel *Havana Red* (London: Bitter Lemon Press, 2005), first published as *Máscaras* in 1997.

Pedro Juan Gutierrez, *Dirty Havana Trilogy* (London: Faber and Faber, 2002).

8: ENTERTAINMENTS AND COMMITMENTS

For the 1950s diplomatic background, see Christopher Hull, *British Diplomacy and US Hegemony in Cuba, 1898–1964* (Basingstoke: Palgrave Macmillan, 2013).

For Havana in the 1950s, see T. J. English, *The Havana Mob: How the Mob Owned Cuba . . . and Then Lost It to the Revolution* (Edinburgh and London: Mainstream, 2009); Peter Moruzzi, *Havana Before Castro: When Cuba Was a Tropical Playground* (Layton, Utah: Gibbs Smith, 2008).

Greene's connections with the SIS are touched upon in Sherry, *Life of Graham Greene Volume Three*, p. 135.

Norman Lewis's entertaining account of his Cuban entanglements is in Lewis, *The World, the World*, ch. 8.

'brothel life': Greene, *Ways of Escape*, p. 184.

For Greene's need to be in places of upheaval and change, see Allain, *Other Man*, p. 108.

Greene's damning verdict on Ted Scott was expressed in a letter to Nicolas Mendoza held at Boston College, John J. Burns Library, Graham Greene papers, Box 73 Folder 12.

Greene dismissed his novel as 'a rather hack job' in a letter to R. K. Narayan, 2 June 1958, in Richard Greene (ed.), *Graham Greene: A Life in Letters* (London: Little, Brown, 2007), p. 228.

Correspondence on film rights: Boston College, John J. Burns Library, Graham Greene papers, Box 58 Folder 17. See also Nicholas Wapshott, *The Man Between: A Biography of Carol Reed* (London: Chatto & Windus, 1990), p. 295.

Greene's letter to Hugh Delargy MP is published in Greene (ed.), *Graham Greene*, pp. 232–3.

Greene's letter to *The Times*, 3 January 1959, is published in Christopher Hawtree (ed.), *Graham Greene Yours etc. Letters to the Press 1945–1989* (London: Penguin, 1989).

10: ADELA

For a searing account of gay life in Castro's Cuba, see Reinaldo Arenas, *Before Night Falls* (London: Serpent's Tail, 2001).

For Fidel's defence of the UMAP, see Ramonet (ed.), *Fidel Castro*, pp. 222–6. Also *La Jornada*, 31 August 2010.

11: THE FORGOTTEN REPORTER

My account in this chapter and chapter 20 of the life of Ruby Hart Phillips draws largely on her own first-hand reporting in the *New York Times* and the three books she wrote: *Cuban Sideshow* (Havana: Cuban Press, 1935); *Cuba: Island of Paradox* (New York: Obolensky, 1959); *The Cuban Dilemma* (New York: Obolensky, 1962).

The New York Public Library holds the Foreign Desk records of the *New York Times* (Manuscripts and Archives Division, New York Public Library, Astor, Lenox, and Tilden Foundations), where I consulted papers relating to Ruby Hart Phillips. These include her extensive correspondence with editors.

For the Herbert Matthews story, see Anthony DePalma, *The Man Who Invented Fidel: Cuba, Castro and Herbert L. Matthews of the New York Times* (New York: Public Affairs, 2006), ch. 6.

13: FILM CREWS AND FIRING SQUADS

My account of the making of *Our Man in Havana* both here and in chapter 16 draws on the following sources:

Alec Guinness, *Blessings in Disguise* (London: Hamish Hamilton, 1996).

Nicholas Wapshott, *The Man Between: A Biography of Carol Reed* (London: Chatto & Windus, 1990).

Maureen O'Hara, *Tis Herself* (London: Simon & Schuster, 2005).

B. J. Bedard, 'Reunion in Havana', *Literature/Film Quarterly*, Vol. 2, No. 4 (1974).

Correspondence held at Boston College, John J. Burns Library, Graham Greene papers, Box 73 Folder 12.

The making of the film is also reported in the *Havana Post* and *Time*.

On the executioner Herman Marks, see Ken Tynan, 'A Visit to Havana', *Holiday Magazine*, February 1960; 'Chief Executioner', *Time*, 13 April 1959; Lewis, *The World, the World*, pp. 183–4.

14: LOVE NOT MONEY

Teofilo Stevenson's story is included in John Duncan's entertaining history of Cuban boxing, *In the Red Corner: A Journey into Cuban Boxing* (London: Yellow Jersey Press, 2000), ch. 8.

The definitive history of Cuban baseball is Roberto Gonzalez Echevarria, *The Pride of Havana: A History of Cuban Baseball* (New York: Oxford University Press, 1999). See also Perez, *On Becoming Cuban*, pp. 255–78.

16: CUBA LIBRE

For references on the filming of *Our Man in Havana*, see notes to chapter 13.

17: ATHENIAN FORUM

For Greene's comments on the Athenian Forum, see 'The Marxist Heretic', in Graham Greene, *Collected Essays* (Harmondsworth: Penguin, 1970), p. 309.

For Fidel's comments on Western and Cuban elections, see Ramonet (ed.), *Fidel Castro*, p. 605.

18: SYMPATHETIC VISITOR

The articles Greene wrote on Cuba in 1963 and 1966 are reproduced in Graham Greene, *Reflections* (London: Vintage, 2014).

For more information on Superman, see Mitch Moxley,

'Superman of Havana', *Roads and Kingdoms*, 16 December 2015, roadsandkingdoms.com.

On the development of Havana's Chinese community, see Kathleen Lopez, *Chinese Cubans: A Transnational History* (Chapel Hill: University of North Carolina Press, 2013).

19: THE CASE OF OSWALDO PAYA

For this chapter, in addition to my own interviews, I have drawn on Angel Carromero, *Muerte Bajo Sospecha: Toda La Verdad Sobre El Caso* (Madrid: Oberon, 2014); Human Rights Foundation report, *Caso Oswaldo Paya*, New York, 22 July 2015.

20: EXILE

For biographical details of Ruby Hart Phillips, see earlier notes for chapter 11.

For Lewis's comments on Ted Scott's expulsion, see Lewis, *The World, the World*, p. 186.

Nicolas Mendoza informed Greene of Scott's departure in a letter of 12 June 1960: Boston College, John J. Burns Library, Graham Greene papers, Box 73 Folder 12.

21: LET'S DANCE

On the Tropical, see Ned Sublette, *Cuba and Its Music: From the First Drums to the Mambo* (Chicago: Chicago Review Press, 2004), p. 478.

22: THE END OF THE AFFAIR

For some outsider observations of 1980s Cuba, see the following:

Pico Iyer, *Falling Off the Map: Some Lonely Places of the World* (New York: Vintage, 1994).

Pico Iyer, *The Man Within My Head: Graham Greene, My Father and Me* (London: Bloomsbury, 2012).

Martha Gellhorn, 'Cuba Revisited', in Bill Buford (ed.), *Granta 20: In Trouble Again* (London: Granta Books, Winter 1986), online edition.

Germaine Greer, 'Women and Power in Cuba', in Ian Jack (ed.), *The Granta Book of Reportage* (London: Granta, 2006).

Reinaldo Arenas's description of the broken Padilla is in Arenas, *Before Night Falls*, p. 216.

Padilla describes his imprisonment in his memoir: Heberto Padilla, *Self-Portrait of the Other* (New York: Farrar, Straus and Giroux, 1999), p. 138.

G. Cabrera Infante's attack on Greene, 'Cain's Cuba', is published in G. Cabrera Infante, *Mea Cuba* (London: Faber and Faber, 1995), p. 93.

For Greene's thoughts on the repression of writers, see Allain, *Other Man*, p. 94.

For Padilla's account of his meeting with Fidel Castro, see Padilla, *Self-Portrait of the Other*, p. 236.

There are two principal sources on Greene's final trip to Cuba in 1983. One is the brief account in Graham Greene, *Getting to Know the General* (London: Vintage Classics, 2011). Gabriel Garcia Marquez's account of the meeting, 'Las veinte horas de

Graham Greene en la Habana', appeared in *El Pais* newspaper on 19 January 1983.

On Greene and 'pornographic' writing, see Allain, *Other Man*, p. 181.

For Greene's comment on his 'good comic novel', see ibid., p. 59.

INDEX

Abreu, Alexander 291
Abreu, Jose 192
Acevedo, Ofelia 258
acoustic attacks 341–2
activism 74–5, 254–6; *see also* Paya, Oswaldo
Ahmadinejad, Mahmoud 19, 20
Aitken, Ian 149–50, 153
Alamar 90–1
Ali, Muhammad 184
American Legion 275, 277
Anderson, Howard 277
anti-corruption 21
Arab Spring 74, 75
Arenas, Reinaldo 100, 296
Armando Mestre Workers' Social Club 285–7

Armas, Liana de 308–24

Baragua 126–9
Barnet, Miguel 239–40
Barrio Chino 249–53
Barroso, Ines 29
baseball 187–93
Batista, Fulgencio 8, 9, 173–4, 316
  and revolution 108, 109, 119–20, 330
Bay of Pigs invasion 279, 318
Benedict XVI, Pope 14, 22, 23, 86, 87–9, 94–5
Biden, Jill 199
Biran 331–2
black market 14, 33, 62–5, 321
  and Internet 72–3, 79

Black Spring 254, 261
Blanco Rico, Antonio 108–9, 315
Bolivar, Natalia 114
books 96–105
boxing 182–7, 193–8
Brazil 213, 214
British West Indians 126–9
building collapse 26–9, 30–1
Bush, George W. 55, 156–7

Cabrera Infante, Guillermo 100, 297
Caimanera 325–6, 329
Calle Lamparilla 37–41
Carcasses, Robertico 236–8
Carpentier, Alejo 245
Carromero, Angel 257–9, 263, 264–5
cars 43
Carter, Jimmy 261
Casa de la Musica 288–9
Casanas, Raul 153
casinos 174–5
Castaneda, Antonio 229, 230
Castro, Angel 331
Castro, Fidel 3–4, 5, 224–5, 331–2
  and assassination plot 178
  and boat landing 329–30, 331
  and Chavez 217
  and counter-revolutionaries 295–6, 297–8
  and death 1, 6–7, 8, 334–6
  and defectors 160
  and doctors 212
  and elections 229, 232
  and gambling 174, 175
  and Greene 9, 115, 246–7, 299
  and Guantanamo Bay 326
  and homosexuals 138
  and the media 141, 142–3, 151
  and religion 86–7, 93
  and revolution 221–2, 332–3
  and speeches 228
  and sport 194, 196, 198
  and Stevenson 182–3, 184
  and USA 203
  and Varela Project 261
Castro, Mariela 130–1, 132, 133–5
Castro, Raul 1, 3, 4, 19–20, 36, 74
  and elections 229, 232
  and Fidel 334
  and Missile Crisis 318
  and Paya 262
  and private sector 17, 55
  and revolution 331
  and USA 201, 202

Catholic Church 81–95, 254–5, 257, 309–11
Cenesex 130, 133
censorship 297
Centro de Prensa Internacional (CPI) 20–1, 22
Cepero, Harold 257, 258
Chanel 44
Chavez, Hugo 67, 210–12, 216–17
Chinatown 249–53
Christian Liberation Movement (MCL) 254, 257
Cienfuegos 67–70
cinema 56–8
clothes stalls 58–9
Cold War 2
Colombia 204–10
Colon cemetery 274–7
communism 1, 87, 88, 229
condoms 125–6
consumerism 52–5, 62–4
convents 81–6
counter-revolutionaries 296–8, 318
Coward, Noel 172, 177, 224
Coyula, Mario 29–30
cricket 127–8, 129
Cuban-Americans 55, 63, 334
Cuban Five 133–4, 235–6

Cuban Missile Crisis 317–18
Cuban Revolution 106–9, 113–15, 119–20, 176–7, 220–2, 315–17
and boat landing 329–31
and the media 141–2
cuentapropistas 55–9, 60–2

Damas de Blanco 87–8, 89, 254–7
dance 285–9, 346–7; *see also* salsa
Daniel, Yuri 245
De Beauvoir, Simone 297
defectors 156–7, 159–60
Diaz-Canel, Miguel 232–4, 236
Diederich, Bernard 116, 150, 298
Dirty Havana Trilogy (Gutierrez) 15, 101, 102, 103, 304
dissidents 74–5, 87–8; *see also* Paya, Oswaldo
doctors 212–16
Dominican Academy 81–6
drugs 46–7
dual currency 17–18

economics 17–18, 339–41
and crisis 98–9, 319, 321–2
Edificio Bolivar 106–8
education 319–20

El Mejunje 234
elections 228–32, 338
emigration 34–5, 161–7
English speakers 126–9
Enriquez, Michel 187, 188–90
Etecsa 76–7
executions, *see* firing squads
exiles 35–6, 278, 295–6
exit permits 155, 156, 161

Farc 204–10
farmers' markets 13–14, 18
Fernandez, Pablo 296
Fernando, Cedric 60–2
firing squads 178–80, 221–2
Fleming, Ian 111–12
Floridita bar 47–51, 180
food 52–3, 59–62, 64–6, 91
football 199–201
Fordham, Stanley 106, 107–8,
    113, 120
foreign travel 161–2
Francis, Pope 94

gambling 174–5
Garcia Marquez, Gabriel 298–9
Gardner, Ava 305
gays, *see* homosexuality
Gellhorn, Martha 146, 294, 295

Getting to Know the General
    (Greene) 298
Gomez, Maximo 84
Gorbachev, Mikhail 233
Granda, Rodrigo 210
Granma (boat) 330, 331
Great Britain 120, 123–4; *see also*
    British West Indians
Grechko, Georgy 302
Greene, Graham 8–10, 25,
    38–42, 46–7, 298–300
    and Castro 224, 228
    and convent 81–2, 83
    and Cuba 241–7
    and film 218–19
    and Floridita bar 48–51
    and Gutierrez 300, 301,
        302–4
    and Hotel Sevilla 111, 112–13,
        116–17
    and *Our Man in Havana*
        118–19
    and revolution 106, 107–8,
        109, 113–15, 119–20, 297
    and Superman 248–9
    and Tropicana 282, 284
Greer, Germaine 40, 295
Gross, Alan 22
Guantanamo Bay 325–9
Guevara, Ernesto 'Che' 232, 330

Guinness, Sir Alec 172, 176, 177–8, 179, 180–1, 224
  and Castro 225
Gutierrez, Pedro Juan 15, 100–3, 293, 300, 301–6

Haiti 212
Hart, Armando 115
Havana D'Primera 290, 291, 339
Havana Pride 130–3
healthcare 214–15
Hemingway, Ernest 26, 48, 224, 304
Hernandez, Adela 132, 134, 135–6, 138–40
homosexuality 130–40, 234, 237, 295–6, 297
Hotel Capri 171–3, 174–6, 177–8
Hotel Inglaterra 300–1
Hotel Manzana Kempinski 337
Hotel Sevilla 109–11, 112, 116–18, 120–1
housing 26–36
Hurricane Irma 343–4

Iglesias, Raisel 191
intelligence 111–12, 315
Internet 22, 64, 69, 70–80, 94–5, 342–3

Iran 19, 20
Iyer, Pico 293–4

John Paul II, Pope 87
Johnson, Armando 191–2

Kovacs, Ernie 218

labour camps 137–8, 245–6
Lansky, Meyer 314
Lewis, Norman 30, 112, 120, 278
LGBT rights 130–40
'Liberty Carnival' 176–7
libreta (ration book) 91
Lineamientos 4, 69
literacy campaign 319–20
literature 96–105, 245

Madonna 44
Malecon 1, 2, 5, 7–8, 30–3, 159–60
Mandela, Nelson 201
Marks, Herman 179–80
Marquez, Ivan 209–10
marriages of convenience 163–4, 166
Marti, Jose 79, 202
Matthews, Herbert L. 141, 142–3, 151, 333–4
May Day 226–8

media 122–3, 141–54; *see also* social media
medics 212–16
Memorial de la Denuncia 345–6
Mendoza, Nicolas 278
Mesa Redonda (TV show) 78–9
Messi, Lionel 189
Mexico 166, 190–1
Miramar 15–16, 270–1
mobile phones 76–8, 79–80
Modig, Aron 257–8, 262, 263–4
Montmartre 314–15
Montpellier, Ela Perez 233
Morrow, Jo 177
mules 62–5, 340
Mulloy, Lucy 155–6, 157–8
Murillo, Marino 88–9
music 236–40, 288–92, 346–7

names 124–5
New York Times 141–54, 279
Nye, Alan 178, 179

Obama, Barack 1, 2, 6, 55, 201–3
O'Hara, Maureen 181, 219, 224–5
oil 21–2, 67, 68
Old Havana 25–6
Old Man and the Sea, The (Hemingway) 304

Olympic Games 182–3, 185–6, 193–4
Operation Peter Pan 84
Otero, Lisandro 113, 298
Our GG in Havana (Gutierrez) 300, 302–3, 304, 305
Our Man in Havana (film) 171–2, 174, 175–8, 218–20, 224–5, 307
and Gutierrez 304, 306
Our Man in Havana (Greene) 9–10, 25, 37, 38–41, 110
and Greene 46–7, 118–19

Padilla, Heberto 245, 296–8, 320
Padura, Leonardo 98–101, 104–5
paladares (house-restaurants) 17, 59–62, 65–6, 340–1
Paya, Oswaldo 254, 257–8, 259–63, 266–9
Pena, Jorge 56–8
Perez, Santiago 330–1
Philby, Kim 111
Phillips, Ruby Hart 108, 141–3, 144–54, 178–9, 270–4
and evacuation 277–80
and revolution 220
Pinera, Virgilio 136

Plimpton, George 180
politics 228–34
potatoes 13, 14
Prado 41–6
Presidential Palace 106–8
prisoners 295, 296
private enterprise 17, 26, 55–9
property 33–6; *see also* housing
Putin, Vladimir 6

Quinquenio Gris (Grey Five
    Years) 297

race 26, 289, 311
Raft, George 172, 174
rafters 155–6, 157–9, 160–1, 321,
    346
Ramon, Jose 31–2
rations 91
Reed, Carol 119, 174, 219, 224
reforms 4, 33–6
reggaeton 238–40
religion 92, 127, 245–6; *see also*
    Catholic Church
restaurants 59–62, 65–6
restoration 25–6
Reyes, Ricards 44–5
Rihanna 44
Roberts, W. Adolphe 59
Rodriguez, Arsenio 289

Rodriguez, Fructuoso 309
Rodriguez, Rodi 327–8
Rolling Stones 123
Romay, Zuleica 104
Russia 6, 340; *see also* Soviet
    Union

St George's school 309–11
salsa 164–5, 238, 284–5
San Juan de Letran 81–2
Sanchez, Jose 328–9
Sanchez, Yoani 21, 74, 75, 156,
    161, 258
Santa Clara 232–4
Santamaria, Haydee 115, 246
Santeria 92
Santiago de Cuba 22–4
Sartre, Jean-Paul 297
Savon, Felix 184, 193–8
Scott, Ted 111–12, 113, 115–16,
    117
  and expulsion 277–8
  and Greene 218–19
  and Hotel Capri 177–8
  and Marks 179–80
  and Phillips 144, 150, 153
Shanghai theatre 46, 112–13,
    175, 178, 248–53, 303–6
shops 52–4, 55, 73
Sierra Leone 212

Sierra Maestra 6–7, 331, 332–4
Sinyavsky, Andrei 245
Sloppy Joe's 222–4, 340
social media 74, 75–6
socialism 89, 90, 132–3, 227–8, 229, 319–20
Soviet Union 49, 183, 245, 293–4, 301–2
  and collapse 98, 233, 321
  and Missile Crisis 317
Special Period 99, 211, 321
spies 111–12
sport 182–98, 199–201
Stevenson, Teofilo 182–5
storms 32, 343–4
Suarez, Sandra 93–4
Superman 46, 119, 248–9, 253, 304, 305–6

technology, see Internet
television 78–9
timba music 238
Torriente, Olga 32
Torrijos, Omar 298
tourism 2, 17, 26, 118, 340–1
Tropical 289–92
Tropicana 69, 109, 119, 247, 282–4, 312–13
Trump, Donald 338, 339, 341–2

Tynan, Kenneth 180
Tyson, Mike 196

UMAP 137–8, 245–6
Una Noche (film) 155–6, 157–9
United States of America (USA) 1–2, 45, 312–14, 118, 221–2, 345–6
  and Bay of Pigs 318
  and embargoes 17, 70, 319
  and Guantanamo Bay 325, 326–9
  and migrants 156–7, 160–1, 162
  and Missile Crisis 317, 318
  and social media 75–6
  and sport 184, 185, 191, 192, 199–201
  see also Cuban-Americans; Obama, Barack; Trump, Donald
USSR, see Soviet Union

Varela Project 260–1, 267
Vargas, Helen 331–2
Vazquez, Lucy 82–4, 85
Vedado 56, 61, 81–2, 308–12, 342
Venezuela 20, 67, 210–12, 216–17
Ventura, Esteban 218, 219, 316

Ways of Escape (Greene) 114
Weeks, Jeffrey 134
West Indies 126–9
white card 155, 156
Williams, Tennessee 180

women 295
Wood, Leta 177, 219
World Series of Boxing 186

Zunzuneo 75–6